Practicing
the Politics of Jesus

The C. Henry Smith series is edited by J. Denny Weaver. As is expected to be true of many future books in the CHS series, volumes published to date are being released by Cascadia Publishing House (originally Pandora Press U.S., a name some of the earlier series books carry) and copublished by Herald Press in cooperation with Bluffton University as well as the Mennonite Historical Society. Bluffton University, in consultation with the publishers, is primarily responsible for the content of the studies.

Practicing
the Politics of Jesus

The Origin and Significance
of John Howard Yoder's Social Ethics

Earl Zimmerman

Foreword by John Paul Lederach

The C. Henry Smith Series
Volume 8

Cascadia
Publishing House
Telford, Pennsylvania

copublished with
Herald Press
Scottdale, Pennsylvania

Cascadia Publishing House orders, information, reprint permissions:
contact@CascadiaPublishingHouse.com
1-215-723-9125
126 Klingerman Road, Telford PA 18969
www.CascadiaPublishingHouse.com

Practicing the Politics of Jesus
Copyright © 2007 by Cascadia Publishing House,
Telford, PA 18969
All rights reserved.
Copublished with Herald Press, Scottdale, PA
Library of Congress Catalog Number: 2007001803
ISBN-13: 978-1-931038-43-0; **ISBN 10**: 1-931038-43-0
Book design by Cascadia Publishing House
Cover photo and design by Merrill R. Miller. Photo
taken at the ancient Church of the Multiplication of the
Loaves and the Fishes in Tabgah, by the Sea of Galilee, Israel.

The paper used in this publication is recycled and meets the
minimum requirements of American National Standard for Information
Sciences—Permanence of Paper for Printed Library Materials, ANSI Z39.48-1984.

Library of Congress Cataloguing-in-Publication Data
Zimmerman, Earl, 1950-
  Practicing the politics of Jesus : the origin and significance of John Howard Yoder's
social ethics / Earl Zimmerman ; foreword by John Paul Lederach.
     p. cm. -- (The C. Henry Smith series ; v. 8)
  Includes bibliographical references and index.
  ISBN-13: 978-1-931038-43-0 (trade pbk. : alk. paper)
  ISBN-10: 1-931038-43-0 (trade pbk. : alk. paper)
  1. Yoder, John Howard. 2. Christian ethics--History--20th century. 3. Social ethics-
-History--20th century. I. Title. II. Series.

BX8143.Y59Z56 2007
230'.97092--dc22

                              2007001803

  16 15 14 13 12 11 10 09 08 07   10 9 8 7 6 5 4 3 2 1

To Ruth,
who has been my constant companion,
conversation partner, and moral support
on this journey

CONTENTS

FOREWORD

John Howard Yoder entered the chronology of my life at an age when I was too young fully to be aware of conversations that at later points would become central to my vocation. In my early grade school years, when my father John Lederach and uncle Ron Kennel were finishing course work at Associated Mennonite Biblical Seminary, I remember some supper-table bantering about various classes and professors. One memory is particularly vivid: They seemed to have a deep respect or even awe for a particular classroom and a set of lectures that I understood later were the beginning drafts of *The Politics of Jesus*. I remember their laughing about how nervously they might ask John Howard a question. Inevitably if a query was posed, the response appeared to be, "That is not quite the right question." Then a new question would be provided that probed the subject matter at different level.

A decade later, around the time my generation was beginning college studies, the name John Howard Yoder and his *The Politics of Jesus* were presented as *fait accompli*. Here was work of such startling insight and importance that it not only recast the internal Anabaptist debates in social ethics and theology, it has done the same in wider Protestant and Catholic circles.

For those of us born during or after the time when Yoder was working through his European postwar experience and embarking on his Ph.D. work, Earl Zimmerman's *Practicing the Politics of Jesus* reads like novel. The cited correspondence, envisioning Yoder as a college and then a graduate student interacting with his mentors—the guiding figures of mid-century Anabaptism—and later doing the same with a range of key European theologians, casts a whole new light on the development of his thought. Zimmerman brings to life a creative mind, one that weaved seamlessly the history of Anabaptism, the relevance of lived experience—particularly during and after World War II—and direct interaction with the most important theological streams and theologians of Yoder's time.

Zimmerman provides insight into the dynamic process of how Yoder's emerging thought developed. I found myself drawn into the narrative unpacking of how a book came to be written, the struggles and ideas that bounced off each other along the way, and ultimately the impact it had decades later. In my reading of Zimmerman's book, *The Politics of Jesus* no longer felt like a well-fashioned product, an essay conclusively wrapping everything up, which of course was the way I absorbed it on my first reading a decade after its first drafts were penned. The journey behind the book came to life.

The significance of *Practicing the Politics of Jesus* lies at several levels. The first contribution, and perhaps most important from the theological perspective for someone like me—a member of a rising younger generation of Mennonite scholars—emerges from the insight that Yoder's contribution through *Politics* provided yet went beyond a less reactive and more ecumenically serious view of Anabaptism for the outside world. I think my generation always understood that Yoder helped recast internal Mennonite debates about social ethics, church polity, and engagement with the world. I think we intuited early on that he put our church history and views on a more equal platform of exchange with mainstream and dominant Christian traditions. What comes clear in Zimmerman's book is the degree to which Yoder through *Politics* accomplished even more. He recast the very nature and framework of the questions and debate with just war proponents, social ethicists, and nonviolent strategists. This recasting made possible a new level of engagement, exchange, and dialogue that even now, some forty years later, provides all of us a platform of greater insight and understanding.

The second contribution, perhaps most important from the standpoint of my vocation as peacebuilder, was the reminder that Yoder's development of *Politics* created the guiding frame of reference for engagement in real world issues and situations by Anabaptist scholars, practitioners, and ethicists. For me, *Politics* did not ask *whether* I, and we as a wider Anabaptist church, should be engaged in the world of tough and inevitably messy social and political issues, but *how* as Mennonites we should engage, without retreat or rejection, the real challenges facing our local and global communities. I understand in new and more significant ways through *Practicing the Politics of Jesus* how Yoder's framing of the questions and the platform he developed—a frame of reference we now take nearly for granted—emerged.

Zimmerman's book places us alongside both a great mind and an extraordinarily relevant and continuing set of challenges that include but certainly go beyond the arena of social ethics as discussed by those professionally engaged in the scholarly world. No matter our walk of life or professional journey, this volume plunges us into the wonderful challenge of how we bring the love of God as an active, incarnate, and relevant presence into our families, communities, and world.

This journey does not simply represent the search for or the testing of the right words and beliefs. *Practicing the Politics of Jesus* requires something of our lives and life vocation. It asks us *who* we will be in this world, the ways we will find to be true to our deepest belief as Anabaptists and Christians, and how that translates into engagement with the real world challenges that surround us.

—*John Paul Lederach*
  Professor of International Peacebuilding, Notre Dame University; and Distinguished Scholar, Eastern Mennonite University

SERIES PREFACE

C. Henry Smith began his teaching career at Goshen College, 1903-13, and then taught history at Bluffton College (now Bluffton University) from 1913-48, except for the 1922-23 year he spent at Bethel College. The first Mennonite in North America to earn a Ph.D. and remain in the Mennonite church, Smith was the premier North American Mennonite historian of his era. He wrote many articles for Mennonite periodicals and was a central figure in planning the *Mennonite Encyclopedia*. He published five major works over thirty-five years, more full-length writings than any other Mennonite historian of his time. Also a church leader, Smith was on the publication board of the General Conference Mennonite Church and the Peace Committee of Middle District.

Producing the C. Henry Smith Series (CHS) with cosponsorship of the Mennonite Historical Society is one dimension of the service Bluffton University seeks to provide the Mennonite church as well as Anabaptists at large and the wider Christian tradition. Smith's historical expertise, commitment to pacifism and nonresistance, commitment to the church, and wide-ranging interests beyond the discipline of history all represent the values and interests that characterize the series bearing his name. Naming the series for an individual of multiple interests and talents signals a vision to publish works that use a variety of disciplines and modes of inquiry to serve Anabaptist and Mennonite churches.

Works in the CHS Series reflect the assumption that a peace church worldview holds potential to shape discussion of any issue. These books present no consensus view, however, since none exists. Instead, they address aspects of Anabaptist and Mennonite studies pertinent to the future of these churches. Precisely that future dimension compels CHS publication.

SERIES EDITOR'S FOREWORD

I grew up in a small Mennonite church where I learned one thing well in Sunday school. It was that "Jesus boys" were supposed to live like Jesus or use Jesus as the model for their behavior. John Howard Yoder learned a version of that same lesson, but he took it much farther. Yoder saw that if that lesson were true, then both ethics and theology should reflect it, and the result could impact virtually all of life and thought. Earl Zimmerman's book reveals that progression. In a word, *Practicing the Politics of Jesus* is an exposition and analysis of how John Howard Yoder developed that early Mennonite Sunday school lesson into his widely known book, *The Politics of Jesus*.

Practicing the Politics of Jesus is the first book-length treatment of the thought of John Howard Yoder that makes use of the voluminous collection of Yoder's papers, now in the archives of Mennonite Church USA at Goshen College. Zimmerman's research in Yoder's correspondence and writings such as committee reports adds important new depth to the understanding of Yoder's thought.

In what is a paradox only at first glance, this book shows how thoroughly Mennonite Yoder's theology was and simultaneously how much more than a Mennonite theologian he was. Zimmerman shows that Yoder was clearly shaped by and a product of his Mennonite upbringing. That ought not to surprise—people do not develop unimpacted by their surroundings. The more significant observation is how Yoder learned to do theology that reflected his peace church background but was accessible to anyone regardless of background and with no need first to run it through a Mennonite filter. Yoder understood that if a denominational view did not make sense first of all as an expression of Jesus Christ, and if it could not be explained in ways that made sense to those outside the denomination—whether or not they agreed with it—then it was not worth saying at all. Zimmerman's book shows how Yoder, a Mennonite theologian, could speak to any tradition.

Just as Yoder wrote in a way that could address the spectrum of Christian traditions, people from any tradition interested in Yoder should read this book. It may be that Mennonites actually need the book more. Mennonite academic writers aside, Yoder's actual thought has not penetrated or spread very far among Mennonites at the congregational level. That is an unfortunate development when one recalls that Yoder is considered one of the most influential theologians of any stripe for the twentieth century and is arguably the most important Mennonite writer since Menno Simons.

Zimmerman's work speaks to many issues in the thought of John Howard Yoder. It shows that for Yoder, rejection of violence is an intrinsic element of Christian profession, even as it is not the only element of Christian profession. That should help readers—both from Yoder's Mennonite tradition and from other traditions—not to shy from a theology shaped by peace church commitments. There has been something of an ongoing debate about whether Yoder's ethics were based on standard Nicene Christology. Zimmerman's work in Yoder's correspondence provides about as close to a definitive answer as one can get to that question. It seems that from early on, Yoder considered his work to be in conversation with but also an alternative to the standard theological line of Christendom.

Some of Zimmerman's most interesting findings come from his analysis of Yoder's graduate study. Related to the question of Yoder's dependence on Nicene Christology is Zimmerman's analysis of Yoder's dissertation. Yoder's choice of a dissertation topic in sixteenth-century Anabaptism was neither a deviation from nor a false start for his later focus on ethics—nor was it an area that he abandoned to pursue theology and ethics. Rather, Zimmerman shows, Yoder used his scholarship in Anabaptism as a way to do theology when his graduate program did not recognize Anabaptist theology as a credible area of study. In addition, with his Anabaptist scholarship Yoder specifically intended to chart a theological path that was an alternative to the standard theology of Christendom.

Zimmerman's analysis of Yoder's graduate work adds a kind of human dimension to Yoder as well. For decades we have marveled at

Yoder's great intellect and tremendous breadth and depth of knowledge, in biblical studies as well as in theology and ethics. What Zimmerman's work shows is where that breadth and depth of knowledge came from. He learned it. In graduate studies, Yoder learned theology from Karl Barth, as is rather well known. But the majority of Yoder's graduate school course work was in biblical studies, and he had more courses from Oscar Cullman than any other single professor. Of course Yoder added to and developed his knowledge beyond his graduate school courses, as does any competent scholar. But Zimmerman's work shows that there was a beginning to Yoder's knowledge, the same beginning as any other scholar. That is both encouraging to the rest of us and also humbling when one considers how far Yoder developed that beginning.

These points and more mean that *Practicing the Politics of Jesus* marks a new stage in the study of the thought of John Howard Yoder. This book should rapidly become a reference point for all further discussion of Yoder's work.

It has been a pleasure to work with Earl Zimmerman in the development of this manuscript. I appreciate his willingness to consider editorial suggestions, and I am grateful for his decision to grace the C. Henry Smith Series with this volume. On behalf of the C. Henry Smith Series, I extend warm appreciation to the individuals who contributed to the publication of this manuscript through the Orie Miller Center of Eastern Mennonite University as well as to the Mennonite Historical Society for its support of this book.

—*J. Denny Weaver, Editor*
The C. Henry Smith Series

AUTHOR'S PREFACE

This book is about practicing the politics of Jesus in our contemporary world. That endeavor is deeply personal, involving one's faith and practice in the company of those who have responded to Jesus and his claims on their lives. This practice also includes collaborating with many others, from different religious and moral traditions, who work for a sustainable world characterized by justice and peace.

This book involves an interdisciplinary conversation between biblical studies, history, theology, ethics, and the social sciences. During different periods of my life I was compellingly drawn to these various disciplines as tools in my quest for understanding and for authentic social engagement. Such an endeavor offers hopeful new possibilities but also poses great risk. It promises new collaborative insights and life-transforming possibilities that can emerge at the intersection of various disciplines. The risk is going beyond one's depth in any discipline and that one's contributions will consequently be superficial at best. Nevertheless, the nature of the challenge to follow Jesus in our contemporary world compels us to attempt such an interdisciplinary endeavor.

My personal search began as a teenager trying to make sense of the Vietnam War and wrestling with how to respond. Like many in my generation, I agonized over the destroyed lives and communities. The United States government claimed that it was a sacrifice that needed to be made for the cause of freedom and democracy. However, the traditional Mennonite community in which I had grown up taught me that all resort to lethal violence was incompatible with Christian faith. I was drawn to that peace position but instinctively knew that a faithful response had to go beyond saying no to war. It had to include active social engagement in the human dilemmas that lead to war in the first place.

18

Such convictions led me and my wife Ruth to take a short-term mission assignment in the Philippines as a young married couple. There we met hardly imagined social oppression, debilitating poverty, struggling grassroots churches, determined revolutionaries, brutal police and military forces, and courageous social activists. This was much more than we had anticipated and changed our lives forever. That encounter shaped my subsequent educational pursuits. On one hand, I was drawn to biblical studies in an effort to figure out how such things relate to the life and vision of Jesus. On the other hand, I was drawn to various academic disciplines that could help me interpret and engage our contemporary world.

Unlike others who are deeply indebted to the thought of John Howard Yoder, I cannot claim that my initial encounter involved an intellectual conversion. Instead, Yoder's formulation of the politics of Jesus gave me the intellectual tools and the courage to continue on the path of nonviolent social engagement I was already traveling. That journey included six more years in the Philippines in the company of evangelicals, mainline Protestants, and Catholics deeply committed to the life of the church and social transformation.

My mature faith was formed there. My mentors were Filipino intellectuals and activists such as Melba Maggay, Jose DeMesa, and Karl Gaspar. They included grassroots pastors such as Gerry Balucas and poor couples such as Paz and Bert Laurio who somehow survived in the slums of Manila. These mentors kept me honest by constantly reminding me that authentic theology and social theory had to come from the ground up and needed to be relevant in communities of the poor and marginalized.

Oddly enough, I again encountered John Howard Yoder's thought when I returned to the United States and began my doctoral studies at The Catholic University of America. I told Joseph Komonchak, my program advisor, that Yoder was the Mennonite theologian and social ethicist I could not ignore. His immediate response was that I should consider doing my dissertation on Yoder.

That is both ironic and hopeful. Komonchak is thoroughly committed to the Catholic just war tradition, yet he encouraged me to pour myself into the study of a Mennonite pacifist thinker. Other members of the faculty, such as Stephen Happel and Cynthia Crysdale, thoroughly enjoyed helping me shape my research project. William Barbieri, the young moral theologian on the faculty, agreed to be my dissertation advisor and spent many hours helping me formulate my research and guiding the long process of writing.

This book is a product of their combined efforts, even though I personally bear final responsibility for what has emerged. I owe them a debt of gratitude and thank all of them for making possible this truly ecumenical project. It is a sign of promising new collaboration in the global church that could not even have happened in the recent past.

I thank my C. Henry Smith Series editor J. Denny Weaver for his skillful and efficient oversight throughout the publication process. His conviction that this would be a significant book was contagious, and he had many helpful suggestions that improved the final product. I thank Michael A. King, the publisher at Cascadia Publishing House, for his commitment to this book and his guidance at various steps in the process. I also thank my colleagues Nancy Heisey, Ted Grimsrud, Mark Thiessen Nation, and Ray Gingerich at Eastern Mennonite University for their encouragement and willingness to read and give feedback on portions of the book.

Most of all, I thank my wife Ruth for her partnership and constant encouragement. I am sure that her practical insights, which grow out of her work as the co-director of the Center for Justice and Peacebuilding at Eastern Mennonite University and our former joint mission assignment in the Philippines, have found their way into this book in ways that even I can no longer decipher. I also thank our three children Krista, Stephen, and Sara for their unwavering encouragement and belief in their dad. Their keen interest in creating communities characterized by justice and peace in the way of Jesus is an inspiration to me. I could not have written this book without the support of my family.

—Earl Zimmerman
  Harrisonburg, Virginia

Practicing
the Politics of Jesus

ONE
CHAPTER

YODER REARRANGES
THE THEOLOGICAL LANDSCAPE:
AN INTRODUCTORY OVERVIEW

The publication in 1972 of John Howard Yoder's classic work, *The Politics of Jesus*, rearranged the landscape of theological ethics in the last third of the twentieth century. The book was translated into ten languages and became one of the century's most influential theological books. It inspired a generation of radical, alternative Christian movements such as the Sojourners community.[1] More broadly, as was stated in his obituary in the *New York Times*, Yoder's "writings on Christianity and politics had a profound impact on contemporary Christian thinking about the church and social ethics."[2] Yoder led mainstream Protestants and Catholics to reassess their understanding of the social and political stance of Jesus in relation to contemporary social ethics. More than a few prominent theologians and social ethicists have said that reading Yoder's book had led to a personal intellectual conversion in how they understand theology and Christian social ethics.[3]

Yoder's "politics of Jesus" challenges and radically reorients common patterns of Christian engagement in the world. At its core, this politics is a call to follow the way of Jesus amid societies that do not specifically recognize him and, in some respects, even contradict his life and message. This politics directly opposes the dualisms that established churches have used to separate religious faith from secular concerns.

Nevertheless, it recognizes that while the common life of the church is shaped by the stories and practices of its faith tradition, it also shares the language and learns from the social and cultural values of the societies in which it lives. Consequently, it also resists the familiar free-church pattern of withdrawal into separate religious communities. Like liberation theologians, Yoder insisted that Jesus' life, death, and proclamation of the reign of God has economic and political implications that are relevant in the contemporary world. He developed this position in a distinctive way that reflected his Anabaptist tradition and his conviction that suffering love and nonviolent social engagement are central norms for Christian life.[4]

The challenge to follow Jesus becomes most acute in the face of socially constructed oppression and violence. Much of Yoder's work grappled with that human condition, especially the problem of war. Christian communities, according to Yoder, are to form and nurture a common life characterized by suffering love, justice, and peace as exemplified in Jesus. The common life of vibrant Christian communities committed to the way of Jesus models new possibilities for human social and political relationships and informs Christian witness and social action within the wider society.

Yoder (1927-1997) had extraordinary mental powers and wrote prolifically. The comprehensive bibliography of Yoder's writings from 1947 until the year of his death covers forty pages.[5] Posthumously published works would extend the bibliography still further. The thickness of this corpus is especially impressive considering all the things he was involved in outside the academy, including various church responsibilities and social action initiatives. He had a remarkable capacity to learn languages and conducted lecture tours in about twenty different countries.[6] Stanley Hauerwas, Yoder's former colleague on the theological faculty at the University of Notre Dame, nevertheless recalls his gentleness and unwillingness to draw attention to himself. According to Hauerwas, Yoder viewed his own life with a godly indifference and saw his unique abilities as gifts for service.[7]

Self-effacing giant that he was, Yoder also had personal limitations. His academic brilliance was not matched with similar social graces. He was shy and socially clumsy. Even more problematically, he sometimes did not recognize or maintain proper social boundaries. Such failures were at times deeply hurtful. The intent here, however, is no to dwell on

Yoder's imperfections but to recognize and learn from the keen social-analytical and theological insights he has given to us.

The "politics of Jesus" that greeted the world in 1972 in *The Politics of Jesus* had a long gestation period. To that end, I trace the development of Yoder's notion of the politics of Jesus in the decades following World War II. The beginning of the evolution of the idea is already visible in an unpublished paper, "Politics of the Messiah," that he delivered at a peace conference in Germany in 1957.[8] When one explores his church background, it is apparent that some roots extend back even farther. Even though the notion that Jesus is the bearer of a new possibility for human social and political relationships is central to his thought, only occasionally in his writings did Yoder use the phrase *politics of Jesus*. The book in hand focuses primarily on the early development of Yoder's thought up to and including the publication of *The Politics of Jesus*. Later chapters, which concentrate on analyzing and applying his thought, draw more extensively on the full corpus of his work.

Yoder's work responded to social issues that dramatically affected churches and local communities in the decades following World War II. Among them were the emergence of the United States as a superpower, a new global economic order, the invention of the atomic bomb, and the onset of the Cold War. Yoder had a pervasive historical and social consciousness. He spoke out of and to his own situation. That makes it important to situate his work within the historical context in which he wrote.

This book is divided into seven chapters. They follow in chronological order, with some historical overlap for topics pursued in more than one chapter. My work is an appreciative inquiry into the development of Yoder's thought. True appreciation recognizes both the strengths and limitations of a given theology. In several short sections (on the margins as it were) I also discuss some limitations and lacunae in Yoder's theology. Critical thinker that he was, Yoder would have welcomed this discussion. That inquiry begins in the second chapter, which explores how the experience of Mennonites in North America shaped Yoder's early thought, leading to his notion of the "politics of Jesus."

To that end, I draw on many of Yoder's unpublished letters and papers, as well as his early published writings. These materials provide a unique window into the life-world that shaped him and his thought. Until the late nineteenth century, Mennonites in North America lived in culturally separate, religious communities. As descendents of the sixteenth-century Anabaptists, they had routinized their beliefs and practices into their communal life, but eschewed active social engagement.

Social changes in the wider society posed stiff new challenges to this posture of withdrawal in the late nineteenth and early twentieth century. Harold Bender (1897-1962), the dean of Goshen Biblical Seminary, was instrumental in using historical research on the Anabaptist movement to help Mennonites recover their radical religious heritage and more adequately respond to the social changes swirling around them. Bender became an influential early mentor to Yoder. Guy Hershberger (1896-1989), a professor at Goshen College who researched and wrote extensively on the questions of war, peace, and human relationships, was another early mentor.[9]

Yoder's personal correspondence during the 1950s and 1960s demonstrates that he was helping Mennonites formulate a more viable and engaged social ethic from an Anabaptist perspective in response to the challenges of the postwar world.[10] Part of that task included responding to the challenge posed by Reinhold Niebuhr (1892-1971), the most prominent American Protestant social ethicist as well as the most formidable theological opponent of pacifism of this era. While Yoder's only direct response to Niebuhr was an article he wrote for the *Mennonite Quarterly Review* in 1955, it is evident that Niebuhr loomed large behind much of his work during those early years.[11] Niebuhr's abstract conceptualizations frustrated Yoder, who believed that they failed to take either Jesus or the church seriously. In 1956, Yoder wrote to two other young Mennonite scholars, "What we should be defending against Niebuhr is not sectarian ethics but Christ."[12] The significance of this statement is that is shows the beginning steps of his development of the notion of the "politics of Jesus."

As a young man, Yoder left for Europe in 1949. The third chapter studies how Yoder's European assignment with the Mennonite Central Committee in the postwar era shaped his thought. His interaction with European Mennonites and with the established European Protestant churches (*Landskirchen*) provided him with a whole new arena for engaging pressing theological and social questions. Americans often overlook the extent to which his early thought was a response to this European context. In these years Yoder was also introduced to ecumenical discussions through the Puidoux theological conferences sponsored by the World Council of Churches, which explored the question of war in the 1950s and the early 1960s.[13] Yoder became a spokesperson for the historic peace churches in those gatherings.

While in Europe, Yoder pursued doctoral studies at the University of Basel. There he studied with Oscar Cullmann (1902-1999) in New Testament and Karl Barth (1886-1968) in theology. Chapter four assesses their influence on Yoder's thought as a doctoral student at the University of Basel. Various scholars have noted Yoder's indebtedness to Barth. Sometimes overlooked is the fact that Yoder's commitment to Anabaptist theology meant that he never had an easy, mutually respectful relationship with Barth. Also overlooked is the contribution that Oscar Cullmann had on Yoder's thought, especially on his formulation of the "politics of Jesus."

Yoder's doctoral work at the University of Basel focused on the disputations between the Anabaptists and the Protestant reformers in Switzerland.[14] Chapter five of this book studies how Yoder's doctoral dissertation shaped his theology. As Yoder scholars Mark Thiessen Nation and Michel Cartwright state, one cannot understand Yoder's central theological convictions without knowing what he was doing in his dissertation on the sixteenth-century disputations between the Anabaptists and the Protestant reformers in Switzerland.[15] My analysis reveals that, in a circuitous way, Yoder's notion of the "politics of Jesus" grew out of his historical research on the sixteenth-century Anabaptists. After studying Yoder's dissertation, one can recognize that his subsequent academic career was a further development and explication of theological themes he found in his Anabaptist research.

After returning from Europe, Yoder began teaching at the Associated Mennonite Biblical Seminary in Elkhart, Indiana, in 1963. Throughout his career, he lectured on peace and justice topics in ecumenical and inter-religious forums. He became a professor at the University of Notre Dame in 1977; there he encountered Catholic moral theology and helped found the Joan B. Kroc Institute for International Peace Studies. Yoder worked at Notre Dame until his death in 1997.[16] While his early years and his European experience were formative in his development of the "politics of Jesus" as a radical constructive effort in theology and social ethics, his mature work was done during the years he taught at the Associated Mennonite Biblical Seminary and the University of Norte Dame.

Yoder's tightly reasoned small book *The Christian Witness to the State* was published in 1964. It articulated a more activist social ethic for Mennonites and shaped Mennonite social practice throughout the rest of the twentieth century.[17] A central argument in the book was that Christ is Lord of all dominion and power (Eph. 1:21). Yoder interpreted this to include contemporary governments and other political entities. Next Yoder carefully critiqued the social thought of his theological mentor Karl Barth in *Karl Barth and the Problem of War*, published in 1970.[18] During this time he kept lecturing and writing on topics related to the social and political stance of Jesus. These materials were published in two books, *The Original Revolution* in 1971[19] and his magnum opus *The Politics of Jesus* in 1972. Much of his subsequent work was a further development and articulation of the "politics of Jesus" and its application to specific social issues.

In many ways the church-state question is formative for Yoder's "politics of Jesus." However, the question of war and lethal violence is never far removed from that formulation; it was the Roman Empire that killed Jesus. Questions of church-state relationships and war were also linked for the sixteenth-century Anabaptists who came out of the Peasants' War. In the following centuries, the question of participation in war defined church-state relationships for pacifist Mennonites. Furthermore, Yoder's experience in Europe after World War II and his dialogue with European Protestants on the question of war made it a living personal issue for him. That deep personal interest in overcoming the scourge of war, usually linked directly with the policies of nation-states, continued throughout his life.

The sixth chapter of this book concentrates on understanding Yoder's mature formulation of the "politics of Jesus." David Tracy's categorization of different theological languages serves as a tool for understanding and evaluating Yoder's thought. This includes what Bernard Lonergan calls the function of dialectics, including comparison and criticism.[20] The chapter describes the lived praxis that informs Yoder's theology, and identifies and discusses the components of his constructive theology via a detailed analysis of his theological language.

The seventh and final chapter of this book considers the application of Yoder's theological ethics by assessing the influence of his thought on religious just-peacebuilding initiatives. To that end, I formulate the basic principles of Yoder's "politics of Jesus" as seen in earlier chapters and drawing on some of Yoder's own applications of his thought to specific social issues. Finally, I relate Yoder's theological ethics to three just-peacebuilding arenas: the dialogue between the pacifist and just war traditions, the social challenges facing churches in the global South and in affluent societies, and the emerging peacebuilding disciplines, including conflict transformation and restorative justice.

Yoder's thought is interdisciplinary and does not fit neatly into a given field of study. In his seminal book, *The Politics of Jesus,* he wrote that his work can be understood as an exercise in hermeneutics in which he seeks to put the social and political meaning of Jesus' life and ministry, as seen in the gospel narratives, into conversation with contemporary theological ethics.[21] Interdisciplinary translation posed some peril, Yoder recognized, but he attempted it to counter our reluctance to consider that Jesus might have had political views that could be relevant to us.[22] In this sense, the "politics of Jesus" is an interpretative endeavor that shaped his theological ethics throughout his long and illustrious career.

For easy reference, the influence of North American Mennonite experience on Yoder's thought is treated in chapter two. Chapter three assesses his postwar European experience. His doctoral studies with Oscar Cullmann and Karl Barth are treated in chapter four. Chapter five analyses his doctoral dissertation on the Anabaptist conversations with the Protestant reformers in Switzerland. An assessment of the mature formulation of his thought appears in chapter six. And finally, chapter seven applies his thought to just-peacebuilding efforts.

NOTES

Please note: The original first editions of John Howard Yoder's classic books *The Christian Witness to the State, The Original Revolution,* and *The Politics of Jesus* are cited in this book because they correspond to the time period being studied. Later printings and editions may have different pagination.

1. Michael G. Cartwright, "Radical Catholicity: Reflections to the Life and Work of Theologian John Howard Yoder," *Christian Century* (January 21, 1998): 44-46.

2. Peter Steinfels, "John H. Yoder, Theologian at Notre Dame is Dead at 70," *New York Times* (January 7, 1998), 16A

3. Cartwright, "Radical Catholicity," *Christian Century,* 44-46.

4. An excellent example of how Yoder addressed the questions concerning Christian faith and culture can be found in John Howard Yoder, "'But We Do See Jesus': The Particularity of Incarnation and the Universality of Truth," *The Priestly Kingdom: Social Ethics as Gospel* (Notre Dame, Ind.: The University of Notre Dame Press, 1984).

5. For the corpus of Yoder's written work, see Mark Thiessen Nation, *A Comprehensive Bibliography of the Writings of John Howard Yoder* (Goshen, Ind.: The Mennonite Historical Society, 1997).

6. Mark Theissen Nation, "John H. Yoder, Ecumenical Neo-Anabaptist: A Bibliographical Sketch," in *The Wisdom of the Cross,* ed. Stanley Hauerwas et al (Grand Rapids: Eerdmans, 1999), 19.

7. Stanley Hauerwas, "Remembering John Howard Yoder," *First Things* 82 (April 1998): 15-16.

8. Mark Thiessen Nation, *A Comprehensive Bibliography of the Writings of John Howard Yoder* (Goshen, Ind.: Mennonite Historical Society, 1997), 16.

9. Albert N. Keim, *Harold S. Bender, 1897-1962* (Scottdale, Pa.: Herald Press, 1998).

10. There are copious personal letters and other materials from that time period in the John Howard Yoder papers in the Archives of the Mennonite Church, Goshen, Indiana.

11. John Howard Yoder, "Reinhold Niebuhr and Christian Pacifism," *Mennonite Quarterly Review* 29 (April 1955): 101-117.

12. John Howard Yoder, letter to Paul Peachey and Lawrence Burkholder, July 20, 1956, John Howard Yoder papers, box 11, Archives of the Mennonite Church, Goshen, Indiana.

13. Donald F. Durnbaugh, "John Howard Yoder's Role in 'The Lordship of Christ Over Church and State' Conferences," *The Mennonite Quarterly Review* 77 (July 2003): 371-386.

14. Mark Thiessen Nation, "John Howard Yoder: Mennonite, Evangelical, Catholic," *The Mennonite Quarterly Review* 77 (July 2003): 357-370.

15. Michael G. Cartwright, "Sorting the Wheat from the Tares," in *The Wisdom of the Cross: Essays in Honor of John Howard Yoder,* ed. Stanley Hauerwas et al. (Grand Rapids, Eerdmans, 1999), 351; Mark Thiessen Nation, "The Ecumenical Patience and Vocation of John Howard Yoder: A Study in Theological Ethics" (Ph.D. diss., Fuller Theological Seminary, 2000), 50.

16. Nation, "John Howard Yoder," *The Mennonite Quarterly Review* 77 (July 2003): 357-370.

17. John Howard Yoder, *The Christian Witness to the State* (Newton, Kan.: Faith and Life Press, 1964).

18. John Howard Yoder, *Karl Barth and the Problem of War* (Nashville: Abingdon, 1970).

19. John Howard Yoder, *The Original Revolution: Essays on Christian Pacifism* (Scottdale, Pa.: Herald Press, 1971).

20. Bernard Lonergan, *Method in Theology* (Toronto: University of Toronto Press, 1971), 153-158.

21. John Howard Yoder, *The Politics of Jesus* (Grand Rapids: Eerdmans, 1972), 5-6. All references in this book are to the original 1972 edition. In the 2nd. ed., published in 1994, the original text was reprinted with only minimal changes but, at the end of each chapter, Yoder added an addendum with additional insights or his response to more recent arguments.

22. Ibid., 11-15.

TWO

NORTH AMERICAN MENNONITE EXPERIENCE

John Howard Yoder's notion of the "politics of Jesus" has roots primarily in his interpretation of the gospel narratives. Nonetheless, even if Yoder's work appears to be straightforward, it involves the reader in a complex conversation with various interlocutors. Exploring the development of his thought thus proves instructive. Nourishing the roots of the "politics of Jesus" in the gospel narrative is Yoder's Mennonite experience. It includes wrestling with the ongoing Mennonite dialectic between separatism and social engagement. His thought owes a debt to Harold Bender and Guy Hershberger, two of his early Mennonite teachers. Finally, it engages ethical issues in American society related to the emerging post-World War II social order.

Until the late nineteenth century, Mennonites in North America, who were spiritual and often direct lineal descendants of the radical sixteenth-century Anabaptists, lived in separate religious communities. As a consequence of the severe persecution Anabaptists experienced in Europe, their Mennonite descendents in North America routinized their beliefs and practices on peace into their daily communal life but eschewed active social engagement. This social posture of withdrawal began to evolve in the twentieth century as the forces of change increasingly impacted Mennonite communities.

These forces of change, in turn, fostered research into the Anabaptist movement as a way for Mennonites to recover and maintain their religious moorings. Harold Bender, dean of Goshen Biblical Seminary, historian, and premier architect of the recovery project, became an influential early mentor to John Howard Yoder. Guy Hershberger, a sociology professor at Goshen College who researched and wrote extensively on questions of war, peace, and human relationships, was another early mentor.[1]

My research studies the conversation of Yoder with these mentors and other interlocutors in the years following World War II. Ironically, it was a cross-Atlantic conversation, even though the gist of it concerned North American Mennonite communities. John Howard Yoder had recently completed his liberal arts education, including various seminary courses, when in 1949 he accepted a church assignment in France with the Mennonite Central Committee (MCC). He was only twenty-one years old and would remain in Europe until 1957, engaged in various church assignments and doing doctoral studies at the University of Basel. Throughout that period, Yoder carried on a regular correspondence with various people about the issues facing Mennonites in the postwar era.[2]

AMSTERDAM 1952

In summer 1952, as a precocious young scholar, John Howard Yoder wrote a letter explaining himself to Harold Bender, his former teacher. He had heard from his friend Paul Peachey[3] that Bender was upset by an ironic and biting essay Yoder had written during a two-week study retreat in Amsterdam. Yoder and six other young Mennonite men working in Europe had met to reflect on their experience and Mennonite realities in the postwar period.

Yoder had been arrogant enough and perhaps comfortable enough with his former teacher to send the sarcastic essay to Bender. Yoder claimed that the essay, woven around the expression "That just about cooks the Anabaptist goose," had no title because it had no message. It poked fun at the distance between Mennonite reality and the claimed adherence to an Anabaptist vision.[4] As both the leading Mennonite churchman of the era and the Anabaptist historian who had crafted the recovery of the "Anabaptist Vision" as a formula for renewing Mennonite churches, Bender could not help but see Yoder's essay as a personal affront.[5] His young protégé had some explaining to do.

The "Anabaptist Goose" essay had been written on a whim at the conclusion of the study retreat that spring in Amsterdam. The young men working and studying in Europe, including John Howard Yoder and Paul Peachey, had come together to gain a better understanding of their experience and current theological issues. They had written various papers exploring questions of Christian discipleship in the postwar world. They sensed that the world had radically changed and that their Mennonite communities in North America were woefully unprepared for those changes. Their reflections conveyed an air of urgency.[6]

European cities had been reduced to rubble during the war, and in the early 1950s whole city blocks still remained in ruins. At the end of the war, MCC had helped resettle thousands of Mennonite refugees from Poland and the Soviet Union into new homes in Canada and South America. Many thousands more had lost their lives as the war swept through their communities.[7] Several of the young men at the study retreat in Amsterdam were still involved in relief and reconstruction efforts. Others were studying in European universities where a consciousness of these realities prevailed. The European world had come apart at its seams.

Paul Peachey's paper on the decline of the West, written for the study retreat in Amsterdam, reflected this apocalyptic perspective. He argued that Christendom in Europe was in decline along with the social structures that had undergirded it for centuries. What this reality called for was a pneumatic Christian fellowship where "two or three are gathered" in primary groups.[8] The European *Zeitgeist* was far from that of secure and prosperous Mennonite communities in rural areas and small towns in the North American heartland. This jarring divide deeply troubled the young men meeting in Amsterdam. It was even more troubling when church leaders like Harold Bender failed to grasp the concerns they wanted to communicate.

In his succinct letter to Bender in summer 1952, Yoder wrote that he was simply trying to state what the sixteenth-century Anabaptists would say if they were speaking to the modern world. He was looking at the contemporary situation in view of their eschatology, their attitudes toward society, and various other questions which he thought could be defended on the basis of logic and the New Testament. He explained:

> What we discovered in our discussion [at Amsterdam] was that
> the revival of American Mennonitism, of which in the last gener-

ation Goshen has become the center, "Anabaptism" a leitmotif, and MCC a practical expression, fails in a number of significant ways to correspond to that consistent Anabaptist attitude. The ease with which the American churches have taken sides in the Cold War is one case in point; their unquestioning allegiance to the American economic system [is] another.[9]

Yoder gave several concrete examples of the compromises that concerned him. One was the willingness of MCC to use funds from the United States Army or the Marshall Plan in the MCC relief and reconstruction efforts without considering the legitimacy of such collaboration in a Cold War setting. Another concern was the North American Mennonite focus on rural community life without confronting their economic relationships to capitalist structures. He argued that such compromises relativized and undermined the Mennonite peace position and made a sectarian hobby out of conscientious objection to military service.[10]

Although John Howard Yoder tried to explain himself to his former mentor, he was not contrite. He ended his letter with this indictment:

> So we almost concluded that the real effect of the revival of the past two generations was not to regain original Anabaptism in the strict original sense . . . but, rather, with the use of Anabaptism as a motto, to make possible a surprising degree of assimilation to surrounding culture and standards on crucial points. That is what my sarcastic essay, written just as I felt it the last day at Amsterdam, tried to say.[11]

The young men meeting at Amsterdam well knew that the European churches, including European Mennonites, had hardly resisted the march toward World War II. They had allowed themselves to be swept along in the nationalistic fervor of their respective countries. At stake was an authentic Christian peace witness that confronted the social forces which had produced such horrific devastation. One place to begin, the young men believed, was with a critical assessment of the peace stance of their North American churches.

North American Mennonites had resisted direct, personal involvement in the war effort. Their resistance included a refusal to buy war bonds or to work in war related industries. More significant was their collaboration with the other historic peace churches, the Quakers and

Church of the Brethren, to organize and run Civilian Public Service camps for their young people as an alternative to military service. However, Mennonites had been slow to get involved in proactive peacebuilding efforts both before and during the war. After World War I, they had largely shunned participation in the peace movement because they feared theological compromise through involvement with groups that did not share their religious convictions.[12]

Now that the war was over, it was especially troubling to the young men at Amsterdam to reckon with the fact that more than half of the Mennonite young men who were conscripted had chosen to enter military service during the war. This occurred despite Herculean efforts by church leaders to have them register as conscientious objectors to war. Even more troubling was the reality that the percentages of young men who served in the military were much higher in congregations most acculturated to North American society.[13] It was such circumstances that prompted John Howard Yoder to warn Harold Bender about making conscientious objection into a sectarian hobby.

A theological perspective was beginning to emerge that would shape all of Yoder's subsequent work. At its core was the conviction that a socially relevant theology needed to take the life and social teaching of Jesus seriously. It would draw on the experience and incipient theological formulations of the sixteenth-century Anabaptists. And it would be credible only to the extent that it was put into practice by faith communities committed to Christian discipleship.

While North American Mennonites tried to avoid overt personal involvement in violence, they had largely eschewed an active peace engagement in American society. Their experience during the war had convinced many of them that they needed to take a more proactive stance. They were increasingly wondering what would happen to their peace tradition as they left their ethnic religious roots and became acculturated into American society—a society with an increasingly materialistic and militaristic bent.

The Anabaptist theology they projected, if it was to have saliency, could not simply reflect the emphasis of a particular denominational body or theological tradition. It had to be ecumenical. Nonetheless, it could learn from the sixteenth-century Anabaptist experience that had so powerfully shaped the original peace commitments of Mennonites. No denominational or theological tradition had exclusive rights to that experience. It belonged to the entire church. This theology, best understood as a distinct hermeneutic, would need to address contemporary social issues. Central among those issues was violence in all its forms as well as related issues of economic justice in a postwar world now dominated by Cold War politics.

The precocious young Yoder at Amsterdam was powerfully shaped by Mennonite experience. That remained true throughout his life. The questions he was asking and the conversations he was engaged in always reflected a Mennonite orientation, even though his constructive work was indebted to various sources and he continually broadened the perimeters of the discussion to include other voices. His teachers at Goshen College and Goshen Biblical Seminary had a deep and lasting influence on his thought. Even before that, his childhood and young adult experience in Oak Grove Mennonite Church (his home congregation in Ohio) contributed to who he was.

American Church and Society in the Postwar Era

While Yoder's thought was shaped by his Mennonite roots, the North American Mennonite communities were themselves profoundly shaped by American society and world events in the postwar era. Much as some might have wished otherwise, Mennonites in the postwar era no longer lived in the culturally and religiously separated communities of prior centuries. They were rapidly adapting to American society. Consequently it is necessary to relate Mennonite experience to the changes that were taking place in the North American church and society in the 1950s.

In 1949, the year John Howard Yoder left for his church assignment in Europe, the Soviet Union exploded its first atomic bomb. American political and military leaders were shocked, thinking a Russian bomb was still years away. Despite the qualms of leading American scientists like Robert Oppenheimer, the United States began pushing for the development of the much more powerful hydrogen bomb. The arms race had begun.

Oppenheimer had spearheaded the development of the atomic bomb during the war. When he expressed his moral reservations to President Harry Truman, however, the president was enraged. Truman told Dean Acheson, his secretary of state and a key architect of the new postwar world, "Don't you bring that fellow around again. After all, all he did was make the bomb. I'm the guy who fired it off."[14] The stage was set for a nuclear arms race that would dominate global relations for the foreseeable future. This is the global context in which Yoder developed his peace theology.

In retrospect, was there any way to have avoided the ideological and military standoff that dominated the world scene in the following decades? Many believed that the Soviet Union would use every means, including American diplomatic concessions, as part of a grand scheme to secure world domination. The other side of this same hypothesis is that the endless demands of the capitalist system for new markets propelled the United States on a course of global intervention. Dean Acheson argued, "We need markets—big markets—around the world in which to buy and sell. . . . We've got to export three times as much as we exported just before the war if we want to keep our industry running somewhere near capacity."[15] John Howard Yoder had these geopolitical realities in mind when he wrote to Harold Bender. North American Mennonites needed to take a hard look at their involvement in these global economic structures. Yoder believed such involvements had a direct bearing on their peace stance, but most Mennonites were largely oblivious to the relationship.

In hindsight, the Soviet Union posed much less of a military threat than many had believed. After the war, it had cut its armed forces from 11.5 to 3 million men, its economy was exhausted, and it had a military budget only half that of the United States. United States strategic planners clearly knew these facts. However, the rhetoric and the politics of Cold War from both sides had attained unstoppable momentum.[16] Even the seminal American theological ethicist, Reinhold Niebuhr, saw the struggle as a battle between good and evil. "We cannot afford any more compromises," he argued. "We have to stand at every point in our far-flung lines."[17] The tragedy is that such thinking left little room for intelligence and flexibility in American foreign policy.

Within American society, the new global political and economic clout brought about astonishing new levels of economic prosperity and consumer spending. According to American historian William Chafe, rarely has a society experienced such rapid and dramatic change. Families previously unable to own a home were now moving to new homes in the suburbs. The advent of television led to new forms of advertising.

First a one-car and then a two-car family became the norm. Soon a ribbon of highways connected the inner cities and the new suburban communities. Interstate highways were being built. All kinds of new household appliances appeared. Middle class families could debate about whether to take a two-week vacation or build an addition to their house. "Between 1947 and 1960," Chafe observed, "the average real income for American workers increased by as much as it had in the previous half-century."[18]

This unprecedented prosperity, however, did not lead to a sense of security for most Americans. In spring 1952, American and allied forces reached a stalemate in the Korean War. It became a war that most Americans wanted to forget, but they were confronted with the distasteful business of negotiating a truce and the repatriation of prisoners with their North Korean and Chinese adversaries.[19]

A Cold War mentality had set in. Sinister enemies were seen and imagined on every front. Senators Joseph McCarthy and Richard Nixon built their careers on fighting alleged Communists and Communist sympathizers in the United States government and other American institutions. The Republicans saw it as their chance finally to win national office and the presidency. Democrats would spend the next thirty years trying to prove they were not soft on communism.[20] It was a most necessary time for American Christians to reexamine their social ethics. Did the social and ethical claims of Jesus have anything to say to such things?

American church leaders were preoccupied with other matters. On the one hand, a mood of optimism prevailed as Americans spread their own conceptions of morality and spirituality to the rest of the world, while other great nations had been physically and spiritually drained by the war. On the other hand, despite the new American prosperity, there were prophets of doom. Cardinal Francis Spellman, the very political Catholic leader who ruled the New York Archdiocese, thought the nation was at war for its very soul against the brutal bludgeon of communism. The editors of the Catholic journal, *America,* suggested that it was necessary to wage "holy war" to keep these forces at bay.[21] Fighting communism, promoting evangelism, expanding institutions, and offering individuals inner security in an atomic age were seen as important priorities.

For several decades the Great Depression and then the war had frozen any plans by the American churches to expand programs and buildings. The move of middle class families to the suburbs added to the pressure to build new churches in these communities. In the postwar era, all the Protestant denominations began to build new facilities. Methodists spent almost half their operating budget on new buildings and improvements. Catholics embarked on major programs that included 125 new hospitals, 1,000 new elementary schools, and 3,000 new parishes. Church membership increased rapidly. A Methodist church study in 1948 showed that membership had increased faster than at any time since 1925. Other denominations also had their largest membership gains in decades.[22]

Will Herberg, an astute interpreter of American religion and society, notes that church membership in the United States grew from about 57 percent of the population in 1950 to about 63 percent in 1958. These figures represented a historical high for church membership in the United States.[23] At the same time religion had little or no influence on politics or business. This pointed to a catastrophic divorce between the public and private spheres in American religion and society. Religion had been relegated to the private sphere. American religion was broadly popular but quite shallow.[24]

What Will Herberg called "The American Way of Life" constituted the common religion of American society. Politically this common religion represented a commitment to democracy; economically it represented a commitment to free enterprise. It honored the values of individualism and pragmatism. In crucial respects, the three predominant religious bodies, Protestants, Catholics, and Jews, undergirded this common American religion. In that respect, American religion and secular society had similar sociological roots.[25]

Mennonites had to figure out how they fit into the American religious and social scene of the 1950s. They faced a perception of unprecedented social change in their communities during the postwar years, even though church membership remained overwhelmingly rural.[26] Mennonite responses included potentially contradictory inclinations toward both separation and engagement. One response aimed toward separation was an explosion of opening new elementary and secondary schools. Another such response was the Mennonite Community Association, which sought to maintain the face-to-face values found in rural America. This Association promoted the conviction that preserving Mennonite faith required maintaining some form of sociological and cultural separation from American society.[27] Such separation is what John Howard Yoder called a "retreat into the rural community" in his blunt letter to Harold Bender in summer 1952.[28]

Meanwhile, Mennonites were also busy constructing new buildings and expanding their denominational infrastructure. Harold Bender, for example, received a pledge of $85,000 dollars to build a new "church-seminary-chapel" complex for Goshen Biblical Seminary.[29] Such building comprised only part of a larger phenomenon that also included new ventures in publishing, missions, mental health, education, and evangelism. Bender believed American Mennonites had come into a golden age, a belief clearly not shared by Yoder and the other conferees from Amsterdam. Writing for a Mennonite periodical in 1954, Paul Peachey noted that the church had become big business. He cautioned, "The 'Church' has never yet survived development into a temporal power structure. Sooner or later, institutional weight crushes the spiritual dynamic of the church as the community of Christ and the saints."[30]

Yoder and the other young men who met at Amsterdam in 1952 were part of a Mennonite movement toward global social engagement—a fascinating movement of Mennonite young people leaving their rural church communities in the American heartland to take up mission and service assignments around the world. Mennonite historian Paul Toews writes:

> By 1970 there were over five thousand MCC alumni. . . . Overall, the majority of MCC volunteers, long-term or short-term, worked in assignments overseas. Many were young people who came with relatively little experience. MCC, missions, and other agencies of volunteer service opened up new worlds. . . . There was hardly a Mennonite congregation without someone who had international experience.[31]

Such overseas service had a powerful impact on a whole generation of young Mennonites. It enabled many of them to become engaged world citizens, while also resisting an uncritical absorption into American society. It gave them a critical perspective on the emerging American economic and military dominance and helped them see through self-serving American ideological rhetoric. It also gave them a critical distance from their own Mennonite communities with their often petty concerns.

Understanding postwar American and Mennonite responses gives insight into what motivated Yoder's theological work. He belonged to a new generation of Mennonite volunteers working on overseas church assignments. Such experience gave them a global perspective that most American church leaders and theologians lacked.

MENNONITE MENTORS AT GOSHEN COLLEGE

Understanding the American religious and social scene during the postwar years provides a useful backdrop to John Howard Yoder's time as a student at Goshen College. He studied there for two years before graduating with a degree in liberal arts in 1948. He was a lanky young man with a mop of black hair and dark-rimmed glasses. Fellow students knew him as a rather strange genius who sat in classes reading a book. Somehow, he was still able to follow the professor's lectures and enter into discussions. His professors respected his brilliance and resisted being drawn into debates with him. He had the reputation of being a formidable debater who could be harsh, even with professors.[32] Harold Bender thought Yoder was probably the only true genius Goshen College ever had as a student.[33]

Yoder was more urbane and sophisticated than most Goshen College students of that era. He came from a family known for its prosperous greenhouse businesses.[34] He had taken classes at Wooster College in Ohio during his senior year of high school. Because he had been accepted into a special program at the University of Chicago, he did not want to attend a Mennonite college. Out of deference to his parents, he went to Goshen College, on condition that he be allowed to put together his own program of studies and finish in two years.[35]

As a student at Goshen, Yoder loved breaking dress conventions. He wore a necktie with a T-shirt or used his necktie as a belt. He was always reading a book, even in the lunch line or as he walked across campus. He soon had a reputation for not having the best social skills; he obviously lived in his own world.[36] That reputation would follow him all his life. He did not always recognize when social and sexual boundaries had been crossed, leading to situations that caused great pain later in his life.[37]

During this era, Goshen College was a center for Mennonite research and writing on the sixteenth-century Anabaptist movement, as well as the Mennonite peace position. Harold Bender had made his reputation as a scholar and interpreter of the sixteenth-century Anabaptists. Guy Hershberger had just written *War, Peace and Nonresistance,* which would become the definitive work on the Mennonite peace position for the next several decades. Yoder's own thought was clearly influenced by both these teachers. He consciously followed in their footsteps throughout his life, even as he struggled to overcome what he saw as real limitations in their positions.

These two mentors had very different personalities. Harold Bender was a dominating church leader who had the political savvy to get what he wanted. He engaged in negotiations with various factions in the church to build the denominational structures he believed would serve the Mennonite communities. He was known for telling his students where they should attend graduate school and then helping to make the connections to get them there. Guy Hershberger, on the other hand, was more self-effacing. He represented an earlier Mennonite cultural and religious ethos shaped by *Gelassenheit* or humility, in contrast to Bender the modern assertive organizational leader.[38]

The difference between Bender and Hershberger can symbolize the changes that were taking place in North American Mennonite communities in the twentieth century.[39] After a legacy of cultural separatism and resistance to centralized organization throughout the nineteenth century, denominational leaders were now making up for lost time. During the first half of the century they had been establishing denominational institutions including colleges, mission boards, relief agencies, and publishing houses. They created a central denominational structure. The organizers claimed that asserting legislative authority over district conferences and congregations was not their intention. Nonetheless, the organizing phrases they used, such as "to centralize" and "to direct," implied centralized control.[40]

The organizational revolution had broad consequences. The familiar associational nucleus of family, farm, and congregation gave way increasingly to denominational institutional centers. This shift created a degree of local and congregational resistance to bureaucratized institutional structures. The denominational process demanded strong leaders with skills to manage bureaucracies as well as the more traditional spiritual gifts. Such rational, goal-directed organizing made Mennonites more like other American denominations, even when these newly found tools were used toward the ends of separatism.[41]

Becoming a denomination gradually changed the consciousness and orientation of Mennonites as a people, allowing them to feel at home among their neighbors in middle class America. They were rapidly loosing the trappings and the identity of a separatist religious sect, a process largely completed by the middle of the century. Harold Bender, perhaps more than any other person, had engineered that transformation.

Harold Bender and the "Anabaptist Vision"

In 1943, amid World War II, Harold Bender, president of the Society, gave the presidential address to the American Society of Church History. His topic was the "Anabaptist Vision" of the church. According to Paul Toews, no other single twentieth-century event or historical writing has so deeply shaped Mennonite self-identity. Toews states, "It became the 'regulative principle' of Mennonite thought, and insofar as ideas can affect practice, it regulated practice as well."[42]

Bender's "Anabaptist Vision" statement interpreted the Anabaptist understanding of the essence of Christianity in relation to three central convictions: (1) discipleship as a complete transformation of life, following the teaching and example of Jesus Christ; (2) the church as a voluntary and gathered community that practices mutuality and accountability; and (3) an ethic of love and nonresistance.[43] This vision was clearly an attempt to help Mennonite communities find their own path between liberal Protestantism and doctrinaire fundamentalism. Bender saw both these alternatives as the grafts of modernity. Not nearly as obvious to Bender and other church leaders was how much their own program was also a modern construct that borrowed as much from mid-century American Protestant organizational models as it appropriated from the Anabaptists or the New Testament. This borrowing would become a bone of contention between Bender and John Howard Yoder.

Bender based his formulation on two underlying assumptions. One was that modernity's threat was more ethical than doctrinal. Mennonites had always considered belief to be important, but the veracity of belief was demonstrated in practice. The other was a deeply held commitment to a distinctive Anabaptist faith tradition. The "Anabaptist Vision" of the faithful church had a confessional stance and was defined in opposition to other traditions. Bender wrote:

For the Anabaptists, the church was neither an institution (Catholicism), nor the instrument of God for proclaiming the divine Word (Lutheranism), nor a resource group for individual piety (Pietism). It was a brotherhood of love in which the fullness of the Christian life ideal is to be expressed.[44]

Bender was pleading for the church to be a distinctive Christian community. He did not, however, call for a radical withdrawal from society nor for reifying past traditional boundaries. He posed the Anabaptist Vision as a strategy for maintaining an ideological and ethical separation but, at the same time, a fuller integration into American society. Toews writes, "It integrated Mennonites into the world but preserved a rhetoric of difference. It brought respect but gave new eloquence to the language of dissent."[45]

Yoder's thought owes a deep debt to Bender's articulation of the church in relation to society.[46] He accepted the basic premises of Bender's Anabaptist Vision and further developed those ideas through his own historical research on the sixteenth-century Anabaptists. The focus on discipleship, on the church as distinct from and yet engaged in society, and on the centrality of Jesus' peace ethic, all became central elements of his theological ethics.[47] As one of the first tasks in his European church assignment, he helped translate Bender's "Anabaptist Vision" into French.[48] Yet Yoder could be sharply critical of Bender and his program. He resisted the way issues were being framed in the postwar era. There was always an undercurrent of significant differences between them.

On one level, these differences can perhaps be attributed to the tensions between generations. Yoder acknowledged as much in his ironic "Cooking the Anabaptist Goose" essay, when he talked about the normal disenchantment that young people experience when they realize the difference between the rhetoric and the practice of their elders. They come to the realization that the world they have constructed and committed themselves to is not as airtight as they had thought. Yoder wrote:

> What was discovered at Amsterdam . . . was that "Anabaptism" had been for some of us just such a sophomoric attachment to an oversimplification, a student fad. . . . We had adopted under that name a set of ideals which went remarkably far toward explaining things, with fruitful and practical applications in some crucial

areas of Christian ethics and sociology. At the same time it could claim to incarnate faithfully much of the sense and spirit of the New Testament. Thus "Anabaptism" united all the advantages a psychological sophomore could want: become academically respectable through the last half-century's scholarship, a synthesis of ethical and social ideas with remarkably few loose ends, which dictated not only a philosophy, but a channel for action. . . . And it put us in the comfortable position of being able to talk back to "compromisers" . . . accusing them of plain and simple disobedience to the pure and clear truth.[49]

Such a coming of age was surely compounded by their exodus from rural communities in the American heartland followed by immersion in the cultural and social traditions of Europe. Calvin Redekop, one of the young men who was in Europe with John Howard Yoder, spoke of it as rural North American Mennonites running up against a society with twenty centuries of history and culture. From this perspective, they could see the sociological and institutional shifts taking place in their North American Mennonite communities in a way that most of their contemporaries could not.[50]

The Clash Over Mennonite Church Polity

The immediate issue on which John Howard Yoder clashed with Harold Bender was Mennonite church polity. The clash also included such related issues as biblical interpretation and the relationship between church and society. Given the broader theological and ethical concerns of both men, it seems like a strange place to lock horns. The conflict reflects, however, how central the life of the Christian community was to their theology. It reflected the Mennonite communal ethos that helped shape them and their concerns. That ethos would have a profound bearing on Yoder's shaping of a relevant Mennonite peace ethic in response to the social changes taking place in American society.

Yoder had a pervasively congregational understanding of the church. Its roots were in his home congregation, the Oak Grove Mennonite Church, which had a strongly independent identity and had experienced significant tensions with denominational leadership structures in Ohio when Yoder was a teenager and young adult.[51] Yoder criticized denominational structures that did not respect the integrity of local congregations. He objected to the movement toward adopting the

Protestant model of a single, seminary-trained, and salaried pastor in Mennonite congregations. He also wanted North American Mennonites to take a more radical and prophetic stance in relation to the emerging postwar social order in the United States.

In a significant way, those concerns put Yoder at cross purposes with Bender. Bender's Goshen Biblical Seminary was an institution committed to training pastoral leaders based on the Protestant model of pastoral leadership. As a modern church leader and the dean of the seminary, Bender had invested his life in that enterprise, and he had worked hard to overcome traditional Mennonite reservations to such changes in congregational leadership patterns. Bender must have found it particularly galling to now be challenged on those same issues by a young scholar in whom he had invested so much time and energy.

Their confrontation, which had all the angst of an intergenerational conflict, centered around an article on the New Testament view of ministry that Yoder had circulated and eventually published in the *Gospel Herald*, the periodical of the (Old) Mennonite Church. In the article, Yoder argued essentially that the New Testament model of church leadership differed significantly from the Protestant model being adopted by Mennonites. He argued that both the hierarchical idea of a bishop, with oversight for several congregations, and the idea of a single salaried pastor were foreign to the New Testament. Instead, he advocated a non-salaried pattern of multiple leaders or elders within a congregation and more congregational autonomy within church structures. Yoder thought this model was more in keeping with the New Testament pattern and had more credence than copying from Presbyterian or Methodist models, which only accentuated the split between the clergy and the laity.[52]

The vehemence of Bender's response to Yoder's article is startling. After he read an early draft, Bender wrote a strongly worded letter to Yoder, stating:

> Contrary to your impressions (and I do not see where you got your impressions) a strong anti-hierarchical and pro-brotherhood trend is evident in the church today. . . . Who "sold you" on exclusive N.T. or Anabaptist congregationalism? . . . Your objection to discipline and church order disturbs me, still more. Are you moving toward a radical individualism? . . . John, what has happened![53]

Indeed, what had happened? Their clash indicated a fundamental difference of opinion about Mennonite church structures and the direction of Mennonite church polity in the postwar period. Yoder was voicing his increasing skepticism about twentieth-century Mennonite denominational structures. He was deeply concerned that, in the desire to fit into the American church scene, Mennonites were uncritically copying from Protestant church models and ignoring the genius of Anabaptist-Mennonite forms of congregational life. Yoder and David Shank wrote a more extended article in *Concern,* an independent publishing venture they had helped to organize. That article further expanded the argument for the primacy of the local church. They argued that even using a denominational name such as "The Mennonite Church" was heretical if this implied that the denominational organization itself was a church rather than a servant of the local church.[54]

Central to the debate was the reality that traditional patterns of leadership within Mennonite communities could be very authoritarian. Simple farmer bishops and preachers, ordained for life, could wield an inordinate amount of influence on many matters, including things like prescribed forms of dress. Face-to-face relationships in small rural communities had always tempered such discipline. The organizational structures created in the twentieth century, however, often exacerbated such authoritarian tendencies.[55] Yoder had experienced such authoritarianism firsthand in his boyhood congregation's struggle with the Ohio Mennonite Conference.

To combine such tendencies with a Protestant model of a powerful trained and salaried pastor who came from outside the congregation had the potential to further exacerbate the problem. Yoder felt this much more keenly than did Bender. Actually, Bender had a hard time understanding what Yoder was talking about. Bender had devoted his life to shaping these new denominational structures. He believed that creating modern organizational patterns actually provided more space for lay participation. Bender found it hard to admit how much he and a small cadre of men ran everything in the North American Mennonite world in the postwar era. Yoder was one of the few people who had the courage to push him on such issues.

Yet, for all the harsh language in their letters, one gets the sense that Bender and Yoder respected each other and strove for mutual understanding.[56] Two issues dominated their conversation. One was what

Yoder saw as the parochialism of Mennonite church leadership. He complained to Bender that many of his former classmates had never studied anywhere but at Goshen Biblical Seminary. Now, their pastoral concerns did not extend further than their own backyards. They could not even understand the questions that Yoder and the other young people in Europe were trying to answer. These seminary trained pastors lacked the ability to confront issues of American economic and military practices in the world. The only response Yoder and those like him received to such questions was a defensive attitude and a desire to end the conversation.[57]

The second issue in the conversation between Yoder and Bender was the impact that American denominationalism had on Mennonite communities. Mennonites had emigrated from Europe to North America as dissenting religious communities. On the American frontier, they had formed religious communities bounded by a distinct Germanic ethnicity, reinforced by separatist theology and communal practices. Yoder sometimes caustically referred to these communities as a *Corpus Mennonitum*. Over the course of the twentieth century, these separatist religious communities had taken on the trappings of an American denominational structure. Yoder believed this situation called for critical evaluation. To what extent, he asked, did these developments faithfully express the nature of the church as seen in the New Testament? To what extend did this situation reflect the Anabaptist origins that Bender claimed as a guiding vision? Such troubling questions had no easy answers.[58]

Yoder went to the New Testament for answers. What he claimed to find there was a focus on the local church and a congregational organizational structure. Harold Bender, on the other hand, argued that the New Testament demonstrated different kinds of church models and was essentially indifferent to types of organization.[59] When he asked Yoder who had sold him on his idea of a congregational New Testament church polity, Yoder replied that it was the New Testament itself, along with the help of Oscar Cullmann and other European teachers.[60]

At first glance, the debate about church polity may seem extraneous to the central concerns which led Yoder to develop the notion of the politics of Jesus. Upon further reflection, however, we can see that it is cut out of the same cloth. Yoder cared deeply about the life of Mennonite communities in North America. Crucial was their ability to embody a distinctive peace ethic centered in the gospel of Jesus Christ. A paramount concern was the ability of these communities to negotiate the transition from a traditional separatist, ethnic embodiment of faith to an expression more acculturated to American society. That transition would take imagination, creativity, and a communally oriented praxis rooted in the gospel. In Yoder's view, borrowing wholesale from Protestant denominational theology and organizational patterns would be the death knell to the kind of community that could live in a prophetic and transformative relationship to American society. That was the issue on which Yoder kept pushing Bender.

A related issue concerned the extent to which North American Mennonite communities, as distinct sociological and cultural entities, embodied the gospel of Jesus Christ. Both Bender and Guy Hershberger were more comfortable with Mennonite cultural distinctives and social structures than Yoder. Yoder always expressed a degree of alienation from Mennonite cultural Christianity, that Corpus Mennonitum. He kept insisting that such cultural Christianity needed to be radically critiqued from the perspective of its originating religious events. His resources for such a critique were historical research and theological reflection on the life of Jesus, the early church, and the sixteenth-century Anabaptists.

GUY HERSHBERGER AND AN ETHIC OF NONRESISTANCE

In many ways Guy Hershberger shaped John Howard Yoder's thought as profoundly as did Harold Bender. Bender's contribution was in historical research and his articulation of the Anabaptist vision. Hershberger's contribution came in working out the implications of Jesus' love ethic and Mennonite peace theology in relation to the social realities of the twentieth century. Like Bender, Hershberger had a profound respect for Yoder's intellectual gifts and his Christian commitment.[61]

In the middle of World War II, Hershberger articulated a peace theology that promised to find a way out of the impasse between a traditional Mennonite nonpolitical and separatist stance and a more proactive, political, and ecumenical stance. To traditional Mennonites and those who had borrowed heavily from American fundamentalism, any peace theology that even hinted at public advocacy or peace activism smacked of liberalism. In contrast, Hershberger argued that, already in the Old Testament period, God's plan was for nations to live in peace.

He believed that a single moral law of love and peace manifests itself throughout the Bible. Such claims seemed suspiciously liberal to Mennonite conservatives who had a strict "two-kingdom" theology with a sharp distinction between God's will for the church and God's will for the nations.[62]

Hershberger was no liberal. He took great pains to differentiate his position from Protestant liberalism and various other kinds of pacifism. On the very first page of his book, *War, Peace, and Nonresistance,* he argued that biblical nonresistance was not the same as Gandhi's campaign of active nonviolence in India. He thought Gandhi's program "was really a form of warfare, since its primary purpose was to bring about the submission of the opposition through compulsion."[63]

Hershberger's argument rested on his distinction between "doing justice" and "demanding justice." Mennonites should submissively do justice in their own individual and corporate lives rather than demand justice for themselves or others. They should seek to do the will of God and be willing to experience suffering rather than demand social justice. Their goal should be to create an alternative community of love and peace—a colony of heaven. Hershberger pointed to the long Christian tradition of contributing to society by building separate, dissident communities. Like his conservative Mennonite critics, he also had a separatist, two-kingdom theology, but one in which Christians clearly contributed to society.[64]

This often acrimonious Mennonite debate has to be understood in relation to the rise of anti-modernist fundamentalism among Mennonites in the first half of the twentieth century. It involves complex issues related to a conservative rural mentality, internal and external cultural changes, fear of their own church-related institutions, increasing pluralism, and the raging battle between liberals and fundamentalists within American Protestantism. There were rumblings of this struggle early in the century, but the storm finally hit after World War I.[65]

In particular, the struggle over anti-modern fundamentalism involved a renewed separatist effort to draw a clear line between Mennonites and American society in the aftermath of World War I. The war experience had caught Mennonites off-guard, unprepared to respond to the difficult questions of military service and to the general public support of the war effort. They were shocked by the hostility they faced from both the government and local communities during the war, in-

cluding mob actions that burned several Mennonite church buildings.
Church leaders were clearly alarmed.[66]

Such anxiety also reflected a general American cultural crisis after
World War I. George Marsden, scholar of American fundamentalism,
sees a relationship between this cultural crisis and the growing fundamentalist theological militancy in America. Premillennialists argued
that Christians should separate themselves from the world, even to the
extent of not voting. During this time, various Mennonites began
adopting similar anti-cultural arguments, along with the accompanying
premillennial theology.[67]

Among Mennonites, fundamentalism also included a renewed emphasis on distinctive plain dress, now defended on clear theological
grounds. The common argument was that nonconformity and nonresistance went together. Nevertheless, even the most strident Mennonite
fundamentalists never completely identified with the larger fundamentalist movement. According to them, Protestant fundamentalists did
not include all the fundamentals, such as nonconformity and nonresistance. The agenda of Mennonite fundamentalists was to arrest the
church's slide into worldliness. John Horsch, a fundamentalist Mennonite leader, wrote in 1921:

> The great war is unanswerable proof that, despite the belief in
> man's natural goodness and the world as God's kingdom; despite
> the "genial culture gospel" of social and moral improvement, of
> education and material advancement, the nature of the world has
> not changed. The world is, in the final analysis, as antagonistic to
> true Christianity as it ever was.[68]

Until the middle of the twentieth century and beyond, this strong
anti-cultural bias permeated Mennonite communities. Ironically
enough, Mennonite experience during World War II began to change
this orientation. That experience differed radically from the Mennonite
experience during World War I. In the second war, Mennonites collab-
orated with Lewis Hershey, the government director of Selective Service, to set up and run Civilian Public Service camps for conscientious
objectors. The historic peace churches financed and ran these work
camps under the general oversight of the Selective Service, as an alternative to military service. Nearly twelve thousand young men served in
these camps set up in various parts of the country. They worked at pub-

lic service tasks such as soil conservation, forest service, and staffing mental hospitals.[69]

Lewis Hershey had encouraged Mennonites to accept this arrangement for two reasons. One was the public respect they would gain by performing service of national importance. The other was that it would enhance the religious service ideals of their own communities. He was right on both counts. Mennonites emerged from the wartime experience with more confidence about their place in American society and with a revitalized sense of their own mission.[70]

These were the tensions Guy Hershberger needed to negotiate in his peace theology. His book, *War, Peace and Nonresistance,* provided a broad and sweeping treatment of the topic. It began with an overview of war in human history. It studied the issue of peace and war in the Bible and argued that Christ's example of self-giving and nonresistant love was God's moral law for Christians. It discussed peace and war in church history, focusing on the experience of the early church and the historic peace churches, especially the Mennonites. The book differentiated Hershberger's position of "biblical nonresistance" from other peace positions and finally addressed the social implications of his position in diverse situations such as industrial conflict, race relations, and economics.

The book tried to do much more than one volume can adequately address. Nevertheless, it laid out the issues in a way that made them accessible to many Mennonites and gave them tools to use in relating their historic peace position to the complexities of the modern world. Yoder's work owes a clear debt to Hershberger's book even when Yoder goes beyond it or refutes Hershberger's positions. Hershberger had defined the issues that the next generation of Mennonites would need to address.

A Developing Peace Theology

While Hershberger saw a single moral law of love in Scripture, he differentiated between God's active and permissive will. To repudiate the law of love was to fall under the wrath of God and become subject to the law of cause and effect. From this point of view, there are two levels of humanity. One is a Christian level that accepts God's law of love and attempts to live according to this law. The other is a sub-Christian level that rejects God's law and lives according to the law of cause and effect.

Even so, God does not forsake them. In that respect, the state's function of maintaining law and order should be understood as part of God's permissive will.[71]

Hershberger's approach spoke to a central problem for pacifists. How could an ethic of love that forbade the taking of human life be reconciled with legitimate government police functions in society? In a letter to the young men who had been in Amsterdam with him, Yoder made an argument that was similar to Hershberger's. One of them had raised the troubling question of one's duty to kill a person to keep him from killing someone else. Yoder responded that the question is worrisome only because we do not "reason on the base of the radical dichotomy between the order of conservation and that of redemption." His response correlates with Hershberger's active and passive will of God. But Yoder did not stop there. In a move that would become characteristic of his ethical thinking, he examined the presuppositions behind the argument. He insisted that the "kill-to-prevent-more-killing" argument involved a crowd of non sequiturs:

- The primary purpose of war is never to prevent other people from being killed.
- The assumption that he is going to kill more people than you are is an unfounded prediction. Especially if your war is successful, you will probably end up having killed more people than the enemy did. This is apparently the case in Korea.
- The whole argument is an attempt to derive ethical means from predicted results. Even if ends could justify means, the prediction that he will kill more people than you is not objectively verifiable.
- My first responsibility is the people I kill, not those whose potential murderers I don't kill. The Christian's first duty is to love, not to coerce others into not committing unloving acts.
- This argument is really a dishonest one. The real motive in war, especially in preventive war such as the argument advocates, is self-defense or self-assertion; the altruism is only pretense.[72]

Yoder returned to his dichotomy between conservation and redemption in his refutation of what he called the kill-to-prevent-more-killing argument. He said the argument was circular and based on the assumption "that killing is bad and a little killing less bad than much killing." He called it good conservation logic. A person committed to a redemptive ethic does not reject the rightness of such logic but refutes its relevance for those of us who aim at something better than the least evil.[73] The task of Christian ethics is to challenge all to live according to God's norm of *agape* or self-giving love.

Yoder continued to develop and refine this ethical perspective. For example, he formed it into a paper for a study conference on "The Lordship of Christ over Church and State" held at Puidoux, Switzerland, in 1955. The paper was then reworked as part of a study assignment given to him by the Institute of Mennonite Studies in 1958-1959. It was finally published as the brief volume *The Christian Witness to the State*.[74]

Hershberger insisted that there was a major distinction between his ethic of biblical nonresistance and other forms of pacifism and nonviolence. Biblical nonresistance meant that Christians would eschew every form of coercion, including nonviolent protests, because these were actually a form of warfare intended to force the other party to accept one's demands.[75] At the same time, Hershberger's biblical nonresistance recognized that, in a sinful society, governments needed to use force to maintain law and order. Nonresistant Christians could witness to the government about their own stance but should never demand that the government itself follow this course. Christians had a duty to submit to government unless they were forced to violate their own conscience. Such considerations ruled out making any demands about how a government would conduct its own affairs.

This separatist ethic reflected the sociology of past generations of Mennonites in rural America who kept clear boundaries between themselves and the larger society. Reflecting a medieval worldview, they thought of themselves as the subjects of a given state rather than as citizens who made their contribution to social policies. Hershberger argued on biblical grounds that this separatist stance was the position of Jesus and the early Christians. The problem with other forms of pacifism, Hershberger believed, was that they did not accept this radical ethic. His critique applied equally to international peace plans, Quaker pacifism, liberal Protestant pacifism, the Social Gospel, Tolstoy, and Gandhi.[76]

Why did Hershberger feel the need to make such distinctions so categorically? One reason was his deep appreciation for the face-to-face relationships as experienced in the rural Mennonite communities he knew and loved. He had involved himself deeply in efforts to save this community ethos. He worked with other Mennonite academics to promote small-scale, rural community life, which coincided with a larger American movement to counter rapid urbanization. Hershberger believed that only such small, face-to-face communities could function without overt coercion. He feared the emerging impersonal, industrial society. He sensed that the rural culture and community structures that had nourished Mennonite nonresistance were being lost under the pressure of modernity.[77]

Second, Hershberger made such distinctions to protect himself against the accusations of Mennonite fundamentalists who would not hesitate to paint his peace ethic with a liberal brush. A third reason was his fear that young Mennonites looking for a more engaged social stance might find these pacifist alternatives attractive. He feared that these alternatives could lead young people far from their Mennonite roots.

Hershberger's ongoing debate with Kermit Eby illustrates this later concern. From a Mennonite and Brethren background, Eby became a labor organizer and later a professor at the University of Chicago. He was devoted to advancing the cause of working people. Hershberger had no quarrel with such social activism, but he had a serious problem with the way Eby used political tactics to further the interests of labor. Eby himself eventually expressed dissatisfaction with such tactics and talked about a cooperative model of justice based on Christian love. Hershberger called it "almost a return to the kingdom"; it deeply frustrated him that Eby still would not return to the nonresistance of his religious heritage. Hershberger gave it a personal twist by accusing the nostalgic Eby of grasping after some of the superficial cultural trappings of his peace church ancestors, such as his grandfather's beard, rather than the basic principles for which they stood.[78]

It is ironic that Hershberger used the arguments of Reinhold Niebuhr to buttress his claim that nonresistance was indeed the position of Jesus and the early Christians. What is ironic is that Niebuhr had moved from a nonviolence position, much like Kermit Eby's, to a Christian realist position. He now understood Christ's norm of love as a transcendent ideal but not as a possibility in finite human existence so dominated by self centered interests and power politics. He argued, "Love which depends upon emotion, whether it expresses itself in transient sentiment or constant goodwill, is baffled by the more intricate social relationships in which the highest ethical attitudes are achieved by only careful calculation."[79]

Hershberger wrote that no one had done a better job than Niebuhr to show the sharp distinction between nonviolence and biblical nonresistance. Niebuhr had demonstrated that the New Testament position is one of absolute nonresistance that makes no compromises with the relativities of politics. Nonviolence, on the other hand, permits various types of coercion as long as it does not take life. Hershberger quoted, with approval, Niebuhr's argument that "there is not the slightest support in Scripture for this doctrine of nonviolence."[80]

Regrettably, Hershberger too readily accepted Niebuhr's argument that the New Testament ethic is completely characterized by suffering and self-giving love that never resists the aggressor. He also too readily accepted the premise that nonviolent action constituted simply another form of power politics that seeks to coerce one's adversary. He apparently had not considered that a key function of nonviolent action is to reveal the violence of oppressors for what it is. Nor had he considered that a central element of nonviolence is its appeal to the conscience of the oppressor as well as the larger society.[81]

It appears that Hershberger did not completely understand Niebuhr. Even though Niebuhr gave a stinging critique of the idealism of liberal pacifists, he did eventually speak appreciatively of nonviolence. He even said that it was one of the greatest contributions the religious imagination could make to political life. He appreciated its ability to recognize and work within the common human strengths and weaknesses of all people, including one's enemies.[82]

Nevertheless, Niebuhr had little use for nonresistance other than as a pure type through which to critique other forms of pacifism. Hershberger was aware of that and said Niebuhr had thrown away this pearl of great price to fool with the dangerous game of politics. He was stung by Niebuhr's rebuke of the nonresistance position as "a form of asceticism and that as such it is a parasite on the sins of the rest of us, who maintain government and relative social peace and relative social justice."[83] He refuted such charges with an extensive argument about the genuine service that Christians who hold the nonresistance position make to society.

YODER'S RESPONSE TO NIEBUHR

John Howard Yoder engaged Reinhold Niebuhr's thought in an article he wrote for the *Mennonite Quarterly Review* in 1955. It is instructive to see how his concerns reflect but also go beyond the formulations of Hershberger, his former teacher. This article and other sources make it quite evident that Niebuhr had powerfully influenced young Mennonite intellectuals in the postwar era. They had either accepted major aspects of his thought or believed he was the one theologian who needed to be refuted from a Mennonite and pacifist perspective.

Yoder began by situating Niebuhr theologically in relation to the dialectical theology associated with Karl Barth that was popular in Europe during that time. Yoder himself was being schooled in dialectical theology at the University of Basel. The basic difference between Niebuhr's theology and dialectical theology, according to Yoder, was that Niebuhr's starting point was anthropology rather than revelation. This was a strong critique in biblicist Mennonite circles.

Next, Yoder dismissively said that people in continental Europe had not heard of Niebuhr because none of his books had been translated into other languages. He then noted that it is difficult to engage Niebuhr on the subject of pacifism because he does not make a distinction between pacifism as a national political policy and pacifism as an ethical principle for Christians. In contrast, Mennonites typically made this distinction—accusing Protestants like Niebuhr of having no developed ecclesiology and of failing to make a distinction between church and society.[84]

Like Hershberger, Yoder complimented Niebuhr for his insight into the spirit of Jesus as self-giving, non-retaliating, non-calculating,and reflecting God's gracious love. Like Hershberger, Yoder thought Niebuhr's grasp of Jesus' radical nonviolence was a great step forward in the dialogue about the appropriate Christian response to violence. His appreciation for Niebuhr's "impossible ideal" of nonresistant love as seen in Jesus was, however, more nuanced than Hershberger's was. Yet, like Hershberger, he used Niebuhr's New Testament exegesis to argue, "Nonviolent resistance remains a means of coercion and of conflict, and is far from being a faithful translation of nonresisting love into social action."[85]

Yoder still accepted Hershberger's position on violence and nonresistance but was beginning to move beyond Hershberger's formulation of the problem. Hershberger had argued that the New Testament had an entirely apolitical outlook and had nothing to say about how the affairs of state should be run.[86] Yoder was beginning to ask how nonresisting love could be understood as a political option and translated into social action. In other words, he was beginning to formulate his own "politics of Jesus" and ask how it applied to social ethics.[87] Most significant is that Yoder began to refute the common argument that Jesus did not have a developed social ethic, a position both Niebuhr and Hershberger inherited from Ernst Troeltsch.[88]

Yoder, however, accepted Niebuhr's argument that a pacifism that considers pure love a simple possibility in politics is wrong. He saw some validity in Niebuhr's argument that the only legitimate type of Christian pacifism is a sectarian one that admits its inability to give practical solutions to political issues and disavows all responsibility for social justice.[89] Yoder did not completely accept that argument, but he agreed that pacifist Christians need to disavow responsibility for running the social order. He also agreed with both Hershberger and Niebuhr that Gandhian nonviolent tactics were actually a means of coercion in class, racial, or political struggles. Yoder worried that if such tactics proved ineffective, they could easily be driven into violent warfare by their own logic.[90]

Though Yoder appreciated Niebuhr's analytical skills, he was deeply critical of Niebuhr's theological ethics. As Yoder saw it, Niebuhr's ethic placed the responsibility for defending Western civilization above the Christian ethic of love. Such a presupposition about what needs to be defended led Niebuhr to pragmatic conclusions, which run the risk of identifying God's reign with a particular social order or a particular strategy. Furthermore, Yoder believed, Niebuhr did not carefully distinguish between policing and war or the escalation of violence in modern total war, leading to a depreciation of the horror and sinfulness of war as we know it.[91]

In a move typical of his moral reasoning, Yoder accused Niebuhr of failing to analyze the presuppositions of his ethical stance. Some of Niebuhr's central, abstract presuppositions were concepts such as *impossibility*, *necessity*, and *responsibility*. Yoder argued that Niebuhr's insistence on the *impossibility* of Jesus' love ethic in a social world, dominated by self-interest and violence, hides the fact that there would be no obligation or need to choose if there were no freedom. Loving action becomes *impossible* only when one willingly sacrifices it to some other value, which one considers more binding. He made a similar critique of Niebuhr's concept of *necessity*. Nothing is *necessary* in itself. It is only *necessary* in view of a given end. And Niebuhr's concept of *responsibility* basically meant an inherent duty to a given social order through means dictated by that social order rather than by Jesus' love ethic.[92]

Yoder's last criticism points to a central premise of his hermeneutic. He insisted that in the Bible the bearer of history is the church and not a particular nation such as the United States or a civilization such as the West. The church, both as a local body and a global community, is before and transcends all national identities and commitments. The problem with Niebuhr's social ethics is his omission of the church. His attempt to construct Christian ethics directly for society itself, without reference to the church, naturally runs into unresolved and impossible tensions and contradictions. This forces him to derive his ethics from the human predicament, rather than God's redemption.[93]

THE DEBATE WITH J. LAWRENCE BURKHOLDER

It frustrated Yoder that many young Mennonites in his generation found Niebuhr's social ethics so persuasive. J. Lawrence Burkholder, a young Mennonite scholar who had accepted much of Niebuhr's argument about the impossibility of *agape* or self-giving love in real social situations, wrote a paper on the relation of *agape* to the social and political order. Burkholder argued that Christian social ethics need to be more than a consideration of given alternatives. They need to be informed by an eschatology that provides a vision for the future. He wrote, "When *agape* is separated from eschatology it loses not only its power but also its theological reality as a component of the Christian religion."[94]

Yoder responded to Burkholder with a letter affirming his move toward eschatology but faulting him for being taken in by Reinhold Niebuhr's and Paul Tillich's abstractions:

> You deal with abstractions like agape, justice, power, structure as if we all knew what they mean. Actually such terms are just as mythological as the "principalities and powers, thrones, dominions. . . . " we have so much trouble with in the New Testament. Biblically, one must not only say that the ontological dimension needs to be complemented by an eschatological dimension as you say. . . we need to say that ontology is bologna, that only history *is*. There is no such thing as "being." . . . I'd rather discuss how many angels can stand on a pinhead with a man who thinks that matters and will relate the discussion to the norms of Christian theology, than discuss ontology with a pinhead who thinks that his defining a quality makes it *be*.[95]

Yoder said he simply could not see the challenges Niebuhr presented to which Burkholder was trying to respond. The one thing he had learned, Yoder said, in his last three years of studying theology in Europe, was that theology and Christian social ethics talk about Jesus Christ. Ethics talks not about human achievements but about what humans *should* achieve because of what Jesus has achieved in his life of self-giving love. He wrote:

> If you believe in the full humanity and the full obedience of Christ I can't see how Niebuhr can bother you. But if you agree to meet Niebuhr with his own ground rules, having to make agape a disincarnate ethical principle for use without faith, you're lost before you start.[96]

Yoder later wrote a letter to Paul Peachey in which he groused about Burkholder's infatuation with Niebuhr and Tillich. He told Peachey that he tried to respond positively to Burkholder but was very disappointed. He thought Burkholder was tripping over Niebuhr's abstract language, which needed more careful analysis.

Yoder thought Burkholder had a feeling of inferiority because of Mennonite inconsistencies in living up to their peace theology. While Burkholder thought that Mennonites did not have the right to talk because of their imperfections, Yoder considered that stance to be both logically illegitimate and theologically heretical. "I don't want to be uncharitable," Yoder concluded, "but I just can't see what is so formidable in the Niebuhr position for anyone who starts with a clear Christian commitment."[97] In a later letter, sent to both Peachey and Burkholder, he argued:

> What needs to be advocated against Niebuhr is not a new systematic ethical philosophy . . . but the reality of the Holy Spirit in the Church, as the condemnation of all possible apologies for compromise. . . . Christ isn't dependent on whether the Mennonites live up to him. What we should be defending against Niebuhr is not sectarian ethics but Christ.[98]

CONCLUSION

John Howard Yoder's response to J. Lawrence Burkholder shows the confidence and zeal of a gifted young theologian who was beginning to formulate his personal response to the theological and ethical issues of his time. It also reflects the ethos of Mennonite intellectuals in the 1950s who, coming from a separatist background, were working hard to formulate their response to theological currents within Christianity. Burkholder later wrote that Mennonite theological leadership during that era was assured and dogmatic. Since he was more impressed by the ambiguity of Mennonite involvement in American social structures, Burkholder himself did not quite fit that assured circle.[99]

For present purposes the significance of this discussion is that it indicates the direction in which Yoder's thought was moving in 1956. Unlike Burkholder, Yoder will not accept Reinhold Niebuhr's "abstract conceptualizations." He will not meet Niebuhr on his own ground. But, he will also not defend separatist Mennonite ethics against people like Niebuhr. In this respect, he went beyond Hershberger, who did carry on that defence. Instead, he will ground his ethic in a careful biblical exegesis of the social and political stance of Jesus and the early church. He will then put this social and political ethic of Jesus into conversation with contemporary social realities and theological ethicists like Niebuhr.[100]

Yoder was acquiring many of the intellectual tools he needed for this task from mentors and colleagues in Europe. The next chapter focuses on the European contributions to the development of Yoder's project in theological ethics.

NOTES

1. Harold Bender's central role in the development of Mennonite theology and church structures in the middle of the twentieth century is amply documented in the extensive biography, by Albert N. Keim, *Harold S. Bender 1897-1962* (Scottdale, Pa.: Herald Press, 1998). In the chapter "Bender and the Concern Group," 450-471, Keim emphasizes Bender's influence on young Mennonite scholars, including John Howard Yoder. Another excellent historical resource on the influence of both Harold Bender and Guy Hershberger on North American Mennonite churches and the young men who studied under them during this era is Paul Toews, *Mennonites in American Society, 1930-1970: Modernity and the Persistence of Religious Community* (Scottdale, Pa.: Herald Press, 1996). Toews also documents the sociological and religious changes that took place in North American Mennonite communities during that era.

2. John Howard Yoder papers (hereafter JHY papers) in the Archives of the Mennonite Church (hereafter AMC) Goshen, Indiana.

3. Paul Peachey, several years older than John Howard Yoder, was the director of the Mennonite Central Committee program in Europe after World War II. He com-

pleted a doctorate in history and sociology at the University of Zurich and taught for many years as a professor of sociology at The Catholic University of America.

4. John Howard Yoder, "Anabaptist Goose" document, JHY papers, box 11, AMC.

5. See the chapter "The Anabaptist Vision," in Albert N. Keim, *Harold S. Bender, 1897-1962* (Scottdale, Pa.: Herald Press, 1998), 306-331.

6. Paul Toews, "The Concern Movement: Its Original and Early History," *The Conrad Grebel Review* 8 (Spring 1990): 109-126.

7. Paul Toews, *Mennonites in American Society 1930-1970: Modernity and the Persistence of Religious Community* (Scottdale, Pa.: Herald Press, 1996), 199-207.

8. Paul Peachey, "Toward an Understanding of the Decline of the West," *Concern* 1 (June, 1954): 8-44.

9. John Howard Yoder, letter to Harold Bender, July 31, JHY papers, box 11, AMC. The year is not included in the date on the letter. I assume it is 1952 because the Amsterdam meeting it refers to took place in the spring of that year.

10. Ibid.

11. Ibid.

12. Paul Toews discussed the growing Mennonite peace activism and peace theology during this era in *Mennonites in American Society, 1930-1970,* 120-128. Another good source on the Mennonite sociological and theological ferment around questions of peace during this era is the chapter "Modern Challenges and Transformations" in the book by Leo Driedger and Donald B. Kraybill, *Mennonite Peacemaking: From Quietism to Activism* (Scottdale, Pa.: Herald Press, 1994), 39-80.

13. Toews, *Mennonites in American Society, 1930-1970,* 154-183. John Howard Yoder's home congregation, the Oak Grove Mennonite Church in Ohio, had posted a list of their young men who were serving either in the military or in Civilian Public Service during the war. In the list of approximately thirty seven men, slightly more than half had signed up for military service. See James O. Lehman, *Creative Congregationalism: A History of the Oak Grove Mennonite Church in Wayne County, Ohio* (Smithville, Ohio: Oak Grove Mennonite Church, 1978), 256-259.

14. David Halberstam, *The Fifties* (New York: Random House, 1993), 35.

15. William H. Chafe, *The Unfinished Journey: America Since World War II,* 3rd. ed. (Oxford: Oxford University Press, 1995), 71-72.

16. Ibid., 73-74.

17. Ibid., 77.

18. Ibid., 111.

19. Halberstam, *The Fifties,* 101-115. See also Chafe, *The Unfinished Journey,* 249-256.

20. Halberstam, *The Fifties,* 49-59.

21. Robert Wuthnow, *The Restructuring of American Religion: Society and Faith Since World War II* (Princeton, N.J.: Princeton University Press, 1988), 41. See also Charles R. Morris, *American Catholic: The Saints and Sinners Who Built America's Most Powerful Church* (New York: Random House, 1997), 219-221.

22. Wuthnow, *The Restructuring of American Religion,* 35-37.

23. Will Herberg, *Protestant Catholic Jew: An Essay in American Religious Sociol-*

ogy (Chicago: University of Chicago Press, 1983), 47.

24. Ibid. See especially chapters 1 and 5.

25. Ibid.

26. Toews, *Mennonites in American Society,* 186-187.

27. Ibid., 208.

28. John Howard Yoder, letter to Harold Bender, July 31, JHY papers, box 11, AMC.

29. Keim, *Harold S. Bender,* 421.

30. Paul Peachey, "Mennonites in 1954: An Appraisal," *Gospel Herald* (March 1, 1955): 193-194, 196.

31. Toews, *Mennonites in American Society,* 208.

32. Interview with Calvin Redekop, August 10, 2001. Mennonite sociologist Calvin Redekop was a fellow student with John Howard Yoder at Goshen College. Redekop also served in Europe with the Mennonite Central Committee in the post-war era.

33. Interview with Leonard Gross, May 21, 2001. Leonard Gross is a retired scholar and archivist at the Archives of the Mennonite Church.

34. Lehman, *Creative Congregationalism,* 171-172.

35. Mark Thiessen Nation, "John H. Yoder, Ecumenical Neo-Anabaptist: A Bibliographical Sketch," in *The Wisdom of the Cross: Essays in Honor of John Howard Yoder*, ed. Stanley Hauerwas et al. (Grand Rapids: Eerdmans, 1999), 13.

36. Interview with Calvin Redekop, August 10, 2001.

37. I have had numerous conversations with people who told me stories of awkward encounters with Yoder. Such awkward encounters became even more problematic as his reputation as a scholar grew. People wanted to talk with him, and this often became uncomfortable, at best. He could occasionally be abrasively blunt and hurtful. People who knew him well said he was shy and socially clumsy, but that he was also caring and deeply sorry when he had caused hurt. See Nation, *The Wisdom of the Cross*, 23. Later in Yoder's life various women accused him of strange and unwelcome patterns of sexual language and behavior. Those allegations led to a church disciplinary process which eventually fostered a degree of forgiveness and reconciliation. See the series of news articles by Tom Price, *The Elkhart Truth* (July 12-16, 1992).

38. For a portrayal of Bender's forceful personality, see Keim, *Harold S. Bender,* 223-242. Various people who personally knew Guy Hershberger, including Mennonite historian Theron Schlabach, talked to me about his more irenic spirit. For a brief account of Hershberger's role in developing a Mennonite peace theology in the middle of the twentieth century, see Driedger and Kraybill, *Mennonite Peacemaking,* 71-80.

39. This claim is especially true of the ethnic Swiss-German Mennonite communities that formed the Mennonite Church, the denominational body to which Goshen College and Goshen Biblical Seminary belonged. The two other largest Mennonite bodies during this time, the General Conference Mennonite Church and the Mennonite Brethren Church, were of Dutch and North German ethnic background.

40. James C. Juhnke, *Vision, Doctrine, War: Mennonite Identity and Organization*

in America (Scottdale, Pa.: Herald Press, 1989), 119-130.

41. For a helpful sociological and historical analysis of the practices and beliefs of North American Mennonite communities in the twentieth century, see Calvin Redekop, *Mennonite Society* (Baltimore: The Johns Hopkins University Press, 1989).

42. Toews, *Mennonites in American Society,* 104.

43. Harold Bender, "The Anabaptist Vision," in *The Recovery of the Anabaptist Vision,* ed. Guy Hershberger (Scottdale, Pa.: Herald Press, 1957), 42. An interesting question is the degree to which Bender's "Anabaptist Vision" is indebted to Dietrich Bonhoeffer, whose book, *The Cost of Discipleship,* was published by MacMillan in 1937. Bender developed a course entitled "Christian Discipleship" at the Goshen Biblical Seminary during the 1950-51 academic year. The textbook assigned was *The Cost of Discipleship* (Keim, *Harold S. Bender,* 418). I personally remember hearing William Klassen, one of Bender's former students, commenting that they studied Bonhoeffer in Bender's classes.

44. Bender, in *The Recovery of the Anabaptist Vision,* 53.

45. Toews, *Mennonites in American Society,* 105.

46. Many of John Howard Yoder's interpreters fail to place his early work within this Mennonite conversation in the postwar era. One example is Craig Carter's dissertation published as *The Politics of the Cross: The Theology and Social Ethics of John Howard Yoder* (Grand Rapids: Brazos Press, 2001). Carter does better than most by devoting one chapter to the historical context of Yoder's thought. Nevertheless, Carter's work relies too heavily on later conversations in published sources rather than historical research on the postwar era and the relationships between Yoder and his Mennonite mentors such as Harold Bender and Guy Hershberger.

47. This can be seen in Yoder's chapter "A Summary of the Anabaptist Vision," in *An Introduction to Mennonite History*, ed. Cornelius J. Dyck (Scottdale, Pa.: Herald Press, 1967), 103-111.

48. Harold Bender, "La Vision Anabaptiste," trans. John Howard Yoder and Marthe Ropp (Montbéliard: Grand Charmont, 1950).

49. Yoder, "Anabaptist Goose" document, JHY papers, box 11, AMC.

50. Interview with Calvin Redekop, August 10, 2001.

51. Oak Grove was a rather large congregation that was more acculturated into American society than the other Mennonite churches in Ohio. Its Amish Mennonite heritage was strongly congregational. Tensions arose when William Detweiler, a radio preacher, became the pastor. Detweiler emphasized evangelism and downplayed the Mennonite peace position during World War II. He accused some influential members of the congregation of having a "modernist" theology and eventually resigned.

Oak Grove then ordained Virgil Gerig, a young Princeton Seminary graduate, over the objections of influential leaders in the Ohio and Eastern Conference who considered Gerig to be too "progressive." The conference then ruled the congregation out of order and expelled it in 1947. Howard Yoder (John Howard Yoder's father) was the chairman of the congregation at the time.

Oak Grove then became an independent congregation that actively nurtured various inter-Mennonite relationships during the next chapter of its history. Almost twenty years later, it became dually affiliated with the General Conference Mennonite Church and the Mennonite Church. It may be that the go-it-alone spirit that maintained Oak Grove as an independent Mennonite congregation for nearly twenty years was reflected in John Howard Yoder, the most famous son of the congregation. See Lehman, *Creative Congregationalism*, 237-255.

52. John Howard Yoder, "The New Testament View of the Ministry," *Gospel Herald* (February 8, 1955): 121-22, 124.

53. Harold Bender, letter to John Howard Yoder, July 2, 1954, JHY papers, box 11, AMC.

54. David A. Shank and John Howard Yoder, "Biblicism and the Church," *Concern* (1955): 55-64. *Concern* was a pamphlet series published by Yoder and other young Mennonites organized around the group that had met at Amsterdam in 1952. This publishing enterprise was controversial because it circumvented official Mennonite channels and was at times sharply critical of church structures. The periodical began in 1954 and continued until 1971.

55. Juhnke, *Vision, Doctrine, War*, 130-132.

56. One example is their constant conversation about Yoder's MCC assignment and his studies in Europe. At one point, Yoder talked about dropping out of further study. Bender responded, "John, whether you ever preach or not, you can be a major servant of the cause of Christ in the next fifty years in the Mennonite church and through the Mennonite Church to the world if you are willing to be such a servant. . . . You can write, and this can and ought to be a major field of your contribution, but you cannot be the best servant to the coming generation without maximizing your enrichment and growth through preparation. You will never have the chance you now have." Harold Bender, letter to John Howard Yoder, January 19, 1951, Bender Papers, box 42, AMC.

57. John Howard Yoder, letter to Harold Bender, July 6. 1954, JHY papers, box 11, AMC.

58. Langdon Gilkey, another American theologian, has raised similar questions about American denominationalism. He argues that American denominational structures are inherently weak. When the formerly separated, ethnic religious community becomes one denomination among others, it preserves no essential area separate from cultural domination. In this new form it can hardly present the possibility of the transformation of the society in which it now fully participates. See Langdon Gilkey, *How the Church Can Minister to the World Without Losing Itself* (New York: Harper & Row, 1964).

59. Paul Peachey, who was back in the United States by this time, was also involved in this discussion. He wrote a letter to Yoder in which he sought to clarify Bender's position. Peachey was concerned that the debate was getting too acrimonious and cautioned Yoder about "the rigorous tone of some of your letters with Brother Bender and others." He said that some people had been hurt and offended. Paul Peachey, letter to John Howard Yoder, July 25, 1954, JHY papers, box 11, AMC.

60. Yoder's letter in response to Bender was as sharp as Bender's letter to him had been, if not more so. He went so far as to tell Bender, "Goshen's effect on me was to

prolong my intellectual adolescence by five years, though the crux of that observation is slightly elsewhere, it is relevant." John Howard Yoder, letter to Harold Bender, July 6, 1954, JHY papers, box 11, AMC.

61. Hershberger wrote a letter to Yoder appealing to him to join the Goshen College faculty. He pleaded, "Please accept this as coming from my inner heart. It is not put on. It is real. We need you." See Guy Hershberger, letter to John Howard Yoder, April 7, 1963, Hershberger papers, box 1-171, AMC.

62. J. Irvin Lehman, "Teachers and Teachings," *The Sword and Trumpet* 11 (July 1943): 28. Lehman was troubled by the suggestion that God did not sanction state violence. His two-kingdom theology argued that God sanctioned the use of violence by the state but not by Christians.

63. Guy F. Hershberger, *War, Peace and Nonresistance* (Scottdale, Pa.: Herald Press, 1944), 1.

64. Toews, *Mennonites in American Society,* 125-28.

65. Juhnke, *Vision, Doctrine, War,* 262-274.

66. Ibid., 218.

67. George Marsden, *Fundamentalism and American Culture: The Shaping of Twentieth-Century Evangelicalism 1870-1925* (Oxford: Oxford University Press, 1980), 141-144.

68. John Horsch, *Modern Religious Liberalism* (Scottdale, Pa.: Mennonite Publishing House, 1921), 280. Incidentally, John Horsch was the father-in-law of Harold Bender.

69. Toews, *Mennonites in American Society,* 129-153.

70. Ibid., 130.

71. Hershberger, *War, Peace and Nonresistance,* 24-25.

72. John Howard Yoder, "Letter to Amsterdammers," June 4, 1952, JHY papers, box 11, AMC.

73. Ibid.

74. John Howard Yoder, *The Christian Witness to the State* (Newton, Kan.: Faith and Life Press, 1964), 4.

75. Hershberger made this argument throughout his book, *War, Peace, and Nonresistance,* and devoted chapter eleven specifically to the issue. It echoes Niebuhr's similar arguments that Gandhi confuses the moral connotations of nonresistance and nonviolent resistance. See Niebuhr, *Moral Man and Immoral Society,* 242-243.

76. Hershberger, *War, Peace, and Nonresistance,* 202-267.

77. Toews, *Mennonites in American Society,* 99-104. See also Leo Driedger and Donald B. Kraybill, *Mennonite Peacemaking: From Quietism to Activism* (Scottdale, Pa.: Herald Press, 1994), 73.

78. Guy F. Hershberger, *The Way of the Cross in Human Relationships* (Scottdale, Pa.: Herald Press, 1958), 273.

79. Reinhold Niebuhr, *Moral Man and Immoral Society: A Study in Ethics and Politics* (New York: Charles Scribner's Sons, 1932), 74.

80. Hershberger, *War, Peace and, Nonresistance,* 224. See also Reinhold Niebuhr, *Christianity and Power Politics* (New York: Archon Books, 1940), 10-11.

81. Reaching out to the oppressor is central to Gandhi's nonviolent strategy. That

becomes especially apparent in his discussion of *ahimsa* or nonviolence. See Mahatma Gandhi, *Non-violent Resistance (Satyagraha)* (New York: Schocken Books, 1951), 40-42.

82. Niebuhr, *Moral Man and Immoral Society,* 254-255. Larry Rasmussen argues that despite Niebuhr's unrelenting polemic against liberalism, he still always saw himself as standing within that tradition which he sought to reform. See Larry Rasmussen, *Reinhold Niebuhr: Theologian of Public Life* (Minneapolis: Fortress Press, 1991), 22.

83. Hershberger, *War, Peace, and Nonresistance*, 298.

84. John Howard Yoder, "Reinhold Niebuhr and Christian Pacifism" *The Mennonite Quarterly Review* 29 (April 1955): 101-104.

85. Ibid., 110.

86. Hershberger, *War, Peace, and Nonresistance,* 49.

87. Given the sharp differences that Hershberger and Yoder had with Niebuhr, it is important to recognize that they all wanted to develop a politically and socially relevant theology without fusing religion and politics. Larry Rasmussen writes about Niebuhr, "On the one hand, he wanted to avoid fusing religion and politics; on the other, to locate the meaning of faith for historically-decisive action, including political action." See Rasmussen, *Reinhold Niebuhr,* 17. The same could be said about Hershberger and Yoder.

88. Larry Rasmussen indicates the degree to which Troeltsch's picture of Jesus influenced Niebuhr's theology. See Rasmussen, *Reinhold Niebuhr,* 25. Arne Rasmusson makes similar observations about Troeltsch's influence on Hershberger. See Arne Rasmusson "Historicizing the Historicist: Ernst Troeltsch and Recent Mennonite Theology," in *The Wisdom of the Cross: Essays in Honor of John Howard Yoder*, ed. Stanley Hauerwas et al (Grand Rapids: Eerdmans, 1999), 213-248.

89. Yoder, "Reinhold Niebuhr and Christian Pacifism," 110-111.

90. Ibid., 111.

91. Ibid., 112, 117.

92. Ibid., 112-113.

93. Ibid., 115-116. Robin Lovin writes perceptively of the different perspectives on social responsibility between Niebuhr and Hershberger, Yoder, and Stanley Hauerwas. He notes that they all agree that biblical faith cannot be related directly to contemporary social ethics. Niebuhr posits biblical faith as an ideal that informs one's ambiguous engagement in the contemporary social arena. Hershberger, Yoder, and Hauerwas posit the church as a polis that mediates the contemporary application of the politics of Jesus. See Robin W. Lovin, *Reinhold Niebuhr and Christian Realism* (Cambridge: Cambridge University Press, 1995), 93-97.

94. J. Lawrence Burkholder, "The Relation of Agape, the Essential Christian Ethic, to the Social and Political Structure," JHY papers, box 11, AMC.

95. John Howard Yoder, letter to J. Lawrence Burkholder, June 12, 1956, JHY papers, box 11, AMC. One should be careful about over-interpreting Yoder's position on ontology and history in this letter. He was not a thoroughgoing historicist as might be implied from his statement that "only history *is.*" What he is objecting to is abstract ahistorical theologizing that ignores or downplays the historical relevance of

the life of Jesus for contemporary Christian social ethics. It is in this respect that "ontology is bologna." Nevertheless, all of Yoder's work demonstrates a profound historical consciousness and he is skeptical of all attempts to ground theology ontologically in logic and abstract reasoning. For a good introduction to Yoder's epistemology, see John Howard Yoder, *The Priestly Kingdom: Social Ethics as Gospel* (South Bend, Ind.: University of Notre Dame Press, 1984), 46-62.

96. John Howard Yoder, letter to J. Lawrence Burkholder, June 12, 1956, JHY papers, box 11, AMC.

97. John Howard Yoder, letter to Paul Peachey, June 23, 1956, JHY papers, box 11, AMC.

98. John Howard Yoder, letter to J. Lawrence Burkholder and Paul Peachey, July 20, 1956, JHY files, box 11, AMC.

99. Rodney J Sawatsky and Scott Holland eds., *The Limits of Perfection: Conversations with J. Lawrence Burkholder* (Waterloo, Ontario: Institute of Anabaptist-Mennonite Studies, 1993), 18-33.

100. For an informative discussion of the theological ferment among Mennonites in the fifties, see Driedger and Kraybill, *Mennonite Peacemaking*, 83-107. Their interpretation of the debate as a dichotomy between sectarian ethics and social responsibility, however, is misleading. All the participants in this debate wanted a socially responsible ethic. They disagreed about what such an ethic entailed. To what extent was this ethic rooted in the life and practice of the church? Did social responsibility simply mean accepting the definitions of American social elites and people like Reinhold Niebuhr? They are especially misleading in their interpretation of Yoder, who they place on a middle ground between withdrawal and responsibility. That way of framing the conversation completely misses the thrust of Yoder's ethic, which insisted that Jesus' social and political stance has something to say to us. Yoder's radically christocentric ethic challenged the basic premises of the prevailing theological ethics in America during that era.

THREE CHAPTER

EUROPEAN EXPERIENCE
AND THE DEBATE ABOUT WAR

In a significant way, John Howard Yoder's notion of "the politics of Jesus" can be seen as his response to the social, political, and religious realities that he faced in Europe after World War II. The European years constituted an ongoing grappling with the question of how the life and teaching of Jesus informs a faithful Christian response to the challenges faced on all sides, both in the European churches and in society. This European context became the arena in which Yoder would first present his theological formulations of the demands of Jesus in relation to issues of war and peace.[1]

The fact that Yoder went to Europe at age twenty-two in 1949 was not a simple coincidence. North American Mennonites sent some of their most capable young people to serve in Europe in the postwar era. They worked in relief and reconstruction efforts with the Mennonite Central Committee (MCC) as well as in other forms of mission service. They constituted the European segment of a movement toward more intensive social and missional engagement that took North American Mennonites far beyond their rural communities. This movement harnessed the restlessness and energy of many Mennonites who wanted to apply their faith in the world.[2] These young people faced formidable challenges in Europe. Those who worked at refugee resettlement in Germany faced the daunting need of thirteen million internally displaced people, in addition to the millions of refugees arriving from Eastern Europe. In practically every major German city, fifty percent or more of the houses had been destroyed.[3]

Among the neediest were the ethnic German people driven from their homes in Eastern European countries. This group included many Mennonites. In Prussia alone, a community of ten to twelve thousand Mennonites was liquidated. Many of these people lost their lives. Others arrived in western occupied Germany as refugees. For months, more than one thousand refugees arrived daily from the Russian occupied territories of Eastern Europe.[4]

The refugee resettlement project at Espelkamp in the British-occupied zone of Germany exemplifies the work of these young North American Mennonites. MCC helped resettle the refugees from Eastern Europe, who were finding their way into western occupied Germany. That work provides one small glimpse into what turned into a devastating human catastrophe for about fifteen million ethnic German people, who fled en masse before the advancing Russian troops. The Russians associated them with the Nazi military machine that had invaded Eastern Europe and Russia. The human exodus began in 1945, and refugees continued arriving in the West into the early 1950s. Emily Brunk, an MCC volunteer at Espelkamp, tells the stories of these people:

> Though the Russians advanced quickly, a fear of defeat spread even more quickly, and the word was carried from village to village, "The Russians are coming, you must flee!" The old and the sick were the first to go; and then the mothers with children, till finally everyone threw his possessions together and fled. But they left their houses in order, their crops in the cellar, and put their keys in their pockets with the thought that this was going to be unpleasant but temporary.[5]

The sheer terror of the flight of these refugees is beyond description. One refugee woman recalls what they went through:

> The streets were hidden by swarms of refugees. One could no longer go forward quickly enough. The Russians, however, drew nearer and nearer. . . . We drove through woods and over fields with the Russians always three or four miles behind us. And because it was bitter cold, many people froze to death. Sometimes just the arm or leg of a child would freeze and would have to be cut off. At every large town the dead were left behind. . . . As we

fled before the Russians, the fighters and bombers were our greatest fear.[6]

Those who could not flee or were overtaken by the advancing Russian troops had even more horrific stories to tell. Villages and entire cities were torched. People could not sleep because of the noise of the battle. Horses, wagons, and food were confiscated. The front line troops functioned like a running, plundering band. Refugees who did not quickly give up their possessions were shot on the spot. Women and young girls were raped—age made little difference. In addition, neighbors turned on people who were identified as ethnic Germans.[7]

It soon became evident that those who had fled would never be able to return. This stream of refugees included Mennonites from Prussia, Poland, and the Ukraine, with the largest number of Mennonite refugees from the Ukraine. The total number from there is estimated at about thirty-five thousand people. About twelve thousand reached Western-occupied Germany. The rest presumably died or were repatriated by the Russians. MCC volunteers were busy with resettlement efforts. By the end of 1949, MCC had helped resettle more than eleven thousand refugees. Most of them migrated to either Canada or Paraguay, two countries that agreed to receive them as a group.[8]

A European Assignment

When John Howard Yoder arrived in Europe, much of the resettlement work was winding up, even though a small trickle of refugees would continue to arrive for many years. This human tragedy shaped the passions and imaginations of the young Mennonites serving in Europe. Throughout the following decade, MCC work in Europe continued to focus on aid to refugees and poor people. MCC set up smaller facilities in Germany and Austria to meet the needs of more recent refugees. With the help of European Mennonites, they also administered children's homes for the many war orphans. Yoder's immediate assignment was to help administer a children's home in Valdoie, France, and to relate to the French Mennonites in the Alsace region.[9]

With his network of connections in Europe and North America, Harold Bender had helped create the assignment. It was not the customary MCC assignment. It concerned Bender deeply that the European Mennonites had lost their peace tradition. Their young men had served in the militaries of their respective countries during World War II. Bender had recently met Pierre Widmer, a French Mennonite minister, who shared his concerns. He wrote about Widmer in a letter to Yoder, "He is a French Mennonite minister, who was a French officer and was in a prisoner of war camp in Germany for five years, but came out as a convinced conscientious objector. He stands almost alone among the French ministers, but is eager for us to help him."[10]

Part of the assignment Bender had in mind for Yoder was to work with people like Pierre Widmer to reacquaint the European Mennonites with their Anabaptist heritage and its peace tradition. An added perk was that this assignment would give his young protégé the opportunity to take some classes in theology, historical studies, and biblical studies at the University of Basel.[11]

The assignment became a social arena that significantly shaped the way Yoder formulated and expressed his distinctive theological ethics. His MCC experience of responding to the horrific devastation of World War II became pivotal in the development of his thought. It framed his lifelong passion to address the morality of war from a Christian perspective. Furthermore, it is important to recognize the extent to which his lifelong ecumenical contacts and relationships began in this European setting.[12] In addition, his studies with prominent Christian scholars at the University of Basel provided a personal intellectual awakening.

Yoder later wrote to Harold Bender about how this experience made him see that his time at Goshen College had only prolonged his intellectual adolescence. He talked about how difficult it was for him and others who served in Europe to communicate with their former Goshen classmates:

> The result of this growth is that we are excommunicated by those of our former schoolmates who in many cases never studied anywhere but at Goshen, and whose pastoral concerns have kept them largely in their own backyards as far as concerns all the varied experiences which led us where we are. The fact that we have faced and tried to answer questions which they never encountered seems to them sufficient grounds for reproach, and for a defensive attitude which seems like a lack of confidence in their own position.[13]

Albert Keim, who served with MCC in Europe during this same time, talks about how this experience shaped these young people's lives. Even in the mid-1950s, whole city blocks still lay in ruins in cities like Frankfurt. Economically, most Europeans were impoverished, and the Americans, even on a MCC volunteer's allowance, were rich in comparison. This offered educational and other opportunities that would not have been available at home. Almost all of them had come from rural America. They could now study at the best European universities. They were thrust into a setting of great need, yet one with an ancient cultural and intellectual heritage that made the Americans feel deficient.[14]

It was hard to know how to bridge these worlds. Orley Swartzentruber, one of the young American Mennonites who served in Europe in the 1950s, talked of standing in front of the Catholic cathedral in Paris, feeling totally inadequate to the task. How could he even begin to relate culturally and religiously to the people he had been asked to serve?[15]

Albert Keim talks about these differences in relation to the European Mennonites they worked with. The French and South German Mennonites were farmers who talked about animals and crops. That was all very familiar. They had a religious piety that the Americans could identify with. The only problem was that they were not pacifists. The Dutch Mennonites were different. They were urban people. To Keim, they seemed to have few religious sentiments. Their worship services were dull. Afterwards they drank coffee, smoked, and went home. Keim attributed the pervasive secularism in Europe to the experience of having prevailed over a great tragedy. They were a group of survivors in a world bereft of mystery.[16]

Service in Europe also gave these young American Mennonites a unique vantage from which to see and understand the superpower standoff between the United States and Russia in the emerging Cold War. Speaking at the first World Council of Churches meeting in Amsterdam in 1948, American diplomat and Methodist layperson John Foster Dulles tried to enlist European Christians in an aggressive stance against communism. European church leaders like Martin Niemöller and Karl Barth, who had led the German church struggle against National Socialism, were not persuaded. The Europeans resented being pawns caught between the two superpowers.[17]

They feared the specter of war between the Americans and the Soviets fought out on European soil. A large Russian army remained positioned on the Eastern Front. After the Soviets developed an atomic bomb in 1949, the fear included fear of a nuclear war. Such fear is exemplified in the arguments of Mennonite leaders when the MCC headquarters were moved from Basel to Frankfurt. Frankfurt was more strategic for their work, but right at the front where Russian tanks could presumably roll across with little advance warning. Those who were more cautious wanted to keep the headquarters in Basel. Such fears were further exacerbated by the tales of repatriated German soldiers who arrived each week by the trainload from Russia. The soldiers were emancipated and destroyed men who told horrific stories of their brutal treatment in Siberia.[18]

The French villages in which Yoder worked had not undergone the kind of devastation experienced by many German communities. In that sense, Yoder did not have the experience of working first hand with people in extreme deprivation. Nevertheless, these French communities were very poor. Other contacts also put Yoder in touch with experiences all over Europe. The European MCC headquarters in Basel was not far away, and Yoder communicated regularly with MCC volunteers and related to their experiences. It also put him in touch with the different European Mennonite communities and their concerns.[19]

Yoder was soon participating in discussions with different European church leaders as they struggled to respond to the aftermath of the war and the emerging Cold War global order. As a very young man, he had been placed on a world stage with all the challenges that entailed. His remarkable linguistic abilities (he was soon fluent in German and French and would later learn other languages as well) and his keen analytical mind enabled him to make the most of this unique opportunity.[20]

The previous chapter showed that Mennonite experience in America and Mennonite mentors like Guy Hershberger and Harold Bender provided significant building blocks for John Howard Yoder's theological ethics. It is just as evident that his notion of the "politics of Jesus" emerged directly out of the ferment of trying to think and act faithfully in the context of postwar Europe. It is important to recognize this European context, because it counters those interpretations that see Yoder's thought as coming out of the comfort of a withdrawn North American Mennonite community and representing its concern for ethical and religious purity.[21] Such interpretations are simply not true. They miss the extent to which Yoder began formulating his ethic in response to the devastating humanitarian, political, and religious crisis in postwar Europe.

It is easy for Yoder's North American interpreters to overlook the powerful influence his European experience had on his theological ethics. This impact includes the way his European social involvements and European social perspectives shaped him. It also includes his sixteenth-century historical research, which until recently has not been accessible in English.[22] Even more overlooked are Yoder's European church relationships. He was intimately involved in the life of the European Mennonite churches and became familiar with their concerns. Sometimes this involvement included conveying their concerns to North American churches and church agencies. He also became familiar with the German church struggle with the legacy of Nazism and their worries about the emerging Cold War alliances.

Through his involvements with the International Fellowship of Reconciliation (IFOR) and the World Council of Churches (WCC), Yoder developed important relationships with various European pacifists and church leaders. Among them was Jean Lasserre, a former colleague of Dietrich Bonhoeffer. Another was André Trocmé, a French Protestant pastor who had organized his parish to rescue Jewish refugees during the war. Both these men made significant contributions to Yoder's theological and ethical thought. He also worked with leaders from the other historic peace churches, such as the Quaker spokesman Richard Ullmann and the Church of the Brethren spokesman, M.R. Ziegler.[23]

Yoder became a Mennonite spokesperson representing the position of the historic peace churches in the WCC debates about the morality of war. As will be shown in more detail later in the chapter, that participation constituted a formative ecumenical involvement for Yoder. The constitutive assembly forming the WCC in Amsterdam in 1948 issued a statement that "war is contrary to the will of God" and urged all Christians to wrestle with the difficulties of this perplexing issue. The historic peace churches and the IFOR prepared several responses but they did not receive much attention in WCC circles. Later, there were more substantive conversations with European Protestants under the auspices of the WCC.[24]

Relating to the European Mennonite Churches

Yoder's MCC assignment involved him directly in the life of the Mennonite churches in Europe in a way that few other MCC assignments did. (He maintained a relationship with European Mennonites for the rest of his life.) Part of his assignment in 1949 was in religious education and youth work with French Mennonite churches in the Alsace region. This plunged him directly into the life of these churches, which in turn led to connections with Mennonites in other parts of Europe.

Mennonite relationships and church structures can be confusing even for insiders. No formal union ever existed between the various sixteenth-century Anabaptist groups in northern Europe. These Anabaptists, the spiritual ancestors of the Mennonites, were soon scattered even more by prosecution, emigration, and internal conflicts.[25] In places like Germany, Switzerland, Holland, France, Prussia, Poland, and the Ukraine, various Mennonite groups evolved in relative isolation from each other in the following centuries. The distance was even greater between the Europeans and the various North American Mennonites groups. Nineteenth- and twentieth-century mission efforts created even more diversity as independent churches were established in Asia, Africa, and Latin America.[26]

It was only in the twentieth century that a loose fellowship of these various and scattered Mennonite groups began to emerge through the creation of the Mennonite World Conference in 1925. When John Howard Yoder arrived in Europe in 1949, these more formal inter-Mennonite relationships were only in the first stages of their development.[27] It was not long before Yoder, as a very young man, had his hands full trying to negotiate the internal dynamics in the insular rural French Mennonite communities as well as the growing global inter-Mennonite relationships.

Yoder and French pastor Pierre Widmer were given the task of teaching about biblical nonresistance and conscientious objection to war. They soon ran into opposition. Other church leaders claimed that Widmer had taught the youth that a soldier could not be saved. He and Yoder both denied that charge. Nevertheless, French Mennonite leaders told Yoder and Widmer to avoid the contentious subject of conscientious objection to war at future youth camps. Yoder said this violated his conscience and the assignment he had been given. Finally, everyone agreed that they would use more discretion in their teaching. It was evi-

dent that most French Mennonites did not want to tackle such controversial social and religious issues.[28]

Yoder quickly learned that the peace theology he had inherited from
his childhood Mennonite community in Ohio and from mentors such
as Harold Bender and Guy Hershberger did not neatly fit the very different situations of European Mennonite churches. American Mennonites faulted the Europeans for having lost their peace witness in the nineteenth century. The charge contained some truth. Historical documen-
tation shows that they had initially resisted but then gradually given in
to the pressures of universal conscription in Europe.[29] What such an interpretation failed to consider, however, was that the Europeans faced a
significantly different social and political situation than did North
American Mennonites.

The difference in contexts became an increasingly controversial
issue for Mennonites working in Europe after the war. Mennonite
church denominational leaders in North America insisted that joining
the military should lead to a forfeiture of church membership, even if it
was noncombatant military service. Young men who entered the military should be excommunicated, even if their only alternative was going
to jail for their convictions.[30] Yoder called for a meeting on the issue. In
preparation for the meeting he wrote a position paper in which he argued:

> The example of Mennonite history does not support entirely the
> American attitude. Refusal of noncombatant service is a recent
> development. Since the inception of universal peacetime con-
> scription Mennonites have: a) migrated; b) accepted noncombat-
> ant service; or c) occasionally paid exemption fees or sent substi-
> tutes. Mennonite history is not full of churches which stayed in
> countries which permitted no civilian alternative service and still
> refused noncombatant service. We Americans are descended
> from people who migrated rather than face the issue, and have lit-
> tle ground on which to stand, either to preach to European Men-
> nonites or to discipline new converts in favor of a position which
> legally must mean long imprisonment.[31]

In preparation for the meeting, Yoder asked for responses to his position paper from various North American church leaders. Harold Bender wrote a lengthy reply. He raised various objections to the way Yoder

had framed the question about Mennonite participation in the military. He thought Yoder had downplayed the struggles American Mennonites had gone through to obtain exemption from military service. Bender faulted European Mennonites for too quickly giving up the struggle for exemption. With reference to German Mennonites he said, "There was an inner decay before the outer surrender to the German state, and this inner decay, not the power of the state, led to the acceptance of noncombatant service." He argued that an issue of such importance should not be left to the individual conscience; it should be a matter of church discipline. Furthermore, while recognizing that each church needs to adapt to its unique national environment, he asked, "Do we want to start a policy of nationalizing our churches? . . . Should we not maintain a common standard across the seas as respects the direct teaching of the Scriptures?"[32]

A group representing several North American mission agencies and European Mennonite churches met to consider the question. Yoder wrote the final report and appears to have greatly influenced the conclusions that were reached. They were as follows: (1) nonresistance is a part of biblical ethics and is rooted in the heart of the gospel and in the very meaning of Christian discipleship; (2) decisions about church discipline are to be made ultimately by the local church; (3) American missionaries and young mission churches should seek counsel from the existing national churches; (4) a distinction needs to be made between what a missionary teaches and what the local church requires through church discipline; (5) there should be no relaxation of our opposition to militarism.[33]

While the primary debated issue concerned the appropriate response to military conscription, church polity was a significant corollary issue. Bender wanted to use institutional church structures to create a common standard enforced by the power of disciplinary measures, including excommunication. Yoder advocated a more congregational polity that respected the local church as the discerning body. He was just as resolute as Bender in his advocacy of a biblical peace position and his opposition to militarization. The difference was that Yoder was unwilling to tie it to a separatist Mennonite ethic, enforced by coercive church discipline. Because nonviolence is rooted in the gospel of Jesus Christ, Yoder saw it as the ecumenical possession of all the churches. He believed it should be presented as persuasively as possible, but with each church, in broad consultation with others, having the freedom to discern what it means to be faithful to this peace ethic.[34]

The relationship of nonresistance to church membership was by no means the only problem the young John Howard Yoder experienced as he attempted to bridge the worlds between American and European Mennonites. He quickly discovered how difficult it was to remain above the fray in the leadership and personal squabbles among the French Mennonites. The American presence complicated and exacerbated such tensions. These tensions became especially problematic when French church leaders tried to use MCC projects and North American funds to personal advantage in these internal struggles. It became apparent that older church leaders had difficulty respecting Yoder because of his youth. He had to appeal to the older Harold Bender, who was respected in French Mennonite circles, to back up his decisions.[35]

Nevertheless, Yoder continued working patiently, in such a way that he eventually gained the deep respect of European Mennonites. They came to claim him as one of their own. He married Anne Marie Guth, a French Mennonite woman, in 1952. He soon identified so closely with the European Mennonites that he became a spokesperson for their concerns to North American church agencies. A repeated complaint through the years was that the North Americans operated on the basis of their own assumptions, on the other side of the Atlantic without considering the needs or interests of the European Mennonite churches. Yoder's ability to communicate across different communities of discourse was first developed and tested as he sought to mediate between the different Mennonite communities with their unique histories and lived traditions.[36]

These European Mennonite churches spanned several different languages, cultures, and social contexts, and were far from a monolithic entity. The Dutch and North German Mennonites shared a similar background and theological perspective. They consisted primarily of wealthy, urban congregations with historical roots in their immediate communities reaching back to the sixteenth century. Religious toleration came early for them in comparison to other Mennonites, who had migrated from community to community in their search for religious freedom. The Dutch Mennonites had their own seminary in Amsterdam and an educated pastoral leadership. They were theologically and socially liberal and quite active in European WCC circles.[37]

In comparison, the French, Swiss, and South German Mennonites had found religious toleration in remote rural communities. They were marked by centuries of social disfavor and even persecution. Their religious life reflected a focus on survival through the maintenance of simple worship patterns, a self-supporting, untrained lay ministry, and a loosely structured conference organization. It evolved slowly into a small, but solid, folk church. Their religious life borrowed extensively from Pietist and European Baptist sources. The Mennonite churches in central Germany bridged these differences between north and south. They had a tradition of a trained and supported pastoral ministry, going back to the middle of the nineteenth century.[38]

To this mix was added the influx of refugees from Eastern Europe who were settled haphazardly across West Germany. Those who had lived east of the Oder-Neisse rivers were resettled in the West. Refugees from what had once been prosperous Mennonite communities in the Ukraine continued arriving throughout the next decades. For all European Mennonites, World War II took a heavy toll.[39]

It is instructive to see how Yoder viewed the European Mennonite landscape of different churches. He recognized every stream as, in some respect, an authentic representative of the Anabaptist tradition. However, he also spoke of their loss of religious vitality and looked for renewal movements in their midst. In the Netherlands he saw a renewal movement that included Bible study, mission efforts, a new peace emphasis, and a more orthodox theology influenced by Karl Barth. He saw another more revivalistic renewal movement in the south, which borrowed from North American evangelicalism and Pentecostalism. He thought this revivalism had led to a sharpening of Mennonite identity, which included a renewed emphasis on peace, nonconformity, evangelism, and interest in Mennonite history.[40]

This positive evaluation of revivalism is intriguing. Historians of North American Mennonite history generally see evangelical and pietistic influences as leading to a dilution of Mennonite identity rooted in Anabaptism.[41] Yoder argued that the American experience does not necessarily apply to the European situation. His work in France put him in contact with a Mennonite renewal group heavily influenced by Pentecostalism. He appreciated their commitment to Jesus and the way they had established a fellowship modeled after the New Testament churches. He saw this group as being less materialistic, less complacent, more peace-oriented, and more radical in their ethical commitments than were the older established Mennonite churches.[42] He was concerned that the older churches were so rooted in their rural culture and folkways that they were ill-prepared for the rapid urbanization and secularization sweeping through postwar Europe. Rapid social change, Yoder feared, was opening a generation gap that threatened the very survival of these churches.[43]

Several developing strands of Yoder's thought come together here. His epistemological commitment to Jesus Christ is central. He understood Jesus as the suffering Messiah who demonstrated the way of peace through his life and teaching. The ethical and communal expressions that flow from the commitment to Jesus find their fullest expression in churches gathered in his name. Over time, churches lose their vitality and become distracted by cultural, familial, economic, political, and social concerns which compete with, and sometimes usurp, this commitment to Jesus. Yoder sometimes referred to such churches, at home in their cultural world, as *Volkskirche*. His more common and better known phrase was a "Constantinian" church. This term primarily referred to politically established churches. But he also used the same moniker to identify cultural establishment as various types of "neo-Constantinianism." He became adept at making this kind of sociological critique. In Europe it applied equally to diverse groups such as the small culturally rooted Mennonite churches and the large, more politically established Lutheran and Reformed *Landskirche* in Germany.[44]

All these established churches had lost their original vitality rooted in the way of Jesus, a vitality he sought to recover. However, it is too simple to call Yoder a restorationist. He knew that one could not, after many centuries of church history, simply restore a church to the New Testament model. Nevertheless, the New Testament model was his lodestar. Consequently, he sought out reform and revival movements within the churches that could help them more faithfully reappropriate their original commitment to the way of Jesus. That is why he was attracted to such movements within the European Mennonite churches. This helps explain why he never wrote these churches off as being hopelessly compromised by their now comfortable relationships within their respective national societies. However, Yoder also never ceased reminding Mennonites that their Anabaptist ancestors had been ostracized and persecuted because of the religious and political stance they took.

CONFRONTING THE MORAL QUESTION OF WAR

The standard North American Mennonite position on biblical non-resistance, as articulated by people like Harold Bender, received a skeptical reception among European Mennonites.[45] Their skepticism was justified to the extent that the American position failed to take the European situation seriously. There was, however, an elephant in the room that was largely ignored. This was the serious problem of European Mennonite (and North American Mennonite) complicity in the war. In the postwar era, Europeans hardly had the physical ability, let alone the spiritual resources, needed to tackle this question. Especially in Germany, the tasks of meeting the needs of refugees and of reconstruction consumed everyone's time and energy. People just wanted to forget and move on with their lives. Hannah Arendt, a German philosopher and political scientist who had fled the Nazis in 1933 and returned to Germany after the war, wrote:

> But nowhere is this nightmare of destruction and horror less felt and less talked about than in Germany itself. A lack of response is evident everywhere, and it is difficult to say whether this signifies a half-conscious refusal to yield to grief or a genuine inability to feel . . . busyness has become their chief defense against reality.[46]

To a great extent, even the Confessing Church movement that had resisted the Nazi politicization of the German Evangelical Church avoided the war question. Many church leaders simply wanted to return to where they had been in 1933 and begin over. Others, however, wanted to view their church's tradition more critically. They wanted to examine how Protestant nationalism, with its coupling of throne and altar, had blinded the church to the dangers of Nazism and made it ineffective in resisting the march toward war.[47]

These European scholars and church leaders became the colleagues and interlocutors with whom John Howard Yoder debated as he began formulating his response to the question of war. From the very beginning, it was an ecumenical conversation. The Europeans entered the conversation with creativity and passion. They knew that for the most part their churches had been swept along in the war fever that had engulfed the world. It was time for critical reflection and soul searching. The historic peace churches, who had wrestled with such questions for centuries, offered a new and exciting resource in the conversation.

The uneasy superpower standoff after the war added another, new dimension to such questions. The German Evangelical Church now straddled the divide between East and West. Church leaders in the Confessing Church who had resisted the Nazis, such as Martin Niemöller and Karl Barth, recognized the extent to which the church's anti-communism had blinded them to Hitler's true intentions in 1933. This earlier blindness now made them especially skeptical of the anti-communist rhetoric of American churchmen, such as John Foster Dulles and Reinhold Niebuhr. Many German leaders believed their nation must become solidly pacifist to finally break with past German militarism.[48]

The only hope for reunification and reconciliation lay in the search for a "third way." Karl Barth saw this way as a middle ground between East and West. He hoped that a dialogue between Christians in this altered European landscape would promote understanding between people living under opposing ideological systems.[49] Others expressed deep frustration with the situation. Herbert Mochalski, a pastor from the Confessing Church, wrote:

> We say that both parts [of Germany], as we have them today, are the occupied colonial lands of the respective victors. One must say that very clearly. We aren't a sovereign state in the Federal Republic, but a colony of the Americans. Don't be shocked. Just as the others are a colony within the entire Soviet empire. . . . We are the spear's end of the western superpowers against the East.[50]

It was difficult for Americans to appreciate or even understand such a point of view. They saw themselves as the liberators of Europe and the defenders of the free world. Reinhold Niebuhr was especially frustrated by Karl Barth's advice that Christians should seek a "third way" in the ideological and military divide that ran through Germany. This tension continued throughout the following decades.

After the Russian army invaded Hungary to put down an anti-communist rebellion in 1956, Niebuhr wrote a scathing article in the *Christian Century* chastising Barth's silence on the matter. He praised Barth for having led in the struggle against Nazism, but then challenged what he called Barth's capricious conclusion that communism was not as bad as Nazism. He argued that Barth's theology was too eschatological, too committed to interpreting everything through the light of the "Word of God," and too lacking in principles to be politically responsible. Furthermore, Barth's political judgment was clouded by "his ill-disguised anti-Americanism and by what he regards as our 'worship of the dollar.'"[51]

Along with other students studying with Barth at the University of Basel, Yoder wrote a letter to the *Christian Century* in defense of Barth. The letter responded to Niebuhr point by point. To the charge that Barth was silent and did not condemn this Russian action, they said that Barth had been asked in a semi-public seminar to make a pronouncement on the Hungarian crisis. He responded that Swiss public opinion was already too agitated. They spoke of Barth's reluctance to encourage Switzerland and the rest of the righteous "Free World" to undertake a holy war against Russia at a time when the West had just as effectively dirtied its hands by using military action in an attempt to wrest the control of the Suez Canal from the Egyptians. They told Niebuhr that Barth was less anti-American than were most Swiss people.[52]

To Niebuhr's charge that Barth's theology was too eschatological to be politically responsible, they argued that Barth's political action had shown that a clear eschatology enables Christians to make a distinctive and independent contribution in political matters. They reminded Niebuhr that Barth's part in the resistance to Hitler demonstrated what he meant in saying, "If the Church is to remain free, above the changing political systems, this very freedom implies that the Church should participate in these events."[53]

More than a year later, Barth penned his own indirect response to Niebuhr in the form of a letter to a pastor from East Germany. He wrote that at that time he had not said a word because Niebuhr had not asked an honest question:

> It was not inspired by the real distress of a Christian seeking genuine conversation and fellowship with another, but it was addressed to me by a hard-boiled politician safe in his castle. He, as is customary with politicians who lead an opponent onto slippery ice, wished either to force me to profess his own brand of primitive anti-communism, or to expose me as a secret pro-Communist, and thus in one way or another discredit me as a theologian. What should I have said to that?[54]

The European social and political context was formative in the development of John Howard Yoder's theological and ethical positions. He imbibed much of the European postwar need to address the moral question of war. It is a question that concerned him for the rest of his life. From the Europeans he also imbibed a profound unease with the postwar economic and political order and the role of the Americans within that order. The European belief that the American role was the raw politics of empire reinforced his inherited Mennonite distrust of such political powers. This distrust shaped his theological commitments. He had a natural affinity with European biblical scholars and theologians who shared such views in comparison to Americans who did not.

THE WORLD COUNCIL OF CHURCHES DEBATE

The assembly at Amsterdam in 1948 marked the beginning of the WCC. The assembly delegates again took up the moral question of war that the ecumenical movement had struggled with as war clouds had gathered in Europe in the 1930s. They now agreed on the statement that "war is contrary to the will of God" but found it impossible to move beyond it to any substantive ethical conclusions. This failure was because they wanted to recognize three competing and contradictory positions, which the assembly recognized as equally valid. These were (1) the pacifist position that participation in war is always wrong; (2) the position that Christians have an obligation to support the wars of their respective national governments; and (3) the position that Christians should only support those wars that met the criteria of a "just war." The assembly called on churches to wrestle with the perplexing difficulties of modern warfare and to produce working documents responding to the issue.[55]

After correspondence from the WCC general secretary, W. A. Visser't Hooft, the historic peace churches decided to take up the challenge. They arranged for the Friends, the Mennonites, and the Brethren to make statements. They also asked for a statement from the International Fellowship of Reconciliation (IFOR). These four statements were published in the booklet *War Is Contrary to the Will of God*. A central premise of the booklet was that Christian pacifism is rooted in the teaching and example of Jesus as recorded in the New Testament. This teaching is intended as a guide for all Christians and is not a minority position only for those Christians given to such a vocation. It called on all Christians to fearlessly preach the gospel of peace and engage the ministry of reconciliation.[56]

The document reflected the different histories, church traditions, and theologies of these peace churches. The Mennonite statement emphasized Christian discipleship and made a biblical argument for the life and teaching of Jesus Christ as the norm through which all Scripture is interpreted. The gospel message of love is then applied to contemporary issues. That message is not a simple humanitarianism that fails to recognize the problem of evil. It is rooted in the realization that God's ways are not our ways, as demonstrated in Christ's victory over evil.

The Friends' statement reflected their more mystical tradition that focuses on being taught by the Spirit of God that moves in the hearts of individuals and groups meeting for worship, prayer, and waiting on God. The Christ who shines in every person is the Christ of the Gospels. This inner light is then brought to bear on questions of human responsibility, the claims of the state, the problem of evil, and the issue of self-defense.

The Brethren statement, which was considerably shorter than the other two, talked about how their church emerged out of the Thirty Years War in Europe and was strongly influenced by the Pietists, who believed that Christianity is primarily a way of life. Consequently, they seek to follow Jesus' teachings as faithfully as possible. His teaching on nonresistance is part of a positive way of life that Christians seek to follow.

The IFOR statement differed from the other three because it did not represent a particular confessional body. Instead, it represented an international Christian peace movement including Lutheran, Episcopalian, and Reformed Christians, as well as people from the historic peace churches. Their statement focused on the call of God in Christ and emphasized a ministry of reconciliation. It argued that Christian pacifism is the positive expression of such a ministry. Especially in an atomic age, the church should renounce war and, in this way, lead the nations in building peaceful relations throughout the world.

The document got mixed reviews from ecumenical leaders at the WCC. They appreciated the attention the historic peace churches had given to the appeal for more study of the question of war but expressed regret that the peace churches and IFOR had not come up with a unified statement. If they could not produce a unified statement, how could the even more denominationally and politically diverse WCC develop an ecumenical statement on the subject?[57] Given that goal, the WCC insistence that the historic peace churches produce a unified statement is understandable. What it overlooks is the reality that the three historic peace churches represent different histories and traditions. Such complexity is lost in a combined statement. Treating them as a single voice simply because they share a commitment to peace can frustrate ecumenical dialogue.

Nevertheless, the Continuation Committee of the Historic Peace Churches decided to take up the task of formulating a unified statement. Various young Mennonite scholars in Europe served on the committee and helped write a document with the title *Peace Is the Will of God*. It was presented to the WCC with the hope that it would be discussed at the next WCC assembly at Evanston, Illinois, in 1954. The preface to the statement expressed the peace churches' own sense of guilt for the absence of peace in the world and their modest evaluation of their ability to address international problems. It also conveyed their belief that they had something to say from the perspective of their ancient peace traditions:

> We do not profess to have a detailed solution to the international problems of today's world, but we believe that our conviction, affirmed by several centuries' experience of the full pacifist position, deserves more thorough consideration than has yet been accorded to it. At the same time we are deeply conscious of our own shortcomings and of the temptations peculiar to our position. We confess our own guilt in the disharmony of our time and share with all Christians a deep longing for peace among the nations.[58]

It is unclear to what extent John Howard Yoder contributed to the actual writing of the document,[59] but a letter he wrote in 1952 indicates that he was part of the group that worked on it. His letter gives his perspective, as a newcomer to the group, on the dynamics in the Continuation Committee of the Historic Peace Churches in Europe. He talked about the administrative and theological difficulties of working together as a diverse and far-flung group, spanning different continents and church traditions. He described two crucial tasks: (1) to come up with a joint statement that did not simply hide their differences; and (2) to create a document on an intellectual level that could get a hearing at the next WCC assembly at Evanston.[60]

Yoder thought that Mennonites would need to carry a big part of the task because they had the resources needed to formulate persuasive biblical, theological, and historical arguments. They also had the necessary organizational resources in Europe. The question was whether they were willing to invest in such a peace witness to Protestant churches related to the WCC.[61] After the document *Peace Is the Will of God* was completed, Yoder wrote an article for the *Christian Century* titled "Let Evanston Speak on War!" He lamented that few theologians had responded to the call to address the moral question of war, which the first WCC Assembly gave at Amsterdam. He noted that pacifists had made several significant contributions to the discussion, including the book, *La Guerre et l'Evangile,* by Jean Lasserre and the document, *Peace Is the Will of God,* by the peace churches. [62]

The article gave two reasons why the WCC should take up the question of war. One was that war is an even greater cause of division within Christianity than confessional and theological differences. He wrote, "The modern nation-state stands first among the non-theological causes of division in the world church." The church is rightfully an international and supernational fellowship. It is heretical when Christians actually go to war against each other because of competing national loyalties. He raised this concern in relation to the American churches:

> Whether the America of McCarthy and McIntire, or for that matter the America of Dulles and Luce, can tolerate the church as a supernational (not only international) fellowship that refuses to endorse national aims and confesses loyalty only to the kingdom of our Lord, will perhaps become clearer at Evanston.[63]

Yoder's second reason was eschatological. He said that we find it easy to make theological arguments that war is contrary to the will of God, while then giving ethical justifications for Christian participation in war. This practice reflects an attitude that Christians have no choice but to participate in the sin of war. Any attitude toward sin is an eschatology, a doctrine of ultimate realities. The contention that the best we can do is to choose the lesser evil is a denial of the resurrection and the presence of the Holy Spirit:

> To deny that redemption, whose central meaning, exegetically, is release from bondage to sin, is a reality for ethics in this world, however incomplete and however in need of a fuller consumma-

tion, is to read backwards Paul's declaration, "If Christ is not risen ye are yet in your sins." By founding all ethical thinking, including thinking on the war question, on the view that "we are yet in our sins," today's self-styled "realists" deny in effect that the power of the resurrection concerns history in our time in any ultimate way.[64]

Such arguments are significant in the development of Yoder's thought. For him the church is always a body that transcends all other human commitments, including national loyalties. Insisting on the primacy of the church and on making a clear distinction between church and society became central components of his ethical argument that following the way of Jesus is paramount for Christian social ethics. Another component is the eschatological distinction between an order of preservation in which nations, often through the use of violence, maintain a semblance of peace and stability, and an order of redemption that follows Christ's way of suffering love through the power of the resurrection.

Yoder's arguments in his *Christian Century* article reflect some of the basic premises of the document *Peace Is the Will of God.* The document expresses agreement with the consensus of Christian faith as expressed at the WCC assembly at Amsterdam. It is on this basis that the peace churches are convinced that Christians should abstain from war. The reason abstaining is not the general position among Christians is that certain pseudo-Christian or secular assumptions have been given axiomatic status alongside Scripture. Some of these extraneous presuppositions are (1) the inviolability of natural social bonds; (2) the medieval concept of society as the *corpus Christianum;* (3) the concept of the "just war" built on the premises of natural theology; (4) the belief that Christian pacifism is a vocation for the few who are called to it; (5) an antinomian concept of grace; (f) the belief that war is sometimes a lesser evil; and (6) the argument that it is possible to kill the enemy in a spirit of Christian love. The document briefly refutes these presuppositions on historical, theological, and scriptural grounds, but the basic rhetorical strategy is to list them together as extraneous to the Christian message.[65]

The document then makes its case for the pacifist position, which is tied to the WCC statement at Amsterdam, that "war is incompatible with the teaching and example of Christ." Pacifism is linked to the cross of Christ as the way of God in a sinful world. The cross, which is at the heart of Christian faith, points to the acceptance of suffering, the denial of self, and the dedication of life to a ministry of redemption. But the cross is not merely exemplary and redemptive. Beyond the cross lie the resurrection and the moral renewal of the believer, through the power of God working in us.[66]

The question of war is not only a matter of individual conscience. It is tied to an understanding of the church as the universal body of Christ. Reflecting what had just happened in World War II, the document insists:

> For Christians to allow themselves to be drawn into taking sides in war is a denial of the unity of the body of Christ. The Christian Church is not provincial or national, it is universal. Therefore every war in which churches on each side condone or support the national effort becomes a civil war within the Church. Is not this state of affairs where Christian kills Christian an even greater breach of ecumenical fellowship than the deplorable confessional differences that have rent our unity? Indeed, can we Christians expect the Lord to restore our unity in worship as long as we put one another to death on the field of battle? Therefore we humbly submit: The refusal to participate in and to support war in any form is the only course compatible with the high calling of the Church in Jesus Christ.[67]

After the argument that war is an ecumenical problem that compromises the integrity of the church, the document addresses the question of the nature of national governments. It recognizes that a task of government is to maintain order. In the language of Romans 13, government is "instituted by God" for that purpose. This biblical text, however, also asserts that "there is no power except from God." The state, therefore, has no metaphysical or mystical quality, no autonomous or ultimate sources or norms of justice. It has only a limited and delegated authority. Furthermore, the New Testament recognizes that the state has a demonic quality that causes it to overstep these limits:

> This element, like a dominant trait in a biological organism, constantly seeks to assert itself, and leads a state, particularly one whose power is growing, to overstep its boundaries, to forget its derivative character, and to abuse its authority, as for example in the prosecution of modern warfare. In the eschatological vision

of Scripture the kingdoms of this world are therefore visited with the righteous wrath of God. The authority which they are given becomes the occasion of their downfall.[68]

Such biblical considerations should not lead to utopian Christian politics or ethics or to an evasion of social responsibility. The document recognizes that the origins of war are intricately woven into the very fabric of social and economic life. We cannot simply say no to war while tolerating other abuses that are equally incompatible with a Christian ethic. Through all legitimate means, Christians will help build the kind of society that can avoid war. While the first task of the church, in its service to the world, is to be the church, this task should not be understood as an evasion of social responsibility. It does, however, mean that we need to be true to the nature of the church as the body of Christ in the manner in which we carry out this responsibility. Saying no to the sinfulness of war is a common Christian task rooted in our unified confession of faith in Jesus Christ.[69]

Even though the Amsterdam Assembly had asked the churches to study the problem of war, the WCC itself did not sponsor a major consultation on the subject in the following years. The efforts of the peace churches to write a unified document on their pacifist position also failed to generate the response they had hoped for. John Howard Yoder's challenge to the WCC, to give major attention to this at the Evanston Assembly in 1954, was not realized. Part of the report on international affairs at Evanston did address the problem of war in a nuclear age, stating that "it is not enough for the churches to proclaim that war is evil. They must study afresh the Christian approaches to peace, taking into account both Christian pacifism as a mode of witness and the conviction of Christians that in certain circumstances military action is justifiable."[70]

The Exchange with Reinhold Niebuhr and Angus Dun

The Evanston Assembly did not move the discussion beyond where it stood in 1948. It also failed to address the document *Peace Is the Will of God* put forward by the peace churches and the IFOR. Consequently, Episcopal Church leader Angus Dun and Reinhold Niebuhr were asked to respond to the peace churches. The journal *Christianity and Crisis* published their response as the article "God Wills Both Justice and Peace."[71]

Dun and Niebuhr did not respond directly to the arguments put forward in *Peace Is the Will of God*. Instead they articulated Niebuhr's distinction between an ethic of love for individuals and the needs of a sinful society. On these grounds, they argued that the pacifist position "distorts the Christian concept of love and tries to apply an individual ethic to a collective situation."[72]

Dun and Niebuhr claimed that the pacifist position is not balanced because it focuses on peace at the expense of justice. According to them, "It makes an absolute of sacrificial love at the expense of social responsibility." They also rejected the claim in *Peace Is the Will of God* that the traditional just war position is too casuistic to be applied to modern warfare. Even the appeal to international law does not work in primitive world affairs, they argued. Instead, they insisted that Christians have a duty, in obedience to conscience, to participate in war waged to defend the victims of aggression and to secure freedom for the oppressed.[73]

The peace churches and the IFOR then asked Paul Peachey, with the help of Yoder and other members of the Continuation Committee of the Historic Peace Churches, to draft a response to the Dun and Niebuhr article. This response called "God Establishes Both Peace and Justice" was later published in a booklet along with the Dun and Niebuhr article and the original document *Peace Is the Will of God*.[74]

The peace church response to the Dun and Niebuhr article begins by welcoming the dialogue. It states its regret that Dun and Niebuhr do not interact with the central arguments in the peace church position nor respond to the peace church effort to put forward a distinctively Christian approach to the problem of war. Instead, they only engage the problem in reference to the concept of the just war. While Niebuhr and Dun fault the peace church position for choosing an individual ethic of sacrificial love at the expense of social responsibility, their own last word establishes the individual conscience as the arbiter of the justice of a particular conflict. They think of Christians as individuals in society at large without reference to the church as a discerning body. In contrast, the peace churches assert that "membership in the body of Christ is membership in a social group whose bonds transcend other impulses of social cohesion." Dun and Niebuhr's response ignores the church and the effort to be faithful to the life and teaching of Jesus Christ.[75]

Conclusion

The social and political issues in postwar Europe, relationships with European Mennonites, ecumenical conversations with European Protestants, and the WCC debate on the question of war, were the significant arenas within which John Howard Yoder first formulated and articulated his theological ethics. It was here that he developed and argued for his understanding of the centrality of the life and teaching of Jesus for Christian social ethics that he would come to call "the politics of Jesus."[76] He learned how to listen to his interlocutors and even enter the conversation on their turf. He also learned to be wary of debating abstract ideas such as "justice" and "social responsibility" when they do not have clear historical referents or directly engage the Christian tradition and the claims of Jesus Christ.

Yoder encountered a similar problem of not taking the claims of Jesus seriously in the broader WCC conversation. In this arena concerns about ecumenical relationships created a reluctance to engage seriously the different positions on the morality of war from the perspective of the Christian tradition. Out of fear of offending anyone, the impulse was to baptize the different positions as equally Christian, even if they were contradictory. There was no deep or sustained commitment to wrestle with the issues in a way that was historically and theologically serious.[77]

Such problems shaped the way Yoder addressed the issues. He insisted that "our ethics are drawn from Christ, whose humanity was perfect obedience." He thought that was simple elementary theology. People should not be baptized if they do not understand it. He chided pacifists who sought to engage others without reference to such basic theological premises.[78] The convictions he developed in such confrontations powerfully influenced his later work, including his articulation of the "politics of Jesus."

As a consequence, Yoder's theology carefully engaged the received Christian tradition. This engagement involves testing the tradition for coherence. He had a preference for historical theology. He worked theologically from the Anabaptist focus on church renewal with reference to its roots in Jesus Christ and the early Christian communities. At the same time, he sought to avoid the ahistorical temptation to read the Bible without reference to later generations. The temptation to work with little reference to Jesus and the received tradition was especially evident in Protestant social ethics. The task he set for himself was to make it impossible for Christians to avoid Jesus Christ and the early church in their social ethics. He wanted them to seriously consider the "politics of Jesus."[79]

The people who gave Yoder the intellectual tools to work at that task were the European scholars he studied under. While he was indebted to various people, the two mentors who shaped him most profoundly were Oscar Cullmann and Karl Barth. The following chapter will study the influence they had on his theological ethics.

NOTES

1. It is important to note the extent to which their assignment in Europe in the postwar era shaped the life and work, not only of John Howard Yoder, but of whole group of young Mennonites who served there. These people, in turn, powerfully shaped the life and thought of Mennonites around the world in the following decades. Included in this group were Irvin Horst, John Miller, Paul Peachey, Albert Meyer, David Shenk, Calvin Redekop, and Albert Keim. All these men made their own significant contributions in academia and in church leadership.

Another significant endeavor that also goes beyond the scope of my research is that several of these young men, including John Howard Yoder, began a publication called *Concern* which was a major avenue of conveying their thought to the broader church. The publication began in 1954 and continued until 1971, when its subscription list and assets were given to *Sojourners* magazine. Yoder helped edit the publication and wrote various articles in it. See JHY papers, box 11 and box 18, AMC. What has since come to be known as the Concern movement was featured in an entire issue of *The Conrad Grebel Review* 8 (Spring 1990). Also see Albert Keim, "Bender and the Concern Group," *Harold S. Bender,* 450-471.

2. Toews, *Mennonites in American Society,* 197.

3. Paul Peachey, "Introduction," in Emily Brunk, *Espelkamp: The Mennonite Central Committee Shares in Community Building in a New Settlement for German Refugees* (Karlsruhe: The Mennonite Central Committee, 1951). At the time, Peachey was the director of the Mennonite Central Committee voluntary service in Europe.

4. Ibid.

5. Emily Brunk, *Espelkamp: The Mennonite Central Committee Shares in Community Building in a New Settlement for German Refugees,* 1.

6. Ibid., 3.

7. Ibid., 4.

8. Frank H. Epp, *Mennonite Exodus, The Rescue and Resettlement of the Russian Mennonites Since the Communist Revolution* (Altona, Man.: Canadian Mennonite Relief and Immigration Council, 1962).

9. *A Guide to the Mennonite Central Committee European Program,* 1957, Historical Library, Eastern Mennonite University, Harrisonburg, Virginia.

10. Harold Bender, letter to John Howard Yoder, August 10, 1948, Bender papers, box 42, AMC.

11. Ibid.

12. A significant historical record of the influence this postwar European experience had on John Howard Yoder is Donald Durnbaugh's edited volume on the discussion on war and peace between the historic peace churches and the European Protestants after WWII. Yoder is rarely self-referential in his writing. However, reading the papers in Durnbaugh's book, including Yoder's contribution to the discussion, impresses one with the impact that this European debate had on Yoder's theological development. One glimpse of the powerful way it has shaped his thought is in his brief epilogue in Durnbaugh's volume. There he traces the evolution of that ecumenical discussion on war and peace with a focus on the way ahead in that conversation. Here Yoder writes of his hope that the record of those conversations "might inspire a new generation to renewed theological seriousness that will recognize a churchly responsibility to renew the dialogue on a level commensurate with the threat to the planet and to the Gospel which is represented by Christian complacency about arms." See Donald Durnbaugh ed., *On Earth Peace: Discussions on War/Peace Issues Between Friends, Mennonites, Brethren and European Churches 1935-1975* (Elgin, Ill.: The Brethren Press, 1978), 390-393.

13. John Howard Yoder, letter to Harold Bender, July 6, 1954, JHY papers, box 11, AMC.

14. Interview with Albert Keim, July 21, 2002. Keim had served in Europe with MCC from 1955 to 1958. He later became a historian and an academic dean at Eastern Mennonite University. He wrote a biography of Harold Bender, which contains several chapters on this postwar European experience. See Keim, *Harold S. Bender 1897-1962*, 351-406; 450-471

15. Conversation with Orley Swartzentruber, July 14, 2002. I met Orley at an ecumenical dialogue ,"Creating Peacemaking Communities for the New Millennium: Catholics and Mennonites Bridging the Divide," at St. John's Abby, Collegeville, Minnesota.

16. Interview with Albert Keim, July 21, 2002.

17. Ibid. For an account of this postwar struggle in the German churches, see Victoria Barnett, *For the Soul of the People: Protestant Protest Against Hitler* (Oxford: Oxford University Press, 1992), 239-255.

18. Interview with Albert Keim, July 21, 2002.

19. Ibid.

20. Ibid.

21. One example is in Richard Miller, *Interpretations of Conflict: Ethics, Pacifism and the Just-War Tradition* (Chicago: The University of Chicago Press, 1991), 241. Miller critiques John Howard Yoder's theology as representing a confessional approach that stresses the importance of religious faith at the expense of publicly accessible phenomena that are open to conversation and debate. Miller has it half right. Yoder always argues from the perspective of his pacifist interpretation of the "politics of Jesus." What he misses is that Yoder developed his thought in conversation with the political and ecumenical ferment of postwar Europe. This conversation shaped

his thought just as profoundly as his confessional commitments. Throughout the rest of his life he had a profound commitment to such conversation. What he would not do was to privilege other kinds of ethical commitments as somehow more publicly or politically available and intelligible than his "politics of Jesus." He was not articulating a separatist ethic that is only relevant to the confessional community. See John Howard Yoder, *Body Politics: Five Practices of the Christian Community Before the Watching World* (Scottdale, Pa.: Herald Press, 1992), vi-vii.

22. Yoder's doctoral dissertation has recently been translated and made available in English. John Howard Yoder, *Anabaptism and Reformation in Switzerland: An Historical and Theological Analysis of the Dialogue between Anabaptists and Reformers*, ed. C. Arnold Snyder; trans. David Carl Stassen and C. Arnold Snyder (Kitchener, Ont.: Pandora Press, 2004).

23. Durnbaugh ed., *On Earth Peace*, 17-29.

24. These conversations had begun shortly before John Howard Yoder arrived in Europe. It is not clear to what extent he participated in formulating some of the first historic peace church responses to the question of war. However, he quickly became involved after he arrived in 1949 and helped to organize of the first ecumenical conference on the topic at Puidoux, Switzerland in 1955. He had also become the principle theological spokesperson for the historical peace churches, delivering the paper "The Theological Basis of the Christian Witness to the State" at the Puidoux conference. See Durnbaugh ed, *On Earth Peace*, 122, 136-145.

25. J. Denny Weaver, *Becoming Anabaptist: The Origin and Significance of Sixteenth-Century Anabaptism*, 2nd. ed. (Scottdale, Pa.: Herald Press, 2005).

26. A helpful guide to this Mennonite story is Cornelius J. Dyck, *An Introduction to Mennonite History: A Popular History of the Anabaptists and the Mennonites*, 3rd. ed. (Scottdale, Pa.: Herald Press, 1993).

27. Ibid., 436.

28. John Howard Yoder, letter to Harold Bender, May 22, 1950, JHY papers, box 8, AMC.

29. Cornelius J. Dyck, *An Introduction to Mennonite History* (Scottdale, Pa.: Herald Press, 1981), 379-382.

30. Such discipline for entering military service was not universally applied in every North American Mennonite congregation. Many young men who were in good standing in their congregation had willingly entered military service. Nevertheless, forfeiting church membership because of military service was the rule rather than the exception within the Mennonite Church denominational structure. Other denominations were more lenient. The General Conference Mennonite Church and the Mennonite Brethren Church generally did not make military service a test of church membership. See Toews, *Mennonites in American Society*, 173-180.

31. John Howard Yoder, "Report on Conscientious Objection and Medical Service," March 3, 1953, JHY papers, box 16, AMC.

32. Harold Bender, "Comments on John Howard Yoder's paper . . . ," March 5, 1954, JHY papers, box 16, AMC.

33. John Howard Yoder, "Report on Meeting in Relation of Nonresistance to Discipline in Mission Congregations in French-speaking Europe," April, 2 1954,

JHY papers, box 16, AMC.

34. The experience of Yoder's home congregation, the Oak Grove Mennonite Church in Ohio, almost certainly influenced his position on this matter. Half the young men in his congregation had chosen military service rather than alternative service during WWII. In 1945, the servicemen who returned from the war were asked to sign a statement professing their belief in the peace principles practiced by the Mennonite Church and expressing their regret for their military service before they were allowed back into full church membership. Few of the returning servicemen were willing to sign the statement. In 1955, the congregation changed its position, saying that the 1945 statement had been too harsh, and welcomed all who had served back into full fellowship. See Lehman, *Creative Congregationalism,* 258-259.

35. John Howard Yoder, letter to Harold Bender, May 22, 1950, Bender papers, box 42, AMC.

36. John Howard Yoder, "Statement on MCC policy and methods . . . ," August, 7, 1952, JHY papers, box 8, AMC.

37. Dyck, *Introduction to Mennonite History,* 382-387. See also John Howard Yoder's extensive study document on American Mennonite mission involvements and relationships that he prepared for a mission study conference at Bienenberg, Switzerland in 1967, JHY papers, box 16, AMC. Through his work as a mission administrator for the Mennonite board of missions until 1965, Yoder kept in close touch with the European churches. Even after that, he remained in informal contact with them.

38. Yoder, "Study Document," JHY papers, box 16, AMC.

39. Dyck, *Introduction to Mennonite History,* 389.

40. Yoder, "Study Document," JHY papers, box 16, AMC.

41. See especially Theron F. Schlabach, *Gospel Versus Gospel: Mission and the Mennonite Church, 1863-1944* (Scottdale, Pa.: Herald Press, 1980).

42. John Howard Yoder, letter to Harold Bender, December, 13, 1949, Bender papers, box 42, AMC.

43. Yoder, "Study Document," JHY papers, box 16, AMC.

44. Ibid. Yoder could give a stinging social and religious critique of contemporary Mennonite life. See John Howard Yoder, "Anabaptist Vision and Mennonite Reality," *Consultation on Anabaptist-Mennonite Theology: Papers Read at the 1969 Aspen Conference,* ed. A. J. Klassen (Fresno, Cal.: Council of Mennonite Seminaries, 1970), 1-46. For his critique of Constantianism, see John Howard Yoder, "The Constantianian Sources of Western Social Ethics," *The Priestly Kingdom: Social Ethics as Gospel* (Notre Dame, Ind.: The University of Notre Dame Press, 1984), 135-147.

45. The phrase *biblical nonresistance* was commonly used by North American Mennonites to describe their position in the 1950s. The phrase was taken from Jesus' command not to resist an evildoer (Matt. 5:39). This description served to distinguish their position from liberal Protestant and Gandhian positions. The term *nonresistance* was also used more broadly by Christian scholars to describe Jesus' response to violence. See Jean Lasserre, *War and the Gospel* (London: James Clark & Co. Ltd., 1962), 35. The problem with the term was that it connoted a passivity with which many Mennonites were not comfortable. It shares that problem with the

more common term *pacifism*, which is used to define a principled opposition to war. In the following decades, Mennonites moved toward more engaged language such as "peacebuilding" and "active nonviolence."

46. Hannah Arendt, "The Aftermath of Nazi Rule," *Commentary* (October 1950): 342, 345.

47. Victoria Barnett, *For the Soul of the People: Protestant Protest Against Hitler* (Oxford: Oxford University Press, 1992), 240.

48. Ibid., 273-274.

49. Karl Barth, *Die Kirche zwischen Ost und West* (Zurich: Evangelisches Verlagshaus, 1949). There is an English translation, "The Church between East and West," in Karl Barth, *Against the Stream: Shorter postwar Writings 1946-52* (New York: Philosophical Library, 1954), 127-146.

50. Cited in Barnett, *For the Soul of the People,* 274.

51. Reinhold Niebuhr, "Why Is Barth Silent on Hungary?" *Christian Century* (January 23, 1957): 108-110.

52. John Howard Yoder, et al., "Barth on Hungary: An Exchange. From Dr. Barth's Seminar in Basel," *The Christian Century* (April 10, 1957): 453-55.

53. In *On Earth Peace: Discussions on War/Peace Issues between Friends, Mennonites, Brethren, and European Churches, 1935-75,* ed. Donald F. Durnbaugh (Elgin, Ill.: The Brethren Press, 1978), 21.

54. Karl Barth, ""Letter to a Pastor in the German Democratic Republic," in *How to Serve God in a Marxist Land,* trans. Henry Clark and James Smart (New York: Association Press, 1959), 46.

55. In *On Earth Peace*, ed. Durnbaugh,19.

56. "War Is Contrary to the Will of God," in *On Earth Peace*, ed. Durnbaugh, 46-49.

57. In *On Earth Peace*, ed. Durnbaugh, 73.

58. Historic Peace Churches and the Fellowship of Reconcilation, *Peace Is the Will of God: A Testimony to the World Council of Churches* (Amsterdam: J. H. De Bussy Ltd., 1953), 3.

59. Paul Peachey recalls that the young Mennonites in Europe were convinced that they could write a joint statement and pushed ahead with the project before they had authorization to do so. Peachey wrote the first draft with input from Yoder and others. He then met at the Friends Center in Oxford England, where Harold Row and M. R. Ziegler for the Church of the Brethren and Percy Bartlett for the Friends, among others, did the final work on the document (telephone interview with Paul Peachey, October 16, 2002).

60. John Howard Yoder, letter to Harold Bender, January 23, 1952, Bender papers, box 42, AMC.

61. Ibid.

62. John Howard Yoder, "Let Evanston Speak on War!" *Christian Century* (August 8, 1954): 973-974.

63. Ibid., 974.

64. Ibid.

65. Historic Peace Churches and FOR, *Peace Is the Will of God,* 6-14.

66. Ibid., 15.
67. Ibid., 16-17.
68. Ibid., 18.
69. Ibid., 20-23.
70. In *On Earth Peace*, ed. Durnbaugh, 91-94.
71. Ibid., 100.
72. Angus Dun and Reinhold Niebuhr, "God Wills Both Justice and Peace," *Christianity and Crisis* (June 13, 1955): 75-78. It should be noted that pacifists generally are not as absolutist in their understanding of sacrificial love as Niebuhr. Niebuhr believed that for an ethic of love to be consistent, it must eschew coercion in any form. Pacifists generally are more nuanced in their understanding and leave open the possibility for some exercise of assertive persuasion and even coercive force. Martin Luther King Jr. gives an insightful contrast between Niebuhr's understanding of pacifism as passive idealism and his own activist understanding of pacifism and nonviolent resistance in "Pilgrimage to Nonviolence," *Nonviolence in America: A Documentary History*, ed. Staughton Lynd and Alice Lynd (Maryknoll, N.Y.: Orbis Books, 1995), 214-215. Walter Wink argues that Jesus is not averse to using coercion but does not employ *violent* coercion. See Wink, *Engaging the Powers: Discernment and Resistance in a World of Domination* (Minneapolis: Fortress Press, 1992), 192. John Howard Yoder, who is actually closer to Niebuhr on this issue, also affirms active nonviolence in *The Politics of Jesus* (1972), 90-93.
73. Dun and Niebuhr, "God Wills Both Justice and Peace," *Christianity and Crisis* (June 13, 1955): 75-78.
74. This booklet was given the title *The Christian and War: A Theological Discussion of Justice, Peace and Love* (Amsterdam: J. H. De Bussy, 1958).
75. "God Establishes Both Peace and Justice," in *On Earth Peace*, ed. Durnbaugh, 109.
76. Of special note in this regard are the two papers "Karl Barth and Christian Pacifism" and "Politics of the Messiah" that John Howard Yoder presented at the second Puidoux Conference, Iserlohn, Germany, in 1957. See Mark Thiessen Nation, *A Comprehensive Bibliography of the Writings of John Howard Yoder* (Goshen, Ind.: Mennonite Historical Society, 1997), 16.
77. Throughout his life, Yoder insisted that one should not ignore differences in ecumenical dialogue. The tendency is to start with what is held in common rather than on issues on which the parties differ. Such a methodology slants the conversation to the agenda of the larger group and pushes to the periphery precisely what it is that makes smaller group different from the larger group in the conversation. See Yoder's posthumously published essay "On Christian Unity: The Way from Below," *Pro Ecclesia* 9, no. 2 (2000): 165-183.
78. John Howard Yoder, letter to Paul Peachey, June 23, 1956, JHY papers, box 11, AMC.
79. For a discussion of how Yoder worked theologically see his "Conclusions Concerning the Discipline of Theology" in John Howard Yoder, *Preface to Theology: Christology and Theological Method* (Grand Rapids: Brazos Press, 2002), 377-405.

FOUR

DOCTORAL STUDIES
WITH BARTH AND CULLMANN

Harold Bender created a European assignment for John Howard Yoder because Bender wanted him to study theology in a European university. He had great confidence in Yoder's intellectual gifts and wanted him to develop them by studying at the best possible theological school. Bender had studied in Europe himself and had many connections on the continent. A year after his arrival in Europe, Yoder received a letter from Bender inquiring about his studies at the University of Basel.[1]

Bender had cause to be worried about Yoder's independent streak. He had earlier tried to get him to come back to Goshen Biblical Seminary for further studies. Yoder had his own ideas about spending a school year taking liberal arts courses at Wooster College, a local college in Ohio, then taking courses at several seminaries in Chicago before leaving for Europe.[2] Now Bender wrote that he had recently heard from Yoder's father that he was not studying theology after all but was registered with the philosophical faculty. He wanted to know what Yoder's future plans were.[3]

Yoder wrote back to inform him that there had been some miscommunication. He was taking one class on the history of Christian philosophy from Karl Jaspers. All his other courses were in theology. He especially appreciated courses he was taking with Oscar Cullmann and Ernst Staehelin. He said that being in this atmosphere made him feel like working on contemporary, updated theology from an Anabaptist perspective (a theological *Vergegenwärtigung*), rather than the historical work being done by most other American Mennonites studying in Europe. But that would take three years and he did not think theology was worth that much time and effort.[4]

Yoder told Bender that his MCC term had really been time off, as far as making any contribution to his future work was concerned. Three more years studying theology, even though enjoyable, would hardly be justifiable because he had no plans to become a theologian. He might, however, spend a semester studying in Geneva before quitting. Any advice Bender had would be appreciated.[5] That got an immediate response from Bender:

> You say that you do not plan to be a theologian, but the trouble is that you are one anyway. You always have been one and you always will be. The only question is what kind of a theologian you want to be. You do not have to be a theologian of the type of any particular school of thought, but among the very few men who have endowments and attitudes which enable them to be the real theologians we need, you are one.[6]

Bender argued that Yoder was still young and had completed his college education so quickly that it justified spending several years studying theology. He thought Yoder should specialize in the history of Christian thought. That would enable him to study a broad range of topics including New Testament, church history, philosophy, and dogmatics. If he liked Oscar Cullmann, he should plan eventually to finish his degree at Basel, which certainly had the best theological faculty in Europe. But it would be good also to study at some other universities. He might want to spend some time in Zurich studying with people like Emil Brunner and Fritz Blanke. He could even spend a semester at some German theological faculty like Göttingen or Tübingen.[7]

Bender, however, did not like Yoder's idea of going to Geneva. He thought it might be worthwhile if Yoder could find some "real" Christian teachers there. Bender wrote to Yoder, "A theological faculty which is still pretty much in the thralls of liberalism or dead in its tracks would not give you very much, except language drill and life in a different environment."[8] It would be interesting to know more about what attracted the young Yoder to Geneva. By that time he surely had his own understanding of the different theological perspectives in Europe.

The reason Yoder gave Bender for studying at Geneva was that he wanted to make contact with a young conscientious objector who had created quite a stir in student circles. But did he also want to study in a setting that exposed him to a different kind of theology? Harold Bender worked hard to get the best education possible for his brightest students, while steering them away from what he considered theological liberalism. This tactic reflected his own conservative theological inclinations but, even more, the reluctance of theological brokers in the Mennonite Church to engage certain theological currents in the postwar era.[9]

In this correspondence, Bender was clearly steering Yoder in a direction that would give him the best intellectual tools while keeping him away from the perceived dangers of theological liberalism. His intervention powerfully shaped the direction of Yoder's academic career and life. Bender, however, did not immediately persuade Yoder. Months later, Yoder wrote to Bender, "I still don't feel much personal interest in the need for theologians." He said that up until then it had been a hobby and pastime. He was afraid that if he did continue studying theology, it would be due to his following not a call but the line of least resistance.[10]

Despite such misgivings, Yoder continued his studies at Basel. The work he did there strengthened his growing conviction that the ethical and political stance of Jesus should be made normative for contemporary Christian ethics. Especially significant were his biblical studies with Oscar Cullmann, his theological studies with Karl Barth, and his doctoral dissertation on the sixteenth-century debates between the Swiss Anabaptists and the Protestant reformers.

The contemporary ethical problem to which he first applied his developing theological convictions was the postwar WCC debate on the morality of war. Yoder was convinced that pacifists needed to answer the American theology and ethics of "responsibility," which are rooted in the Reformed tradition. In his doctoral dissertation he traced such ethics back to Ulrich Zwingli and other early Reformed theologians. A related task was to work constructively on the question of church and society in relation to Christian social action. These various pieces were beginning to come together for Yoder. It would be a difficult task, but he saw the possibility of making a significant contribution to Christian theological ethics from a peace church perspective.[11]

From 1950 to 1957, Yoder studied in a doctoral program with the theological faculty of the University of Basel in Switzerland to help prepare him for that task.[12] He was working at his doctoral studies during the same time period as all his other activities that were seen in the previous chapter. As will be seen, his doctoral studies helped shape his thought as it relates to his notion of "the politics of Jesus."

Karl Barth taught systematic theology at Basel during those years and significantly influenced Yoder's theological thought. One can identify the imprint of Barth's theology on Yoder's work, especially as it relates to social ethics. For this reason I pay special attention to Barth's writings on current social issues. I also pay close attention to Yoder's own interpretation of the strengths and weaknesses of Barth's theology.

Oscar Cullmann was on the New Testament faculty at Basel when Yoder was a student there. Little has been written about the influence that Cullmann had on Yoder. I intend to correct that. It would be difficult even to conceive of Yoder's "politics of Jesus" without Cullmann's prior exegetical work in the New Testament. In particular, Yoder appropriated three things from his work. One is Cullmann's articulation of the "reign of Christ" as a way to overcome the deficiencies of traditional two-kingdom theologies. Second is Cullmann's work on Jesus' relationship to the Romans and the various Jewish parties in first-century Palestine, especially the Zealots. Third is Cullmann's work on the politics of Paul and the early Christian communities.

The Theology of Karl Barth

Karl Barth was Yoder's theological mentor at the University of Basel. Yoder took numerous classes, colloquiums, and seminars with Barth during the years he studied there.[13] Much has been made of the influence Barth had on Yoder's theological ethics. Painted in broad strokes, Barth's contributions include the following perspectives: (1) reading the Bible as a narrative centered in Jesus Christ; (2) making the particular story of Jesus decisive for discipleship and ethics; (3) rejecting natural theology as a source independent of the story of Jesus; and (4) drawing a distinction between the church and the world for all social and ethical reflection.[14]

One should, however, not overemphasize Yoder's indebtedness to Barth. Similar theological commitments are also central to Yoder's Anabaptist tradition. What he owes to Barth is the ability to use the energy and dynamism of such convictions in a way that could engage the imag-

inations of Christians from various ecumenical perspectives. It also
needs to be recognized that systematic theology was only one of various
tools that Yoder used to construct his thought.

As a student at the University of Basel, Yoder actually took more
courses in Old Testament (44 credit hours) than in any other subject. He
took a total of 72 credit hours in biblical studies as compared to 34 credit
hours in theology and 31 credit hours in church history. That concentration helps explain the rich and imaginative biblical exegesis that he
brought to the field of theological ethics. He was a capable biblical
scholar.[15]

The most courses Yoder took with any one person were with Old
Testament professor Ernst Eichrodt (27 credit hours). That was followed by New Testament courses with Oscar Cullmann (23 credit
hours), church history courses with Ernst Staehelin (22 credit hours),
and systematic theology with Karl Barth (13 credit hours). He also took
several courses in ethics with Hendrik van Oyen and one course in philosophy with Karl Jaspers.[16]

It would be simplistic to try to determine the relative importance
each area of study had for Yoder by counting the number of courses he
took in it. Nevertheless, this range of courses, with heavy concentrations
in biblical studies and church history as well as theology, indicates the
breath of his interests. It also indicates the interdisciplinary way in
which Yoder would work at the theological task throughout his life.

There is no question that Barth's theology greatly influenced Yoder.
In Yoder's personal papers there is an outline of part of Barth's *Church
Dogmatics*. On the back these words are written in Yoder's handwriting,
"Don't know what God is, only that God is in Christ; my knowledge of
God is relative because my knowledge of Christ is relative. But God re-
ally is what he is in Christ."[17] One can imagine Yoder jotting that down
during one of Barth's lectures. That christological focus may well be the
crux of what Yoder learned from Barth.

Motifs in Barth's Theology

George Hunsinger, an interpreter of Karl Barth, has isolated various
motifs that characterize Barth's theology. These motifs can also be seen
in Yoder's work. They help us appreciate his indebtedness to Barth without insisting on a theological congruence that is not there. Some of these
motifs are more pronounced than others in Yoder's work, but they are all

present. They are (1) thinking primarily in terms of events and relationships rather than substances; (2) moving from the particular to the general, rather than from the general to the particular; (3) proceeding with
the conviction that theology is objective in the sense that it does not
begin with the human predicament but with our understanding of God
as revealed in Jesus Christ; (4) insisting that such theological objectivity
does not deny but rather establishes our personal encounter with God;
(5) reading biblical narratives through the lens of a "biblical realism"
that does not understand them as "factual reports" or as "mythological
pictures" but rather as "legendary witnesses"; and (6) understanding
faith in biblical revelation as the basis upon which rational reflection in
theology must occur.[18]

In his elucidation of these motifs, Hunsinger says that Barth did not
think in terms of the "real" and the "ideal," but rather in terms of the
"real" and the "unreal." He makes a helpful comparison between Karl
Barth and Reinhold Niebuhr, which also applies to Yoder. For Hunsinger, Niebuhr exemplifies the kind of theology that thinks in terms of
the real and the ideal:

> Niebuhr thought of love . . . as representing an unattainable ideal.
> Although impossible to attain, the love ideal had at least two im-
> portant functions. It served constantly to remind us of human
> sinfulness, and it stood as a warning against identifying any
> human achievements or institutions with the absolute. It was a
> critical standard which . . . disclosed that human beings, no mat-
> ter how hard they might try, would always fall short. Love, for
> Niebuhr, thus had to be described as an "impossible possibility,"
> for human nature as such determined what could be called
> "real."[19]

Whereas Niebuhr's thinking about reality was anthropocentric,
Barth's was theocentric. For Barth, God's love as revealed in Jesus Christ
set the terms for what was real and what was unreal:

> Anything opposed, hostile, or contrary to the reality of God was
> "unreal" by definition. Therefore for Barth the "impossible possi-
> bility" was not love but sin. Sin (and sinful human beings) existed
> in a netherworld of unreality. Sin's origin was inexplicable, its sta-
> tus was deeply conflicted, and its destiny was to vanish. Mean-
> while, it was actually there and had somehow to be taken into ac-

count, but (being essentially absurd) it could only be described in paradoxical terms.[20]

As I noted in chapter one, this discussion of the counterpart to love was also the basic disagreement between Yoder and J. Lawrence Burkholder. Yoder had studied with Barth and understood this difference as crucial for a Christian social ethic rooted in the gospel. Burkholder, on the other hand, had done his doctoral studies at Princeton and was deeply influenced by the thought of Reinhold Niebuhr. Consequently, he thought of love as an impossible ideal in real social situations. (Yoder had also studied Niebuhr's work, but was more critical of the way he framed theological and ethical questions.)

For Burkholder, the dialectic between love and justice was a problem that needed to be answered from a pacifist perspective. He wrote a paper that sought to address the problem by using Niebuhr's understanding of the distance between the real and the ideal. The Christian always falls short of the ideal of agape. Structured human society always includes some degree of coercion. He answered this by arguing that the church is an eschatological community that points us toward the ideal, even though it is imperfect.[21]

Yoder, following Barth, rejected that way of posing the problem. He insisted that theology does not begin with the human predicament but with what we know of God in Jesus Christ. He was particularly unhappy with Burkholder's claim that, "Jesus never told us in so many words the exact structural form love would take. Jesus had no ethic in terms of a social blueprint." Consequently, Burkholder asked if love can be "structuralized."[22] Yoder thought that way of posing the problem was wrongheaded. He retorted:

> What do you mean by can? What I can do or what God can do? The question is whether it should be; if it should be, then God can. Whether I can depends on whether I believe and obey, which is not a question within the field of Christian ethics.[23]

Here, Yoder is forcefully articulating an ethic of obedience, following Barth's understanding of the possibility of an objective knowledge of God. Christian ethics becomes a matter of following the way of God, who is revealed in Jesus Christ. That is what is real.[24] Anything that deviates from it is unreal and caught up in the paradoxical "impossible possibility" of sin. Yoder concluded:

Our disagreement with Niebuhr is not so much in individual content or doctrinal affirmations as in what we mean by faith, ethics, and theology. For Niebuhr ethics is for the nonbeliever and theology is applied anthropology. For us ethics is for the believer and anthropology is applied theology.[25]

This basic difference explains how controversial both Barth and Yoder could be in the guilds of professional theologians and ethicists. Both adamantly affirmed the primacy of theology based on the revealed word of God in Jesus Christ. They always worked from that premise. Beginning at any other place than with revelation ran the serious risk of distorting the gospel. Yoder was notorious in classroom discussions for telling his students, "You're not arguing with me, you're arguing with Jesus."[26] One might be tempted to see such extemporaneous statements as Yoder's failure to recognize that every understanding of Jesus, including his own, is always an interpretation that needs to be tested.

Yoder was, however, too astute a biblical scholar to make such a mistake. It is better to understand such statements as reflecting his conviction that "God really is what he is in Christ."[27] Careful and creative biblical exegesis and historical research can give us an even greater understanding of such revelation. There are things that can be known and said with confidence. Scholars should proceed on this basis in their theological and ethical reflections. One may still want to argue with Yoder about his hermeneutic, but it is not a biblical naiveté unaware of hermeneutical issues. Instead, it reflects the realist convictions he shared with Barth.

A European Social Perspective

Another thing that Barth and Yoder share is seeing the world from a European perspective. This, of course, is also true for the other European scholars and church leaders who contributed to Yoder's thought. Yoder's interpreters have not given enough attention to how the postwar European context shaped his work. The influence of that context can easily be lost if one only concentrates on the formal content of his theology. However, after becoming sensitized to his European perspective, one can see it emerging in various places throughout his work. Postwar social issues posed the crucial questions that European theologians were asking. The church struggle to define itself in relation to Nazism, communism, the horrors of World War II, and the emerging Cold War shaped the work of both Barth and Yoder.

One can learn about Barth's perspectives on such matters by studying his pastoral writings such as "The Church between East and West" and his "Letter to a Pastor in the German Democratic Republic." In these writings he addressed the contemporary questions of what it meant for the church to seek the "third way" in the postwar ideological divide. He warned that the East, with its communist ideology, should not be seen as the only adversary of Christianity. The West, with its capitalist ideology, was also an enemy. They both sought to dissuade the church from being the church. Both attempted "to silence the fearless, resounding proclamation so alien and so disturbing to the world, that God's rule is close at hand and will ultimately be revealed to the whole earth, that his kingdom is supreme and victorious over all economic, political, ideological, cultural, and also religious realms of life."[28]

As Barth was writing such words, some thinkers were already beginning to talk about this new situation as the end of Christendom, the centuries-long era in which the church had been closely allied with the reigning political powers. Barth was wary of such theoretical formulations of history but could see the possibility that a *Volkskirche* or national church was a thing of the past. Consequently, he saw that the churches in East Germany had the potential to exemplify a people that trusts in God alone, putting Westerners to shame, while at the same time encouraging them to be faithful. Thus Barth encouraged the Christians in East Germany, "Might it not be your special calling to be a living example for the rest of us of how a church lives that seeks for and perhaps has already entered upon a new way, of a church *for*, not of, the people—the church in 'God's beloved (deeply beloved!) East Zone?'"[29]

In this context Barth encouraged the Christians in East Germany to consider the prophet Jeremiah's advice to the Jewish exiles in Babylon to see exile as a cultural mandate that was appropriate to their situation. Jeremiah told the exiles to put down roots and make their home in this alien land. They were told, "Seek the welfare of the city where I have sent you into exile, and pray to the Lord on its behalf, for in its welfare you will find your welfare" (Jer. 29:7). It was a way of existing as a people who maintained their distinct religious identity, yet were willing to give themselves for the society in which they lived.[30]

Barth saw the Cold War as a global political struggle for power. Russia and America, two children of old Europe, had grown into giant rivals and now each of them in its own way, "would like to be teacher, patron, protector, benefactor—or, to put it more frankly, the master of their old mother, Europe, and with that the rest of the world as well." The church, on the other hand, is the living congregation of our living Lord Jesus Christ. It should respond to the struggle as a community that transcends these rival power blocks. Christians should not take part in the conflict:

> As Christians, it is not our concern at all. It is not a genuine, not a necessary, not an interesting conflict. . . . We can only speak in favor and support of every relaxation of the tension, and do what we can to increase the remaining fund of reason which may still be at the disposal of notoriously unreasonable humanity. With the gospel in our hearts and on our lips, we can only go through the midst of these two quarreling giants with the prayer: "Deliver us from evil! . . ."[31]

Barth believed that Christians in the West should not identify with the cause of the West merely because they live in the West and have inherited Western traditions. Such traditions do not necessarily make it God's cause any more than the East is God's cause. Barth saw a difference between this struggle and the struggle against Nazism ten years earlier. At that time, even though people feared it, there was a strange European fascination with the Nazi cause and a susceptibility to its ideology. At that time, the church had to say an unequivocal "No." The present situation was different. There was little danger of the West becoming infatuated with Russian communism. The danger for Christians in the West came from their susceptibility to capitalist ideology and their failure to acknowledge the atrocities of the Western powers in various other parts of the world. Barth warned that the battle cry Christians were being asked to join was not completely honest because it was directed against only the East. Therefore, they should not make it their own.[32]

Christology and the Church in the World

Like Barth, Yoder made God's revelation in the life and ministry of Jesus Christ central for his theology. Yoder saw a growing maturity in Barth's Christology. He said that Barth's initial understanding of Jesus, based on the Nicean Creed and Chalcedonian formula, had served as little more than a cipher for revelation. This later developed into the human figure of the gospel narratives.[33] Yoder thought Barth's mature Christology more fully recognized the implications of the claim that

Jesus, in his humanity, is a manifestation of God and God's way in the world. Accordingly, one recognizes that the crucifixion occurred as the consequence of the life Jesus lived. The resurrection and the presence of the Holy Spirit creates the church as the body of Christ, which is the bearer of a different way of being in the world—living in the presence and the hope of God's new world coming.

Consequently, Yoder understood the church as the living congregation of the living Christ. Christian theology and ethics speaks to and from this community. Yoder was fond of saying that, epistemologically, church precedes the world. As we have just seen, Barth's admonition to the Christians in the East (and in the West, for that matter) was based on that premise. Yoder appreciated Barth's free-church sympathies. One indication of those sympathies is visible in Barth's preference for the German word *Gemeinde,* which in English means the gathered congregation, rather than the magisterial word *Kirche,* which has more the meaning of church structure and polity.[34]

Yoder went considerably farther in that direction than Barth. Yoder believed this was the direction Barth's thought was moving, and that Barth should be understood and interpreted in terms of a free-church trajectory.[35] For Yoder, drawing on his Anabaptist tradition, that free-church trajectory led him to resist every political and social establishment of the church. The Constantinian era had been a mistake. It produced ingrained habits of thought and practice with disastrous results for Christian social ethics. Such establishment took many forms, ranging from the political establishment of magisterial churches in Europe to the cultural and social establishment of separatist Mennonite enclaves.[36]

Yoder took his argument for the shape of an authentic Christian presence in the world from Barth's advice to the Christians in East Germany, which followed Jeremiah's admonition to the Jewish exiles in Babylon (Jer. 29). Yoder developed the idea further, into the model of a distinct religious community that sometimes cooperated with and sometimes resisted the society in which it lived. It should not be a self-serving community but should seek the welfare of all human society.[37]

At the same time, Yoder could be quite critical of Barth. He was especially troubled by Barth's dialectic, which he believed could undermine serious ethics.[38] Yoder considered it especially problematic in Barth's discussion of the morality of war. As a student, Yoder heard Barth's lectures on this topic in 1950-51. He recalls:

[Barth's] argument was categorical, condemning practically all the concrete causes for which wars have been and may be fought. The students became more and more uneasy, especially when he said that pacifism is "almost infinitely right." Then came the dialectical twist, with the idea of a divine vocation of self-defense assigned to a particular nation, and a war which Switzerland might fight was declared—hypothetically—admissible. First there was a general release of tension in a mood of "didn't think he'd make it," then applause.[39]

What was most significant, according to Yoder, was the difference between what Barth had said and what the students understood. He had condemned all wars except for an "exceptional case" or *Grenzfall* and was himself a nuclear pacifist. But, what the students heard was that Karl Barth was not opposed to war.[40]

Barth had introduced the concept of the Grenzfall to protect the sovereignty of God. If it had been simply a reminder of the limit of human knowledge and the freedom of the commanding God, Yoder could agree with Barth. But it limits God just as much to affirm that God will command killing as to say that one does not know of any exceptions to the rule. The finitude of human knowledge is no ground for assuming that God will command war in an exceptional case. Further, the idea of Grenzfall contradicted the distinction between church and state that ran through all of Barth's theology. It made a nation-state such as Switzerland the primary locus for thinking and acting in Christian ethics.[41]

Writing in a circle letter to other young Mennonites who had been in Europe with him, Yoder could be even more categorical in his condemnation of Barth. He thought Barth's dialectic bypassed serious exposition of Scripture. With a rhetorical flourish he wrote, "The only Spirit I want to listen to is God's and he doesn't bypass the Bible as do the spirits of Tom, Dick, and Harry, of Karl Barth and George MacLeod."[42]

In the end, any understanding of Yoder as a Barthian theologian needs to be carefully nuanced. Yoder finds Barth a helpful and sometimes problematic theological mentor and conversation partner, but his real passion is to work at theology from within the Anabaptist and free-church tradition. This is clearly evident in a letter he wrote to Paul Peachey in 1954. Here he struggled with the relationship between his Anabaptist tradition, biblical studies, systematic theology, and ethics. In a fascinating effort to fit these sometimes congruent and sometimes disparate pieces together, Yoder wrote:

> It is my growing conviction that there exists a consistent biblicism of discipleship, parallel to Anabaptism not only in ecclesiastical separateness from Calvinism, but in its entire rejection of medieval carryovers in doctrine as well as in life. Which means that as Grebel and Manz [two Anabaptist leaders] were the most consistent humanists, carrying the principle of respect for the sources to the point of throwing out all doctrine which would get between them and the Bible, so in a sense we should be consistently *wissenschaftlich* [or scholarly], since the more the Bible talks for itself without Anselm or Augustine in the way, the more it talks [about] discipleship. . . . There is a widening gulf between the exegetes (Cullmann) and the systematikers (Barth), for while the exegetes, digging deeper and deeper into the text, are discovering discipleship, the systematikers, swinging back fad-wise to conservatism, have less and less to do with man's real need, and the professional ethikers who reject discipleship (Niebuhr) have less and less vital Gospel.[43]

Yoder saw two sides to Barth's theology. Decades later, in 1986, he reflected on this in an essay he wrote in the book, *How Karl Barth Changed My Mind,* a collection of essays by theologians who were influenced by Barth. This essay, written when he was a mature theologian, still demonstrated the same ambivalence about Barth's theology that had appeared in his much earlier letter to Paul Peachey. One side to Barth's theology, according to Yoder, was a conservative creedal orthodoxy, with which he was uncomfortable. The other side to his theology was a movement toward a radical discipleship and commitment to a free-church vision, which Yoder affirmed. Yoder said that Barth's *Church Dogmatics* remained a torso and never fully completed this vision. Nevertheless, a faithful interpretation of Barth's work, Yoder believed, should not see him as rehabilitating orthodoxy or establishment. It should focus on the movement of his thought toward the vision of radical discipleship, rooted in the human figure of Jesus in the evangelical gospel accounts.[44]

From Yoder's conversation about Barth, it becomes clear that a big part of the task, as Yoder saw it, was biblical exegesis, which could provide the foundation for Christian discipleship. Systematic theology and theological ethics need to be in conversation with such scholarship to have integrity in their own disciplines. Yoder attempted to be a bridge where such conversation could take place. That was the task he set for himself with his comprehensive study of the "politics of Jesus."

OSCAR CULLMANN AND BIBLICAL STUDIES

Yoder was convinced that biblical research on the life of Jesus and the early church was vital to recapturing the meaning of discipleship. The biblical exegesis of people like Oscar Cullmann excited him. Such biblical scholars were studying the social and political situation in first-century Palestine, and were asking how Jesus and the early Christian communities related to their world. Yoder wanted to put such biblical exegesis into conversation with contemporary theological ethics.

Yoder appropriated several significant things from Cullmann. One was the work Cullmann did on the relationship of Jesus and the early Christian communities to the Roman Empire. To do this, Cullmann examined the teaching of Jesus in the Gospels, the teaching of the apostle Paul, and the perspective of the Johannine Apocalypse. European Protestants, during the postwar era, had a great interest in reexamining their theological understanding of the relationship between church and state. Central to this task was a new historical examination of the biblical sources.

Such interest is evident in the conversation between the historic peace churches and the established European Protestant churches at the Puidoux Theological Conference held in Switzerland in 1955. The theme of the conference was "The Lordship of Christ over Church and State." Cullmann could not attend the conference, but participants discussed two of his papers related to the conference theme.[45]

One of Cullmann's papers concerned "The Kingship of Christ in the Church in the New Testament."[46] It was an exegetical study of the concept of the "reign of Christ" and the confession among the early Christians that "Jesus Christ is Lord." The other paper was titled "The State in the New Testament."[47] It was an abbreviated version of material later published in a book with the same name. The time and energy the conference put into discussing Cullmann's biblical exegesis indicates how important they believed such research was for the difficult task of rethinking the role of the church and the state in the aftermath of the war.[48]

Wrestling with Traditional Two-Kingdom Theologies

The European Protestants were especially interested in overcoming the deficiencies of traditional two-kingdom theologies that made a clear distinction between the spiritual, eternal realm of the church and the temporal, political realm of the state. According to this conceptualization, the church served as the earthly custodian of the spiritual realm and the state served as the earthly custodian of the temporal realm. It was built on an ethical dualism in which the clergy and religious followed a counsel of perfection involving a commitment to a life of poverty, nonviolence, and celibacy. The laity or ordinary Christians, on the other hand, needed to participate in mundane affairs and were not expected to follow such a strict ethic.

According to this doctrine, God had charged the church with preaching the gospel and the state with ensuring the political order. Such traditional two-kingdom theologies have their roots in the Constantinian era. Pope Gelasius I had formulated the thesis in 495. It is instructive to follow this formulation of the relationship between distinctive spiritual and temporal realms through subsequent church history. During the medieval era, there was an assumption of the primacy of the spiritual realm. This primacy provided the basis by which the church could intrude into the affairs of the temporal realm while resisting state intrusion into church affairs.[49]

This way of conceptualizing the relationship between church and state changed during the Protestant reformation. Luther rejected the dual morality of the medieval two-kingdom theology, but, tragically, he introduced another dualism by transferring it to the life of each individual. According to Luther, we all live with the tension between being a Christian and a citizen of a given state. As a Christian, one follows the example and teaching of Christ, while as a citizen one follows the natural law, which God has implanted in our hearts.[50] It was such ethical dualisms that had helped undermine Christian resistance to the secular totalitarian state in the modern world. That undermining had become painfully apparent to European theologians and church leaders in the postwar era as they reflected on German Christian responses to the Nazis.

It had become evident that such theological formulations, at their worst, had divinized the state and left the church impotent in the face of totalitarian schemes. As a result, the conversation at Puidoux in 1955 turned to the limits of Christian obedience to the state. Oscar Cullmann recognized that the state, within its own sphere, sometimes ceases to be founded on law and actually reverses any criterion of justice in the civil order. He was very cautious, however, when it came to making judgments about when a state had crossed this line and no longer remained within God's plan. He said that, from the perspective of the New Testament, one clear criterion of such demonic folly was the imposition of emperor worship.[51]

Jean Lasserre, a French Reformed pastor and scholar, was frustrated by such caution. The issue that French Christians faced under the Vichy government during the war was not overt emperor worship. Surely, Lasserre argued, theologians and ethicists should be able to draw up some criteria for determining when the state has exceeded its bounds. He gave several examples of situations where the state obviously asked people to do things that were unjust. Must a German woman obey the Nazis who required her to divorce her non-Aryan husband? Must a policeman obey when he is ordered to interrogate a woman by stripping her and burning her breasts with cigarettes? Lasserre exclaimed, "So the church of Jesus Christ has absolutely nothing to tell believers faced with problems of conscience such as I have evoked, but leaves them entirely to their own resources: this seems to be yet another sign of a church which is no longer faithful and has given up the struggle."[52]

The Reign of Christ

While Cullmann was reluctant to challenge government authority, he was a gifted biblical scholar. It was here that he made his contribution to the discussion. He claimed that the problem of church and state was rooted in the very nature of Christianity from its beginning. The New Testament referred to the *reign of Christ,* which Cullmann insisted was distinct from the church or the future kingdom of God. He built his argument on the apostle Paul's discussion of the reign of Christ (1 Cor. 15:23 ff.), which was the basis upon which the early Christians proclaimed that Jesus Christ is Lord (Rom. 10:9). Christ's kingship extends to all creation (Phil. 2:10). Cullmann claimed:

> It is, therefore not true that Christ now exercises his kingship only in heaven or the invisible world. Christ also rules on earth and over the state as well as the Church. Admittedly, he does not rule over the states of this world directly, but only through the

mediation of the "powers and authorities" which he has subjected and which are provisionally attached to him. These invisible powers are active on earth.[53]

The New Testament uses various terms for such invisible powers, which were believed to be behind the state authorities who executed Jesus. Herod and Pilate were merely the human functionaries they used for their purposes. If these powers had known God's plan of salvation, they would not have crucified Jesus because this led to their own defeat (1 Cor. 2:7-8). Though they have been conquered, their power still persists through the terrible power of the *sarx* (body or unregenerate human nature) and the *last enemy*, which is death. Even though the divine Spirit is already at work, it will only transform these enemies at the end (1 Cor. 15:35 ff.). Even so, it is a mistake to think that these powers can escape the rule of Christ. In other places, Paul uses the image of *head* to describe Christ's rule over the invisible and visible creation, including every *ruler and authority* (Col. 2:10).[54]

Accordingly, Cullmann insisted that the reign of Christ must not be identified with the church. Nevertheless, the New Testament concentration on the church as a definite point within creation signifies that it is the heart and center of the reign of Christ. What happens in the church has a decisive influence for all of creation. The church itself, however, must resist any theocratic aspirations, because such aspirations belong to the future in heaven (Phil.3:20).[55]

On the other hand, Cullman argued that the state does not have any independent right of its own. Governments function as God's servants within the reign of Christ (Rom. 13:6). As such they are entitled to our obedience and active support. But, when they become disengaged from the reign of Christ, they are extremely questionable and become demonic. In this sense, Cullmann claimed that the earthly state, though not ultimate and divine in itself, is nevertheless a member of the reign of Christ by the will of God. But there is a crucial difference between church and state within the reign of Christ. Cullman wrote:

> The fact that the members of the church are conscious of all this, they know that Christ rules, and are therefore members of the kingdom of Christ consciously, is what distinguishes them as a Church from all the other members of the *Regnum Christi* [or reign of Christ] who may be its servants unconsciously.[56]

Even though Lasserre criticized Cullmann's cautious reluctance to say when the state had overstepped its limits, he accepted Cullman's premise that government officials were God's servants within the reign of Christ. In his own presentation at the Puidoux Theological Conference, he had this to say about the role of such people:

> Their function, as God sees it, is in no way placed outside the Revelation as though they enjoyed some kind of autonomy that they had to themselves. Very much to the contrary, they carry out a ministry—extra-ecclesiastical, to be sure—which is integral to the framework of Redemption. I think that the picture of Cullmann, who speaks of two concentric circles representing the Church and the *Regnum Christi,* is right. In the plan of God, the magistrates are placed, not in the circle of the Church, but in the larger circle of the "Reign of Christ." But they are always under the control of Revelation.[57]

There was general agreement on this way of formulating the relationship between church and state among the theologians and church leaders at Puidoux. It was on this basis that they could argue that Christ was Lord of both church and state while still maintaining a distinction between them. It was on this basis that the church could witness to the state about the will of God as understood in Christ. It enabled the church to maintain its own freedom in relation to the state. They could insist on a certain primacy of the church in God's economy. Christian social and political ethics should always begin from the premise of the reign of Christ.

Such a conceptualization of the relationship between the church, the state, and the "powers" under the reign of Christ became central to the way Yoder worked at social and political issues. We cannot understand his theological ethics apart from this conceptualization.[58] It became the basis on which he would prod Mennonites out of their separatism and toward a more engaged witness to the larger society. It was also the basis on which to prod American Protestant proponents of "social responsibility" toward taking the church seriously in their ethics.

Like Lasserre, Yoder criticized Cullmann's reluctance to define the limits of the state's authority, short of emperor worship or self-deification. He argued that it was more than the vagueness of the criterion that makes it suspect. Most German Christians had not even seen such extreme self-deification in Hitler. There is no evident reason why violating the first commandment of the law should be understood as more grievous than violating any of the other commandments. Idolatry need not become cultic to make it rebellion against God. The problem with making the extreme case of self-deification the criterion for such rebellion is the implication that there can be an exercise of violent domination that is not intrinsically self-glorifying, that there can be a nationalism that is not prone to idolatry, or a total war that is not indicative of the state's self-aggrandizement.[59]

An early contribution to the discussion was Yoder's paper "The Theological Basis of the Christian Witness to the State," which he presented at the Puidoux Theological Conference. In this paper Yoder argued that Christianization of the world is possible in the sense that there is a Christian influence on what happens in the world. The important question, however, is *how* one exercises that influence. His paper makes various references to the work of Jean Lasserre, who presented an earlier paper at the conference. It is also deeply indebted to Cullmann's exegetical work on the reign of Christ.[60]

In his paper, Yoder addressed the relationship between church and state and the problem of traditional two-kingdom theologies. He defined the difference between the church and the world on the basis of their respective responses to the invitation of God in Jesus Christ. The church says *yes* to God while the world says *no*. God respects the world's freedom to say *no*. Therefore, in the world, which includes the state, God's requirements are adapted to that *no*. Accordingly, all that can be counted on is a basic ethical minimum that is valid despite humanity's *no*. His paper was a heuristic attempt to formulate and test the duality that results from humanity's *no* to God, while recognizing that there is ultimately only one ethic established in the reign of Christ.[61]

The church is where humanity's *no* is overcome through God's grace. Consequently, Yoder argues, "In speaking of the Church, we must say that the meaning of history and the significance of everything that happens in the world is not the fate of Western culture, of civilization, of the human community of justice, or of the world, but the formation and building of the body of Christ."[62]

Such distinctions, grounded in his understanding of the reign of Christ, became the basis of Yoder's argument against an ethic of responsibility rooted in the life of a given nation-state. It is not the nation but the church that carries the meaning of history. That is why the Christian must, at some point, make a break with human continuity rooted in family, ethnic identity, social identity, and national identity to place her or his faith in the church, which is the resurrection body of Christ.

While the church has an immediate relationship to God through Christ, the world, including the state, has a mediate relationship through the "powers" (*exousiai*). These "powers," though originally part of God's good creation, are fallen in the sense that they resist God. In this sense, pragmatically speaking, the state is also fallen because it is always less than submissive to God. Since it is never as submissive as it could be, it is with reference to relative degrees of submission that we can say that a given state is Christianized. Hence, we could say that a relatively democratic and nonviolent state is more Christian than a brutal totalitarian state. But, a state is never so submitted to God's rule that we can do anything but make such relative comparisons.[63]

Finally, according to Yoder, the reign of Christ over the "powers" and over the states is conservative rather than redemptive. The purpose is not to bring in the kingdom of God but to keep things from falling apart so that the church can do its redemptive kingdom work. For that reason, Yoder said, "There is always this distinction between these two areas, or orders, and the duality is defined in that one is redemptive and the other conservative."[64]

Having laid this theological groundwork, Yoder tackled the question of the church's witness to the state. It is not true that Christians who follow Christ's way of self-giving and nonviolent love have nothing to say to the state. If they recognize that the state is not an abstraction but various people doing different tasks, they will address them as individuals. The first message to these people is an invitation to become Christian, which means being a disciple who follows Christ's way of nonviolent love. Government officials who are Christians should be reminded that it is not a government office but being a disciple of Jesus that defines their actions.[65]

Even if the statesperson does not accept the challenge to become a Christian, Yoder insisted, it does not free the officeholder from responsibility before God. If these persons choose to say *no* to this invitation of God, they are still under the *yes* of God that reaches out to them. They are still under the reign of Christ, and God still has claims upon them. For those who say *yes* to God in Christ, the demand is to bear the cross, and those who say *no* to this invitation are still called to do justice. Correspondingly, the concept of a just war has some value in defining the demands of justice for such people, even though it becomes less and less useful as governments keep building more and more sophisticated weapons of mass destruction.[66]

Yoder insisted that the state is not autonomous nor an authority to itself. But even if it functions as an autonomous authority, we can always challenge it to make a particular choice with reference to justice. Because of its frame of reference, we cannot ask the state to be perfectly just, but we can ask it to be more just. We can ask the state to live up to its own concept of justice. For example, we can ask France to take seriously its commitment to liberty, equality, and fraternity. Because each state is already committed to some understanding of order, Yoder said, we can appeal to it to live up to its own principles.[67]

Using Cullman's biblical exegesis, Lasserre and Yoder were both working at defining a single Christian morality to overcome the easy dualism of traditional two-kingdom theologies. Lasserre wrote:

> In the New Testament . . . there is no duality between the good which concerns civil society and the good which concerns the Christian's so called "private" life: one's difficulty in finding adequate terms is in itself significant. No, there is only a single Christian morality, only a single good in the eyes of the God of Jesus Christ; and the ultimate norm of that good is that it glorifies God in *Jesus Christ.* There is no good which denies Jesus Christ, contradicts Him, or even leaves Him out of account.[68]

While they basically agreed, Lasserre made the point about the need for a single morality more forcefully than Yoder did. That most likely reflects their respective theological traditions. Lasserre, from his Reformed tradition, was more comfortable with a less nuanced single morality. Yoder, from his Anabaptist tradition, wanted to maintain a clear distinction between church and state. However, they both sought to overcome the artificial dualism of traditional two-kingdom theologies. They both wanted to avoid the mistake of collapsing church and state into a kind of Christian theocracy. To do that, they relied on Cullman's study of the reign of Christ, which was understood to determine the roles of both the church and the state. Their effort was only a beginning and, even today, still needs more work.

Limitations

The issue of the relationship between church and state has been an ongoing tension throughout Christian history. That tension was already present in the life and ministry of Jesus and the early church in relation to the Roman Empire. What's more, the issue defies easy or permanent resolution because of the evolving cultural and sociological forms of the various historical states and churches. The contexts within which the issue is addressed throughout the centuries of the church's existence vary enormously. The social realities in the first century differ significantly from those in the fourth century. The same goes for the sixteenth or twentieth centuries. Even more, the contexts shaping the relationship between a given church and state within any historical era differ markedly. The issue is more complex than getting the theology right.[69]

Lasserre and Yoder built their case against two-kingdom theologies on a biblical theology centered on the apostle Paul's teaching on the reign of Christ. That argument would be stronger if augmented with more historical and theological work, including more practical and pastoral application. Turning specifically to Yoder, one needs to raise some questions about the limitations inherent in his dependence on Cullmann's exegetical research on Paul, given Cullmann's reluctance to challenge the established political order. Cullmann framed the conversation on an exposition of Romans 13:1 and Paul's admonition to be subject to the governing authorities. Making that text central and then attempting to harmonize it with the rest of the New Testament made it difficult to create space for a principled Christian opposition to oppressive governments.

A second limitation is that Yoder's understanding of the church, in his paper at the Puidoux conference, was an abstraction, or even an idealization, that he did not flesh out. Is the church simply a pneumatic people of God? If it has a structural form, in what sense is it also a manifestation of the "powers?" In what sense is it also fallen, with at least some characteristics similar to those of the state? In such respects, the sociological distinction between church and state is not as clearcut as it might seem from Yoder's argument. Finally, Yoder's primary concern was the problem of war. Christian ethics includes other equally pressing social and economic issues. War is never isolated from such human problems and is always a consequence of our failure to courageously respond to them.

It is not fair to say that Yoder could have adequately dealt with those issues in a single paper at the Puidoux conference. However, pointing to these questions demonstrates the need to address more fully the historical and sociological dimensions of the problem. Furthermore, one needs to raise questions about the extent to which Yoder's subsequent work on this topic reflects some of these same limitations. To what extent did he keep grounding his theology in Cullmann's exegetical work on the reign of Christ without substantially reexamining the basic premise of his social ethics? Cullmann's reign of Christ is a metaphysical idea which needs to be rooted in the life and experience of real communities if it is to have validity. These challenges still need to be worked at in order adequately to address the question of the relationship between church, state, and other social entities. Such work is especially pertinent for people who are deeply indebted to Yoder and his approach to social issues.

Jesus and the Jewish Religious Parties

John Howard Yoder's theology also owes a debt to Cullmann's insights from biblical research on the relationship between Jesus and the various Jewish religious parties in first-century Palestine. Biblical scholars during that time (especially Oscar Cullmann, Martin Hengel, and S. F. Brandon) were researching the relationship between Jesus and the Zealots.[70] The Zealots were a loosely defined group of Jewish revolutionaries committed to the violent overthrow of the Roman occupation of Palestine. Cullmann identified at least five of Jesus' disciples as Zealots and said that Jesus had to continually come to terms with the Zealot question throughout his ministry.[71] Yoder was less interested in the immediate question of Jesus' relationship to the Zealots than he was in the broader question of Jesus' political stance in relation to the various options available to him in first-century Palestine.

Cullmann was clearly Yoder's mentor in such research, even though Yoder pursued the question farther than Cullmann had. Cullmann set the question of Jesus' relationship to the state in the context of the Jewish theocratic ideal as espoused by the Maccabees. Such theocratic aspirations were a significant source of political unrest in Palestine under the imperial occupation of the Romans. The Zealots, a potent revolutionary force, espoused such a theocratic ideal. Cullmann, however, argued that Jesus and the early Christians rejected theocratic aspirations as demonic. He tied the struggle to Jesus' temptation in the wilderness, where he rejected Satan's offer of world domination (Luke 4:5-8). In doing so, Jesus rejected the state in any sense as a final or divine institution. Cullmann thought the temptation account demonstrates that Jesus accepted the state and rejected any revolutionary attempt to overthrow it.[72] The Romans, according to him, had not understood Jesus when they crucified him as a revolutionary. Cullman did not consider that Jesus might nevertheless have posed a real threat to the established social order in Palestine, even though he rejected violent revolution.[73]

The Original Revolution

In his own interpretation of Jesus' political involvements in first-century Palestine, Yoder followed the general outline of Cullmann's work. Like Cullmann, Yoder made the temptation story central to the interpretation of Jesus' political stance. Like Cullmann, Yoder focused on Jesus' relationship with the Zealots, but he also went beyond Cullmann to look at the other political options available to Jesus. Like Cullmann, Yoder understood Jesus' execution by the Romans as definitive for our understanding of who Jesus was. But, unlike Cullmann, Yoder did not think the crucifixion involved a misunderstanding of Jesus by the Romans. He saw Jesus as a real threat to the political powers in first-century Palestine. Yoder wrote:

> Both Jewish and Roman authorities were defending themselves against a real threat. That the threat was not one of *armed,* violent revolt, and that it nonetheless bothered them to the point of their resorting to illegal procedures to counter it, is a proof of the political relevance of nonviolent tactics, not a proof that Pilate and Caiaphas were exceptionally dull or dishonorable men.[74]

Yoder's portrait of the historical Jesus was more socially and politically involved and considerably more radical than that of Cullmann. Yoder's more popular book on Jesus and the early church that preceded *The Politics of Jesus* was titled *The Original Revolution*. Here he wrote, "If we are ever to rescue God's good news from all the justifiable but secondary meanings it has taken on, perhaps the best way to do it is to say that the root meaning of the term *euangelion* would today best be translated 'revolution.'"[75] He insisted that Jesus' message involves real social and political choices that are revolutionary in nature if we take them seriously. He was convinced that Jesus is "the bearer of a new possibility of human, social, and therefore political relationships."[76] It is this political Jesus, found in the gospel narratives by biblical exegetes, whom Yoder placed in conversation with contemporary social and political ethics.

The Politics of Paul and the Early Church

Additionally, one needs to ask how the revolutionary nature of Jesus' life and message formed the life of the early churches. It can be argued that there is a radical break between Jesus' proclamation of the reign of God and the worship of the heavenly Christ in the Gentile churches during the following decades. To counter such an interpretation, Yoder drew on the themes of discipleship and imitation found in the epistles. Through a careful study of these themes, he was able to argue that the way of the cross should not be understood as literally following Jesus' lifestyle or an existential identification with suffering in itself. Instead, the cross points to the concrete social meaning of Jesus' political stance in relation to dominant structures of power in our world.[77]

The big question for this argument was whether the apostle Paul's stance toward the Roman Empire differed significantly from that of Jesus. Cullmann worked on this question as it related to Paul's counsel to Christians to submit to the governing authorities because they have been ordained by God (Rom. 13:1-7). Various two-kingdom paradigms have claimed this passage as the central basis for the argument that God has ordained government to function as a distinct authority rooted in natural law rather than in the gospel of Jesus Christ. Christians should obey governing authorities in matters pertaining to national citizenship such as waging war.[78]

Cullmann insisted that such interpretations misunderstand this Scripture passage and Paul's stance toward the Roman Empire. The only way Romans 13:1-7 could be interpreted as unequivocal support for the state is by taking it out of context. Both in chapter 12 and in the rest of chapter 13, Paul is speaking directly to Christians about their responsibility to act out of love, not to resist evil with evil but to do good to one's enemies. The Roman state, as Paul knew it, often did the exact opposite. Nevertheless, Christians are to accept the state as an institution despite that reality. But Paul is not suggesting, Cullmann argued, that Christians should participate in the retributive aspects of state vengeance against evildoers. Instead, he calls for a positive expression of the Christian love ethic in relation to the state. While he does not explicitly explain how that is possible, Paul argues that the state is also a servant of God as long as it does not exceed its bounds.[79]

According to Cullmann, one needs to recognize that Paul is talking about Nero's regime. Christians had reason to feel animosity toward this tyrannical government. Paul is encouraging them to not reject the validity of the state as a matter of principle. Paul needs to be explicit about that point because the retributive nature of the state makes it less than self-evident. Nevertheless, they are to subordinate themselves to the state as long as it functions within its proper sphere and does not demand that which belongs God. Even when it demands more than it rightfully should, the Christian response should still be guided by the love ethic. It is the same stance toward the state that Jesus had.[80]

This stance becomes even more evident when we examine other passages where Paul addresses Christian relationships to the state. He chastises the Christians in Corinth for filing lawsuits against each other in Roman courts of law (1 Cor. 6:1ff.). They should settle their quarrels within a congregational discernment process, rather than relying on punitive government institutions. When Paul tells the Corinthians that they will someday judge the world, it is clear that he understands the state to be a temporary institution whose scope is limited.[81]

Finally, Cullmann emphasizes Paul's recognition of a demonic element in the state. Paul tells the Corinthians, "None of the rulers of this world understood the wisdom of God; for if they had understood it they would not have crucified the Lord of glory" (1 Cor. 2:8). The phrase "rulers of this world," like the expression "authorities" or "powers" (*exousiai*) in Romans 13:1, refers not only to political figures but also to invisible spiritual powers that stood behind them—a common understanding of power within the first-century Jewish worldview. References to authorities and powers have a double meaning, referring to both the state and such invisible spiritual powers. Jesus conquered these powers through his death and resurrection (Col. 2:15). Cullmann wrote:

> Against the background of this belief in the vanquished powers at work behind earthly happenings it becomes especially clear that the State is now a temporary institution not of divine nature but nevertheless willed by God; that we must remain critical toward every State; that we must nonetheless obey the State as far as it remains within its bounds.[82]

Accordingly, Cullmann sought to make a distinction between a state that lived within the bounds of Romans 13 and a state that moved outside these bounds (the demonic state of Rev. 13). Christians had an obligation to obey the state that stayed within its bounds, but not the state which moves outside these bounds by becoming totalitarian and self-deifying.[83]

Yoder followed the general argument of Cullmann's exegetical work. Cullmann sought to harmonize a vast and disparate body of New Testament material dealing with the question of church and state. This material ranges from the Gospels, though the Pauline Epistles, to the book of Revelation. Yoder began by recognizing that the New Testament contains different strands of thought concerning the state, but then followed Cullmann in the effort to demonstrate that Paul's argument in Romans 13:1-7 is consistent with these other materials.

Cullman and Yoder try to harmonize too much difference. Other biblical scholars have even raised questions about Romans 13:1-7 being a later interpolation because it demonstrates a much more positive assessment of government than the rest of the New Testament and even the rest of the Pauline material (e.g. 1 Cor. 2: 6-8). This tension does not necessarily mean we must assume Romans 13:1-7 is an interpolation, but it certainly has a much more positive attitude toward Roman imperial rule than do other New Testament materials. The New Testament did not have a univocal understanding of how Christians should relate to the state. Even Paul apparently was not completely consistent in his attitudes toward imperial Roman government.[84]

There is a crucial difference between Cullmann's and Yoder's understanding of the threat that Jesus' ministry and community organizing posed to Roman rule. As seen earlier, Cullmann begins with the belief that Jesus had not posed a threat to the Roman Empire. He writes, "Jesus was in no sense an enemy of the State on principle, but rather a loyal citizen who offered no threat to the State's existence."[85] Yoder had a considerably more radical and revolutionary Jesus. Jesus' nonviolent community organizing in Palestine did pose a real threat to the ruling authorities. In its own way it was an even greater threat than violent insurrection.[86]

The most important common agenda of Cullmann and Yoder is that both sought to discredit the two-kingdom theologies that had been prevalent until the postwar era. Yoder said that the basic premises of such theologies (built on Rom. 13:1-7) had not been questioned until the crisis of Nazism made it necessary to re-examine them. Before this crisis, these verses had served as a sort of capsule, guiding the Christian statesperson (punishing evil and rewarding good) and the Christian citizen (obeying state authorities). Within such a theological construct, the government that wields the sword by divine decree was exempted from the general prohibition against killing. All that remained were some borderline questions concerning things such as determining what constituted a just war.[87] Yoder made it clear that he was challenging the tradition of two-kingdom theology at its very core:

> Let us then put most precisely the challengeable claim of the tradition we intend to challenge; it is that by virtue of the divine institution of government as a part of God's good creation, its mandate to wield the sword and the Christian's duty to obey the state combine to place upon the Christian a moral obligation to support and participate in the state's legal killing (death penalty, war), despite contrary duties which otherwise would seem to follow from Jesus' teaching or example.[88]

The first part of Yoder's argument was that Romans 13:1-7 is not the center of New Testament teaching about the state. The New Testament speaks in many ways about the problem of the state. A strong strand of teaching in the Gospels even sees the state as demonic. Following Cullmann, Yoder argued that Romans 12 and 13 constitute a complete literary unit. Therefore Romans13:1-7 should not be understood by itself. It becomes a static or conservative underpinning of the present social order only by refusing to take its larger literary context seriously.[89]

Revolutionary Subordination

Next, Yoder tackled the question of Christian submission or subordination to the state. Such subordination, he said, merely recognizes whatever power exists or whatever structure of sovereignty happens to prevail. This subordination does not imply recognition of a particular government as divinely instituted. Yoder rejected Cullmann's argument that governments living within the bounds of Romans 13:1-7 are instituted of God in a way that other governments are not.[90] This point is significant for understanding Yoder's basic stance toward government authority. With reference to Romans 13:1-7 he wrote:

God is not said to *create* or *institute* or *ordain* the powers that be, but only to *order* them, to put them in order, sovereignly to tell them where they belong, what is their place. It is not as if there was a time when there was no government and then God made government through a new creative intervention; there has been hierarchy and authority and power since human society existed. Its exercise has involved domination, disrespect for human dignity, and real or potential violence ever since sin has existed. Nor is it that in his ordering of it he specifically, morally approves of what government does. . . . God does not take responsibility for the existence of the rebellious "powers that be" or for their shape or identity; they already are. What the text says is that he orders them, brings them into line, that by his permissive government he lines them up with his purpose.[91]

Another central aspect of Yoder's position involves his understanding of what it means for Christians to be subordinate to government authorities. Paul was calling the early Christians away from any notion of violent revolution or insubordination. Instead, he was asking them to take a position of nonresistant love toward tyrannical Roman rule. Yoder explained that subordination does not mean compliance or acquiescence in evil, but rather the suffering renunciation of retaliation in kind. It does not rule out other kinds of resistance to evil.[92] In this sense, Christians should be subordinate but also rebel against all forms of government. Yoder argued that such subordination is actually a Christian form of rebellion because, in doing so, we share God's patience with a system we have basically rejected.[93]

Yoder shared Cullmann's understanding of the limited scope of appropriate government authority. Accordingly Yoder said that the appropriate government functions, to which Paul calls Christians to be subject, are the juridical and police functions of the state. These functions cannot include such things as the death penalty or war. It certainly cannot mean that Christians need to participate in the military or even in police service. Yoder made a distinction between war and police action, which is more than a matter of the degree of violence:

It is a structural and a profound difference in the sociological meaning of the appeal to force. In the police function, the violence or threat thereof is applied only to the offending party. The use of violence by the agent of the police is subject to review by higher authorities. He applies his power within the limits of a state whose legislation even the criminal knows to be applicable to him. In any orderly police system there are serious safeguards to keep the violence of the police from being applied in a whole-sale way against the innocent. The police power generally is great enough to overwhelm that of the individual offender so that any resistance on his part is pointless. In all of these respects, war is structurally different.[94]

Yoder understood just war theories as attempts to extend these limits on violence within policing into the realm of war. He saw some logic in such just war patterns of thought but little realism. When one thinks honestly and carefully about it, one can recognize that, as far as any real war is concerned, it is not possible to fit such action under the authority given to governments in Romans 13:1-7.[95]

Accordingly, Yoder argued that Paul does not believe governments are self-justifying or that whatever they ask of their citizens is automatically good. Paul is not asking citizens to mindlessly obey government authorities but to be subject to them. Christians who accept their subordination to government nevertheless retain their moral independence. Yoder followed Cullmann in seeing an allusion to the words of Jesus (Mat. 22:21) in Romans 13:7 where Paul instructs the Roman Christians to "pay to all what is due them." This change means giving to Caesar what is his (taxes and a certain amount of respect and honor), but giving their primary allegiance to God. This stance follows the example of Jesus, who accepted subordination and humiliation from the hands of government authorities.[96]

Subordination is one of the most misunderstood parts of Yoder's theology. He claimed that subordination was not simply a calculated recognition of the strength of the powers that are operative in our world. It is not a passive acceptance of one's lot nor a willingness to suffer passively. It is actually a strategy of engagement and resistance. He wrote:

> The willingness to suffer is then not merely a test of our patience or a dead space of waiting; it is itself a participation in the character of God's victorious patience with the rebellious powers of creation. We subject ourselves to government because it was in so doing that Jesus revealed and achieved God's victory.[97]

OTHER EUROPEAN CONVERSATIONS

Yoder's contribution to the debate about the relationship between church and state was the way he made Jesus' social and political stance normative. He effectively challenged the centuries-old two-kingdom theologies, which made Paul's teaching in Romans 13: 1-7 the center of their understanding of the distinctive roles of both church and state within their respective spiritual and temporal realms. Such theologies had been conceptualized within the worldview of a unified European Christian society. The twentieth-century experiences of secular totalitarian governments and two brutal world wars made theologians recognize that these suppositions no longer held.

European theologians were already working on the question of state-church relations when Yoder began his doctoral studies at the University of Basel. He brought both his intellectual abilities and his pacifist, free-church tradition to the discussion. Studying the biblical texts through his pacifist, free-church lens gave them a congruence that they did not have when viewed from an established Christendom perspective. That helps explain why Yoder saw Barth moving in a free-church trajectory in what was obviously becoming a post-Christendom era. The contribution he made needs to be understood within this unique confluence of factors.

Yoder was a gifted student who learned from mentors such as Karl Barth and Oscar Cullmann. His indebtedness to them is obvious when one traces the development of his thought in relation to their work. As has been seen, his understanding of Jesus' social and political ethics and the relationship between church and state owes a deep debt to Oscar Cullmann's exegetical work. The theology of Karl Barth and his struggles with the question of a church now divided between East and West is also central. It provided the theological structure for his work. But it is a mistake to understand Yoder as a student who continued working in the school of either Cullmann or Barth. Yoder worked much more broadly than that and he also obtained aspects of his thought from other European scholars and church leaders.

Yoder's indebtedness to Jean Lasserre has been seen. He was also indebted to André Trocmé, another Reformed French church leader. Trocmé was a pacifist pastor who had organized his parish in the French village of Le Chambon to protect Jewish refugees and resist the Vichy government during World War II. When Yoder made his acquaintance, Trocmé was serving as the European secretary of the International Fellowship of Reconciliation.[98]

Yoder's activist and radical understanding of Jesus is at least partly indebted to Trocmé, a capable biblical scholar, even though he made his biggest contributions as an activist and a pastor. Trocmé wrote a booklet arguing that Jesus' concept of the reign of God was deeply immersed in the Hebrew prophetic tradition of the jubilee year.[99] Yoder incorporated this idea into his own thought and freely adapted parts of Trocmé's work in the chapter "The Implications of the Jubilee" in the *Politics of Jesus*.[100]

Yoder's work also owes a debt to the Dutch theologian Hendrikus Berkhof, who studied the phenomenon of the "powers" as conveyed in biblical language. Yoder found Berkhof's work so significant that he translated it into English. He later incorporated much of Berkhof's thought into the chapter "Christ and Power" in *The Politics of Jesus*. Berkhof had first presented this material as a lecture at a theological conference in Germany in 1950, where it spoke to the devastated situation of a divided Germany during that time. After a series of delays, Berkhof had tried to have it published in 1955 in the series Theologische Studien, which Barth edited. After some initial enthusiasm, the manuscript was turned down because editors believed that Berkhof was mythologizing the "powers" too much. Berkhof also attributed the rejection of his manuscript to the changing social situation in Germany, where tensions had significantly subsided and the general welfare of the population was rapidly rising.[101]

The question about the contemporary relevance of New Testament language about the "powers" emerged in the postwar era as theologians were able to reflect on the emergence of secular ideologies such as Nazism, communism, and capitalism. The language of "powers," which had been seen as an untranslatable carryover of a first-century worldview, now took on fresh meaning. Protestant theology had become existential and focused on the individual. Because of that focus, it had little capacity to address structural evil. Berkhof and Yoder, in turn, recaptured the relevance of the biblical "powers" language in relation to contemporary institutions and ideologies and incorporated it into their theological ethics.

CONCLUSION

As seen in this chapter, John Howard Yoder's "politics of Jesus" owes much to European mentors and colleagues such as Oscar Cullmann, Karl Barth, Jean Lasserre, André Trocmé, and Hendrikus Berkhof. Cullmann especially contributed to his political understanding of Jesus. Barth provided the theological tools that Yoder used to such great effect. Lasserre was his colleague in the struggle against two-kingdom theologies. Trocmé gave Yoder insights into the function of the jubilee year in Jesus' social agenda. Berkhof gave him the language of "powers" in reference to social structures. Despite such valuable teachers and conversation partners, Yoder's concerns would also direct him on his own path.

Yoder's agenda had two foci. One, which we have already seen, is his ongoing debate with the dominant American Protestant ethics of social responsibility as articulated by people like Reinhold Niebuhr. Yoder would not accept the characterization that the pacifist chooses personal faithfulness or eschatology over social responsibility. To follow in the steps of Jesus and Paul is to be socially responsible.[102] The other focus is that he remained a Mennonite theologian and social ethicist, building on the work of his earlier Mennonite mentors, especially Guy Hershberger and Harold Bender. For that reason, he did his doctoral dissertation on the sixteenth-century conversations between the Swiss Anabaptists and the Protestant reformers. The next chapter explores the contribution this research made to Yoder's theological ethics.

NOTES

1. Harold Bender, letter to John Howard Yoder, December 6, 1950, Bender papers, box 42, AMC.

2. John Howard Yoder, letter to Harold Bender, August 16, 1948, Bender papers, box 42, AMC.

3. Harold Bender, letter to John Howard Yoder, December 6, 1950, Bender papers, box 42, AMC.

4. John Howard Yoder, letter to Harold Bender, January 12, 1951, Bender papers, box 42, AMC.

5. Ibid.

6. Harold Bender, letter to John Howard Yoder, January 19, 1951, Bender papers, box 42, AMC.

7. Ibid.

8. Ibid.

9. For a fuller description of the ways Bender did this and the conservative theo-

logical environment in the Mennonite Church in the 1950s in the midst of rapid social change see Albert Keim, *Harold S. Bender,* 415-418; 504-511.

10. John Howard Yoder, letter to Harold Bender, March 3, 1951, Bender papers,
box 42, AMC

11. John Howard Yoder, letter to Harold Bender, January 23, 1952, Bender papers, box 42, AMC.

12. John Howard Yoder, "Courses Taken by John H. Yoder in the Theological
Faculty of the University of Basel, Switzerland," Mark Thiessen Nation, Yoder Collection at Eastern Mennonite Seminary, Harrisonburg, Virginia.

13. In 1950-51 John Howard Yoder took two classes in which Barth lectured on
what became the *Church Dogmatics,* vol. 3, part 4 on ethics. Yoder also participated
in two Barth colloquiums for English and French speaking students. In 1954-55
Yoder took another class with Barth in which he lectured on what became the
Church Dogmatics, vol. 4, part 2 on "Jesus Christ, the Servant as Lord." That year
Yoder also took a seminar with Barth on "Luther and the Enthusiasts" and another
colloquium. In 1955-56 Yoder took another colloquium with Barth. In the summer
of 1957 Yoder took a seminar with Barth on "Calvin and Pedobaptism." See John
Howard Yoder, "Courses Taken by John H. Yoder in the Theological Faculty of the
University of Basel, Switzerland," Mark Thiessen Nation, Yoder Collection at Eastern Mennonite Seminary, Harrisonburg, Virginia. John D. Godsey, a fellow student
with Yoder at Basel during those years gives an insightful reminiscence of what it was
like to study with Karl Barth. See John D. Godsey, "Reminiscences of Karl Barth,"
The Princeton Seminary Bulletin 23, no. 3 (2002): 313-324.

14. Craig A. Carter, *The Politics of the Cross,* 89. Carter interprets Yoder as a
Barthian theologian. This can be helpful but, as I will demonstrate, does not do justice to the broad compass of a seminal thinker like Yoder. He borrowed from many
different sources to create his distinctive theology and social ethics.

15. John Howard Yoder, "Courses Taken by John H. Yoder in the Theological
Faculty of the University of Basel, Switzerland," 1-2, Mark Thiessen Nation, Yoder
Collection at Eastern Mennonite Seminary, Harrisonburg, Virginia.

16. Ibid.

17. John Howard Yoder, "handwritten note," JHY papers, box 81/21 AMC.

18. George Hunsinger, *How to Read Karl Barth: The Shape of His Theology* (Oxford: Oxford University Press, 1991), 27-64.

19. Ibid., 38-39.

20. Ibid., 39.

21. J. Lawrence Burkholder, "The Relation of Agape, the Essential Christian
Ethic, to the Social and Political Structure," JHY papers, box 11, AMC.

22. Ibid., 9-10.

23. John Howard Yoder, letter to J. Lawrence Burkholder, June 12, 1956, JHY
papers, box 11, AMC.

24. Such an ethic of obedience to God's command should not be misunderstood
as a casuistic exercise in seeking to understand the command of God as a prescribed
text that is then applied to life. Both Barth and Yoder had a deep appreciation of the
revelation of God in the person of Jesus and of the ongoing activity of God's Spirit in

the life of the community of faith. In that sense it involves a commitment to act and think within a received tradition with a confident faith that God still has more things to reveal through this Word. For a discussion of the kind of issues involved in theological ethics, see Karl Barth, "The Problem of Special Ethics," *Church Dogmatics,* vol. 3, part 4, ed. G. W. Bromiley and T. F. Torrance (Edinburgh: T. & T. Clark, 1961), 1-31.

25. Ibid.

26. Personal conversation with Ray Gingerich, June 19, 2002. Ray Gingerich is professor of theology and ethics at Eastern Mennonite University, and a former student of John Howard Yoder at the Associated Mennonite Biblical Seminary in Elkhart, Indiana.

27. John Howard Yoder, "handwritten note," JHY papers, box 81/21 AMC.

28. Karl Barth, "Letter to a Pastor in the German Democratic Republic," in Karl Barth and Johannes Hamel, *How to Serve God in a Marxist Land* (New York: Association Press, 1959), 1-52.

29. Ibid., 65.

30. Ibid., 71.

31. Karl Barth, "The Church between East and West," *Against the Stream: Shorter Post-War Writings 1946-52* (New York: Philosophical Library, 1954), 127-131.

32. Ibid., 135-141.

33. John Howard Yoder, "Karl Barth: How His Mind Kept Changing," in *How Karl Barth Changed My Mind,* ed. Donald K. McKim (Grand Rapids: Eerdmans, 1986), 170-171.

34. Ibid.

35. Ibid.

36. Yoder made this argument in many places in his writings throughout his life. One place that he makes it most clearly is in John Howard Yoder, "The Constantinian Sources of Western Social Ethics," *The Priestly Kingdom: Social Ethics as Gospel* (Notre Dame, Ind.: The University of Notre Dame, 1984), 135-147.

37. Yoder especially developed this strain of thought later in his life. It was his answer to H. Richard Niebuhr's classic book *Christ and Culture.* See John Howard Yoder, "How H. Richard Niebuhr Reasoned: A Critique of Christ and Culture," in *Authentic Transformation: A New Vision of Christ and Culture,* Glen H. Stassen, D. M. Yeager, and John Howard Yoder (Nashville: Abingdon Press, 1996), 31-89. Yoder also became fascinated with the Jewish Diaspora as a model for how religious communities can relate to their larger social context. This can especially be seen in John Howard Yoder, "See How They Go with Their Face to the Sun," *For the Nations: Essays Public and Evangelical* (Grand Rapids, Eerdmans, 1997), 51-78. That chapter has also been included in John Howard Yoder, *The Jewish-Christian Schism Revisited,* ed. Michael G. Cartwright and Peter Ochs (Grand Rapids: Eerdmans, 2003), 183-202. A former student of Yoder's, Duane Friesen, has more recently developed this diaspora model into an Anabaptist theology of culture in his book, *Artists, Citizens, Philosophers: Seeking the Peace of the City* (Scottdale, Pa.: Herald Press, 2000).

38. John Howard Yoder, letter to Harold Bender, January 23, 1952, Bender papers, box 42, AMC.

39. John Howard Yoder, *The Original Revolution: Essays on Christian Pacifism* (Scottdale, Pa.: Herald Press, 1971), 87-88. During that time, Barth was lecturing on ethics in what in what became *Church Dogmatics,* vol. 3, part 4.

40. Ibid., 88. For Barth's argument about protecting the territorial integrity of Switzerland as an exceptional case, see *Church Dogmatics,* vol. 3, part 4, 462.

41. John Howard Yoder, *Karl Barth and the Problem of War* (Nashville: Abingdon, 1970), 71-73. For a helpful discussion of Yoder's objections to Barth's concept of the *Grenzfall* see Carter, *The Politics of the Cross,* 83-88.

42. John Howard Yoder, letter to the Concern Circle, July 15, ?, JHY papers, box 11, AMC. The year is not included in the date of this letter. From the context I assume that it was approximately 1955. I also assume that he is referring to George MacLeod, the social activist and founder of the Iona Community in Scotland. It is not clear what connection, if any, that Yoder and the Concern Circle had with MacLeod.

43. John Howard Yoder, letter to Paul Peachey, June 15, 1954, JHY papers, box 11, AMC.

44. McKim ed., *How Karl Barth Changed My Mind,* 168-171. In this sense, A. James Reimer is correct when he calls into question Yoder's commitment to traditional creedal orthodoxy. See A. James Reimer, "The Nature and Possibility of a Mennonite Theology," *Conrad Grebel Review* (Winter 1983): 43. Another way of saying this is that Yoder will not allow establishment orthodoxy to reduce Christology to a cipher for revelation in a way that obscures the full import of the gospel narratives. For an affirmative assessment of the ways that Yoder's Christology goes beyond the formulations of creedal orthodoxy see J. Denny Weaver, "The John Howard Yoder Legacy: Whither the Second Generation?" *Mennonite Quarterly Review* 77 (July 2003): 451-71.

45. MCC Peace Section – Conferences, Puidoux I – Reports 1955, box 1/38, AMC.

46. Oscar Cullmann, "The Kingship of Christ and the Church in the New Testament," Albert J. Meyer papers, box 1/40, AMC. This paper is extracts adapted from *Königsherrschaft Christi und Kirche im Neuen Testament* (Zollikon-Zürich, 1950). It was later published as a chapter with the same title in *The Early Church: Studies in Early Christian History and Theology* (Philadelphia: Westminster Press, 1956).

47. Oscar Cullmann, "The State in the New Testament," Albert J. Meyer papers, box 1/40, AMC.

48. An interesting question that reaches beyond the scope of my research concerns the significance of Cullmann's exegetical work for various political theologies, including liberation theology. For instance, Gustavo Gutiérrez draws on Cullmann for his theological work. See Gustavo Gutiérrez, "Jesus and the Political World," *A Theology of Liberation: History, Politics, and Salvation,* rev. ed. (Maryknoll, N.Y.: Orbis Books, 1988), 130-135.

49. Luigi Sturzo, *Church and State* (Notre Dame, Ind.: University of Notre Dame, 1962), 37-43.

50. Bainton, *Christian Attitudes Toward War and Peace* (Abingdon Press, 1960), 136-138.

51. Cullmann, *The State in the New Testament*, 78.

52. Jean Lasserre, *War and the Gospel*, 120-121. Jean Lasserre was a friend of Dietrich Bonhoeffer and a longtime French IFOR leader. See Durnbaugh, ed., *On Earth Peace*, 22. John Howard Yoder worked closely with Lasserre in the Puidoux conferences and wrote the preface to the English translation of his book, *War and the Gospel*. Yoder always demonstrated a deep respect for him and his work.

53. Cullmann, *The Early Church*, 120. Cullmann apparently thinks of these invisible powers as platonic, spiritual entities which are the real forces behind every human or natural phenomenon. He does not develop a sociological analysis of how they are embodied in concrete government structures or other social entities. In his thought, they largely remain disembodied spirits.

54. Ibid., 122.

55. Ibid., 126-128.

56. Ibid., 128.

57. Jean Lasserre, "The 'Good' of Romans 13:4," in *On Earth Peace*, ed. Durnbaugh, 133.

58. For two examples of the way Yoder conceptualized the relationship between the church, the state, and the "powers," see Yoder, *The Christian Witness to the State* (1964), 16-35 and *The Politics of Jesus* (1972), 135-162.

59. Yoder, *The Christian Witness to the State* (1964), 37-38.

60. John Howard Yoder, "The Theological Basis of the Christian Witness to the State," in *On Earth Peace*, ed. Durnbaugh, 136-143.

61. Ibid., 136-139.

62. Ibid., 140.

63. Ibid., 141.

64. Ibid.

65. Ibid., 142.

66. Ibid., 142-143.

67. Ibid., 143.

68. Lasserre, *War and Gospel*, 136. The chapter "Political Morality and Gospel Morality," from which this quote is taken, is still one of the most helpful discussions of the issue that is available from a pacifist perspective.

69. A classic work on the historical relationship between church and state is Lugi Sturzo, *Church and State*. American Catholic Theologian John Courtney Murray, who is indebted to Sturzo's historical research, has perhaps worked at this issue more than any other twentieth-century theologian. Murray's essential writings on the issue are in *Religious Liberty: Catholic Struggles with Pluralism*, ed. J. Leon Hooper (Louisville: Westminster John Knox Press, 1993). An excellent article discussing Murray's work on a public philosophy of church and society is by Joseph Komonchak, "John Courtney Murray and the Redemption of History: Natural Law and Theology" in *John Courtney Murray and the Growth of Tradition*, ed. J. Leon Hooper and Todd David Whitmore (Kansas City, Mo.: Sheed & Ward, 1996), 60-81. These resources represent a tradition of historical and theological wrestling with the issue that can profitably be put into conversation with John Howard Yoder's theological ethics and give more depth to the debate.

70. Scholars were already working on the subject in the 1950s and various books appeared in the 1960s. Cullmann included a brief chapter on the Zealots in *The New Testament and the State*. He later wrote *Jesus and the Revolutionaries* (New York: Harper & Row Publishers, 1970). Other scholars working on this were Martin Hengel, *Die Zeloten* (Leiden: E. J. Brill, 1961; and S. G. F. Brandon, *Jesus and the Zealots: A Study of the Political Factor in Primitive Christianity* (Manchester: Manchester University Press, 1967.

71. Cullmann, *The State in the New Testament*, 17. Some more recent scholars including Raymond Brown, Richard Horsley, and John P. Meier have questioned the belief that there was a smoldering Zealot insurgency during Jesus' lifetime. See Raymond Brown, *The Death of the Messiah*, Vol. 1 (New York: Doubleday, 1993), 679; Richard A. Horsley, "The Death of Jesus," in *Studying the Historical Jesus*, ed. Craig Evans and Bruce Chilton (Leiden: Brill, 1994), 395-422; John P. Meier. *A Marginal Jew: Rethinking the Historical Jesus*, Vol. 2 (New York: Doubleday, 1994), 1040. Others, including N.T. Wright and Ben F. Meyer depict a more turbulent social situation during Jesus' lifetime, creating periodic surges in the number of poor people, emigrants, Zealot revolutionaries, bandits, and beggars. See N.T. Wright, *Jesus and the Victory of God* (Minneapolis: Fortress Press, 1996), 150-151. See also Ben F. Meyer, "Jesus Christ," *The Anchor Bible Dictionary*, vol. 3 (New York: Doubleday, 1992), 777. For a careful historical argument that Jesus rejected the option of joining a Zealot revolutionary cause see William Klassen, "Jesus and the Zealot Option" in *The Wisdom of the Cross*, 131-149.

72. Cullmann, *The State in the New Testament*, 8-23.

73. Ibid., 41ff.

74. Yoder, *The Politics of Jesus* (1972), 59. N.T. Wright agrees with Yoder's understanding of the politics of Jesus in first-century Palestine. Wright argues, "Anyone announcing the kingdom of YHWH was engaged in serious political action. Anyone announcing the kingdom *but explicitly opposing armed resistance* was engaged in doubly serious political action: not only the occupying forces, but all those who gave allegiance to the resistance movement would be enraged." See Wright, *Jesus and the Victory of God*, 296.

75. Yoder, *The Original Revolution* (1971), 15.

76. Yoder, *The Politics of Jesus* (1972), 63.

77. Yoder, *The Politics of Jesus* (1972), 132-134.

78. This way of stating the problem especially reflects traditional Lutheran theology. Roman Catholic and Reformed theologies have their own variations of this two-kingdom theological formulation.

79. Cullmann, *The State in the New Testament*, 57.

80. Ibid., 58-59.

81. Ibid., 60-62.

82. Ibid., 69-70.

83. Ibid., 73 ff.

84. One recent study that can fit the general interpretation of Cullmann and Yoder, but is more mindful of the tension between this passage and other New Testament materials, is by Neil Elliott, "Romans 13:1-7 in the Context of Imperial Pro-

paganda," in *Paul and Empire: Religion and Power in Roman Imperial Society,* ed. Richard A. Horsley (Harrisburg, Pa.: Trinity Press, 1997), 184-204.

85. Ibid., 54.

86. Yoder, *Politics of Jesus* (1972), 59.

87. Ibid., 193.

88. Ibid., 194-195.

89. Ibid., 194-198.

90. Ibid., 202, note 11. Yoder is also arguing against Karl Barth, who takes a position similar to that of Cullmann.

91. Ibid. 203. Yoder does not refer to the opinion of any other biblical scholar to help substantiate his interpretation of God "ordering" the powers. Nor does he examine the possible range of meanings of the Greek word *tasso,* which he translates as *order* instead of *ordain.* This can fit his translation but is more easily understood as actively *ordained* by God. It has the basic meaning of placing or stationing a person or thing in a fixed spot; to appoint or establish in an office; to put someone over or in charge of someone or something. Other uses of this word in the New Testament are in Mat. 8:9 and Luke 7:8, where the centurion tells Jesus that he is a man *placed* under authority. The other place is in Acts 15:2, where Paul and Barnabas are *appointed* to go to Jerusalem. See Bauer, Arndt, and Gingerich, *A Greek-English Lexicon of the New Testament and Other Early Christian Literature* (Chicago: The University of Chicago Press, 1979), 805-806. Instead, Yoder makes a logical historical argument about the formation of governments. He also makes the argument from the Old Testament that God did not approve morally of the brutality with which Assyria chastised Israel (204). He apparently assumes that these arguments in themselves substantiate his interpretation. This is a good example of Yoder's burden to explain too much in his need to harmonize this text with other New Testament materials.

92. Yoder, *The Politics of Jesus* (1972), 204, note 13. Yoder makes it clear that such resistance can include various forms of civil disobedience. For him, personally, such civil disobedience included war tax resistance.

93. Ibid., 202, note 10.

94. Ibid., 206-207.

95. Ibid., 207.

96. Ibid., 211-213.

97. Ibid., 213.

98. For a perceptive account of Trocmé's resistance to the Nazis and the Vichy government during World War II, read Philip Hallie, *Lest Innocent Blood be Shed* (New York: HarperPerennial, 1994).

99. André Trocmé, *Jèsus-Christ et la Revolution Non-violente* (Geneva: Labor et Fides, 1961).

100. Yoder, *The Politics of Jesus* (1972), 64.

101. Hendrikus Berkhof, *Christ and the Powers,* trans. John H. Yoder (Scottdale, Pa.: Herald Press, 1962),8-9. Through the translation process, Yoder and Berkhof developed a personal friendship. They remained in correspondence for many years. Their correspondence can be seen in the JHY papers, box 48, AMC.

102. Yoder, *The Politics of Jesus* (1972), 213-214.

CHAPTER FIVE

DISSERTATION ON THE SWISS ANABAPTISTS

Many young Mennonite scholars in the 1950s were doing historical research on the sixteenth-century Anabaptist movement, but few were working in theology. History was a safer endeavor because most North American Mennonite churches held to traditional or fundamentalist understandings of the Bible and distrusted theology. The anti-modernist volume, *Doctrines of the Bible,* which had borrowed heavily from Protestant fundamentalism, still functioned as a kind of catechism in many Mennonite communities.[1]

That cultural and religious ethos was slowly changing. Mennonite scholar John C. Wenger had recently written *Introduction to Theology,* which moved away from the Bible doctrines motif.[2] However, the book was still a conservative Protestant theology that incorporated various Anabaptist beliefs, and it could be argued that it actually moved Mennonites closer to conservative Protestantism. Thus a real need existed for theological work from within the Anabaptist tradition. Given his talents and interests, it is understandable that John Howard Yoder wanted to do that. But it was risky.

In view of that risk, it is a little surprising that the first real resistance Yoder experienced came from an entirely different source. His desire to concentrate his doctoral studies in constructing an Anabaptist theology encountered difficulties when he began formulating his dissertation proposal.[3] He discovered that it was almost impossible to find a theologian in a European university who would allow him to work from an Anabaptist perspective. If he wanted to have an Anabaptist focus, he would need to do historical research. Dr. Fritz Blanke, from the University of Zurich, was a European professor especially known for his work on the Anabaptists. Yoder was in conversation with Blanke and wrote to Paul Peachey about it:

> The reason for not working with a theologian is that in Blanke's estimate they really aren't open-minded enough to let something they basically disagree with through, so the *Dogmengeschichte* lets you write on the same questions but with a broader-minded professor. If the thesis itself tried to be systematic the professor would be obliged to call in a systematiker, and none . . . would let Anabaptist stuff through.[4]

Consequently, Yoder decided to do historical work under the direction of Dr. Ernst Staehelin from the University of Basel, where he was studying. Blanke would serve as an outside consultant.[5] Even so, the work he did for his dissertation was divided into two sections. Only the first section, which was historical, was submitted for his doctorial examination in 1957. He did not submit the second section, a historical theological examination of his primary historical research.[6]

Yoder carefully chose the topic of his dissertation, focusing on the early conversations between the Anabaptists and the Protestant reformers in Switzerland. That choice allowed Yoder to study the theology of the sixteenth-century Anabaptists as it emerged in those conversations. In this way, he was able at least partly to work around the barrier to his desire to do a theological dissertation. In addition, it allowed him to further the historical project of Harold Bender, who had done his own doctoral work on the Swiss Anabaptists. Like Bender, Yoder was not interested in sixteenth-century historical research as an end in itself. Bender's project was to create a historical renaissance that would provide Mennonites with what Mennonite historian Paul Toews calls a "usable past." Toews writes:

> Bender's vision provided twentieth-century Mennonite people with a way of linking the church to the heroism of the sixteenth century. Anabaptism rather than fundamentalism came to define the center of twentieth-century American Mennonites. A rediscovery of the past permitted a different future.[7]

Awareness of Bender's agenda is crucial for an adequate understanding of Yoder's thought. Yoder spent the formative years of his intellectual life studying the theology of the Anabaptists as it emerged in Switzerland in various disputations between the Anabaptists and the Swiss Protestant reformers. His historical research and his theological examination of the sixteenth-century issues that emerged enabled him to develop the theological structure that informed his "politics of Jesus." That structure became central to his lifelong theological project.

As we will see, Yoder understood many of the central concerns that he addressed in his "politics of Jesus" as issues that had already emerged in the sixteenth-century disputations between the Anabaptists and the Protestant reformers. One set of issues came from Anabaptist ecclesiology, with its focus on the local congregation and its distinction between church and society. This focus informed his understanding of the church as a distinct community of discernment within society and his argument against the Constantianian synthesis of church and state. Accordingly, Yoder would argue that the very possibility of tolerance and religious freedom follows the Anabaptist understanding of the relationship between church and state.

Another set of issues emerged from Yoder's understanding of Christian social ethics as following the "earthly way of Jesus." As will be seen, Yoder believed he had discovered this radical commitment to Christian discipleship in his Anabaptist research. Discipleship is not just a matter of imitating Jesus' actions but of being fully present in the world in the same way that Jesus was. Such presence means being willing to experience the same kind of persecution and suffering that Jesus experienced.

In this respect, interpreting Yoder as a Barthian theologian,[8] as a proponent or critic of creedal orthodoxy, or as a Mennonite apologist, easily become diversions for other theological agendas.[9] Such interpretations tend to obscure the central passion that gave life to Yoder's theology. In some ways, he was all these things, but none of them adequately defines his "politics of Jesus," which was rooted in his Anabaptist theological commitments and his passion to have the church take Jesus seriously in social ethics. His "politics of Jesus" really needs to be understood as his creation of a contemporary Anabaptist theology. His doctoral dissertation on the Anabaptists was a central part of that task.[10]

Yoder's primary theological convictions, and the way he formulated them throughout his life, draw from his historical theological research on the Swiss Anabaptists. Michael Cartwright, a scholar who has extensively studied and written on Yoder's thought, concurs: "Throughout his career, Yoder has drawn on the results of his early research as an historical theologian, but most readers have not recognized how central Yoder's historical scholarship is to his ethical analysis."[11] One reason is that Yoder's historical research was written in German and only recently has become available in English.[12]

Mark Thiessen Nation, the compiler of Yoder's comprehensive bibliography and an able interpreter of his work, makes a similar argument about the centrality of Yoder's historical theological research:

> One could argue . . . that John Howard Yoder's whole academic career was committed to communicating in ecumenical terms what he learned through his studies of sixteenth-century Anabaptism in the early to mid-1950s in Europe. For it was through those studies that he came to the central convictions that he would subsequently spend a lifetime articulating.[13]

Yoder's doctoral research on the Swiss Anabaptists was central to the formulation of his distinctive theology. His basic theological orientation, however, was already formed before his doctoral research. It was already present in his desire to write an Anabaptist *Vergegenwärtigung* (a contemporary, updated Anabaptist theology) as a young student. The real stimulus and direction of Yoder's doctoral research came from Bender's articulation of the Anabaptist Vision.

While Yoder was committed to Bender's project of recovering a usable past for Mennonites, he was even more committed to articulating an Anabaptist social and political ethic in ecumenical circles. He was convinced that this theological ethic was not merely a Mennonite distinctive that other Christians could easily dismiss. It was the gospel and belonged to the heritage of the ecumenical church.

Where did Yoder get his creative reading of the Anabaptists that went beyond customary separatist interpretations with which both Mennonite and Protestant scholars were content to work? Stated another way, where did Yoder get the insight which enabled him to change the questions that have shaped received ways of thinking and living?[14] One obvious answer is that he received it from his careful, elicitive reading of the early Swiss Anabaptist movement. His historical research focused on the formative stage of the movement before Anabaptism had crystallized into small, persecuted, separatist, religious communities on the margins of European society.

In his historical research on the disputations between the Anabaptists and the Protestant Reformers, Yoder was impressed that it was the Anabaptists who almost always initiated the discussions. He was equally impressed with their non-defensive stance in those discussions and their willingness to change their position in light of new evidence. Even to enter into conversation with their powerful adversaries, who could rely on government religious sanctions, was a considerable risk that they were willing to take because of their commitment to share and proclaim the gospel.[15] Those conversations took place during a fertile and epoch-shaping decade that affected subsequent Christian history in the West. Focusing his historical research on those conversations gave Yoder the ability to revisit the crucial issues they raised.

As seen in my earlier chapters, the events and conversations that Yoder engaged in during the post-World War II period provide other sources of creative insight. They include North American Mennonite conversations about separatism and social engagement and the debate with the North American Protestant ethics of social responsibility. They also include (1) Yoder's mission and service involvements in Europe and his relationships with European Mennonites; (2) the conversations with European Protestants and the World Council of Churches about church and society; and (3) the problem of war. Furthermore, he was shaped by the exciting new biblical research on the historical Jesus and the early church by scholars such as Oscar Cullmann. A synergy existed between those postwar events and conversations and Yoder's Anabaptist research, which enabled him to change the questions that had shaped the conversation in theological ethics for centuries.

HISTORICAL ANABAPTIST RESEARCH

Yoder's historical research focused on the developing events and issues that eventually led to the break between the Swiss Anabaptists and the Protestant Reformation in Switzerland. In particular, he researched the disputations between the Swiss Reformer Ulrich Zwingli and emerging Anabaptist leaders, such as Conrad Grebel. He traced the development of Anabaptism, especially through the influence of Michael Sattler, and the crystallization of the Anabaptist position in the articles of the *Brüderliche Vereinigung* or Brotherly Union, often known as the Schleitheim Confession. Through such research he sought better to understand the theological commitments of the early Anabaptists.

Swiss Anabaptist Dependence on Zwingli

Yoder made the historical argument that the Swiss Anabaptists emerged out of the Zwinglian reformation. He insisted that they had no direct connection with other earlier dissident movements such as the Waldensians. They also had no direct relationships with other Protestant Reformers or Anabaptist leaders, such as Martin Luther, Andreas Carlstadt, or Thomas Münster. Conrad Grebel, a key Swiss Anabaptist leader, had said that Zwingli had brought them into this matter.[16] Beginning from that premise, Yoder examined the conversations between the Swiss Anabaptists and the Swiss Reformers with the goal of clarifying Anabaptist theological and ethical commitments.[17]

To that end, Yoder carefully reconstructed the formal disputations and other conversations between the Anabaptists and the Reformers that could help identify the crucial issues that eventually caused them to go separate ways.[18] He quickly dismissed the idea that what separated them were differences in temperament, maturity, or patience. It is too simplistic, he argued, to say the Anabaptists wanted to push forward with the reforms more rapidly than Zwingli did.[19]

Yoder noticed that there are actually more recorded conversations between the Reformers and the Anabaptists than between other groups in the sixteenth century. That can be partly explained by the fact that the Anabaptists were both geographically and theologically in the immediate neighborhood of the Reformation. Another reason is that the other religious parties were geographically separated from each other because regional governing authorities had mandated the state religion for their respective territories. Anabaptists, however, ignored such territorial boundaries. As seen before, Yoder was impressed that the Anabaptists had initiated the conversations with the Protestant reformers.[20] In turn, throughout his career, he emphasized the importance of ecumenical dialogue.

The fact that the Swiss Anabaptists were originally followers of Zwingli was a key element of Yoder's historical argument. He noted that their spiritual and intellectual indebtedness to Zwingli can be seen in various ways:

Even when they separated themselves from him and had to go another way, they could only go in the directions that he had already shown them: discipleship as the formal principle of ethics, the local congregation where valid church action is located, the questioning of infant baptism; all this they had from Zwingli.[21]

In view of that beginning relationship with Zwingli, Yoder asked how it was that that their differences became so great that the Zwinglian party eventually banned the Anabaptists' existence. Zwingli later claimed that the Anabaptists had only joined him for a time so that they could create the support they needed to establish their own church. The Anabaptists claimed that they wanted nothing more than to be Zwingli's followers, but that he had lost his courage and abandoned them in the face of opposition.

The first section of Yoder's historical research begins with what he calls a "pre-history of Anabaptism," showing their dependence on Zwingli.[22] It is followed by a section on the disputations with the Zürich City Council, leading to the banning of the Anabaptists and the subsequent introduction of believers baptism, which created a separate Anabaptist community in January 1525. Following sections trace the development of Anabaptism in relation to the writing of the Brotherly Union or Schleitheim Confession in 1527 and various discussions with Swiss Reformers in the following decade. The last section summarizes the significance of his research for understanding Anabaptism.[23]

The issues debated by the Anabaptists included matters such as the propriety of charging interest, the reformation of the Mass, and infant baptism. Yoder maintained that it was not the issues themselves that became intractable. There was initially a broad agreement as all parties worked together at the task of reforming the church. What complicated matters, and eventually led to the parting of ways, was the role of the city council in implementing the reforms. Yoder insisted that it was Zwingli's move from reform based on tolerance to mandatory reform applied to all citizens through government enforcement which created the intractable division between Zwingli and those who had been his followers. He wrote:

> By thus seeing the basic nature of Zwingli's shift in position we have at the same time found the crux of Grebel's clash with him. To place the unity of Zürich above the faithfulness of the church

is not only to abandon the church; it is also the demonization of the state, for persecution becomes a theological necessity.[24]

As a consequence of their rejection of government authority in religious matters, the Anabaptists were beginning to rethink the role of government, including the use of force. During this time of ferment, they wrote letters to three major reform leaders—Martin Luther, Andreas Carlstadt, and Thomas Müntzer—exploring the possibility of mutual understanding and working together. The letter addressed to Thomas Müntzer chastised him for his willingness to use revolutionary violence. They also began to rethink the use of the oath, which served as a religious underpinning of government authority.[25] In this struggle the Swiss Anabaptists were gradually developing their own congregationally based ecclesiology in opposition to the emerging Zwinglian Reformed ecclesiology, which made the state sovereign in matters of ecclesiastical discipline.[26]

The Legacy of Schleitheim and Michael Sattler

The subsequent persecution by the Zwinglians threatened to destroy the budding movement. Conrad Grebel died prematurely, and other key leaders were either executed or driven into exile. Internal dissensions also threatened the new movement. In response to that crisis, a group of Anabaptist leaders met in the village of Schleitheim near the Swiss-German border in 1527. There they drew up the Brotherly Union articles of faith, often referred to as the Schleitheim Confession.[27]

According to Yoder, those articles of faith represented a further development in Anabaptist congregational ecclesiology. Baptism, communion, and church discipline were understood in relation to their distinction between the church and the national society. All these practices now fit together as a whole. Their rejection of violence and the oath were not just literal citations of New Testament passages but were underpinned theologically by this ecclesiology.[28] According to Yoder, Schleitheim "must be recognized as the coming of age of a distinct, visible fellowship taking long-range responsibility for its order and its faith."[29]

The influence of Michael Sattler, the former prior of St. Peter's Benedictine Monastery in the Black Forest, appears in the theological commitments of Schleitheim. Yoder called Sattler the most significant first generation leader of the Anabaptists. Sattler brought a distinct

Benedictine influence to the Anabaptist movement. Such influence is evident in Sattler's focus on the Christian life as an outworking of the divine nature of Christ and the polarity between Christ and Belial, which is played out in the world. Yoder was intrigued by this connection with the Benedictines, which he described as the West's oldest renewal movement.[30]

Sattler had not been directly involved in the disputations with Zwingli in 1523 and 1524. In 1526 he was in Strasbourg, but it is not clear what his relationship was with Martin Bucer and Wolfgang Capito, the leading Reformers in that city. By that time, he had clear Anabaptist convictions and could not agree with ways they were implementing reform in Strasbourg.[31] He left of his own volition, writing a letter explaining his reasons for leaving and briefly stating his theological convictions. As in Zurich, the fundamental disagreement concerned the Reformers' commitment to a uniform reform program enforced by government authority versus the Anabaptist congregationally based, voluntary reforms. Sattler especially opposed use of force against religious dissidents. He pleaded with the Strasbourg Reformers to exercise leniency:

> Be mercifully considerate, I pray you, of those who are in prison and do not permit a merciful judgment to be superseded by a blind, spiteful, and cruel one. Those who are in error (if that they were) are not to be coerced but after a second admonition to be avoided. Christians admonish benevolently, out of sympathy and compassion for the sinful, and do not legalistically coerce persons this way or that.[32]

Bucer and Capito always spoke well of Sattler and considered him a Christian martyr when Austrian authorities burned him at the stake on May 20, 1527. Sattler and other Anabaptists were captured in the town of Horb, less than a year after he left Strasbourg. He was quickly tried for heresy and executed.[33] Capito wrote a letter to the Council of Horb condemning that action, even though he thought Sattler was in error on several points. One of those errors, according to Capito, was that, "He wished to make Christians righteous by their acceptance of articles and an outward commitment. This we thought to be the beginning of a new monasticism."[34]

Nevertheless, Capito considered Sattler a true Christian and condemned his persecution along with other members of the Anabaptist congregation in Horb. He wrote, "I tell you it is true, what you do to these poor ones, that you have done to Christ, who suffers with them."[35]

The legacy of Schleitheim and Michael Sattler is significant for understanding Yoder's own theological commitments. He believed that Sattler and the Swiss Anabaptists were the most authentic representatives of the sixteenth-century Anabaptists. Their core beliefs, which he discovered in his historical research, became building blocks of his constructive theology.

THE CORE OF ANABAPTIST BELIEFS

John Howard Yoder called the second part of his dissertation a dogmatic-historical examination of the discussions between the Swiss Anabaptists and the Reformers. A central purpose of his inquiry was to discover the central elements of sixteenth-century Anabaptist beliefs that he could use to construct what he called his "theological *Vergegenwärtigung*" (a contemporary, updated theology of Anabaptism).[36] It was the "usable past" that he would use in his theological project.

Yoder wanted his theological project to have ecumenical significance. For that reason, it was necessary to explore the disagreements as well as the places of agreement between the Anabaptists and the Reformers. He thought the disagreements were actually more instructive and should not be covered over out of a shortsighted desire for church unity that ignores real differences. The tragedy of Reformation history, Yoder thought, is not that there were differences, but that no constructive way was found to deal with them. When they could not be resolved theologically, the Reformers resorted to police action.[37]

The challenge, for Yoder, was to find the center that defined these differences. His problem was not only that insufficient resources were available on the Anabaptist position, but that the Anabaptists had no center of their own which held together by itself. Anabaptists understood the existence of their communities as a necessary consequence of the failure of the Reformation churches to bring about the needed changes. They believed that the Reformation churches had failed to complete the reforms they had initially embarked on. In Yoder's analysis, the Swiss Anabaptists were in basic agreement with the initial teachings and objectives of Zwingli and believed they were implementing those teachings in the life of their communities.[38]

In his work of reconstructing the Anabaptist distinctives, Yoder followed earlier attempts to find deeper assumptions behind the confrontations over specific issues such as infant baptism. He was building on the work of Harold Bender, who had defined the Anabaptist vision in terms of discipleship, a voluntary church, and an ethic of love and nonresistance. Yoder said that trying to understand such Anabaptist distinctives systematically is made more difficult because the Anabaptists did not think in systematic categories.

According to Yoder, the opposition between the Anabaptists and the Reformers did not grow out of competing theologies but out of the implementation of a common body of belief associated with the Reformation in Switzerland. In discussions with their opponents, the Anabaptists kept insisting, rightly or wrongly, that the Bible alone should be the norm. Few of them were trained theologians, and they had neither the time nor the educational resources needed to develop a sophisticated theology.[39]

Because of those factors, Yoder believed that any theological reconstruction of their thought could only be an interpretation and a hypothesis. He said that we need to ask if we are dealing with the legitimate possibility of a theology that is worthy of interpretation. The implied answer was "yes," but only the expressed opinion and believability of the Anabaptists can provide that answer. In such a reconstruction, central Reformation issues such as justification by faith will not occupy the center of discussion. Instead, other issues will emerge. One should guard against too quickly deciding what is central. Yoder wrote:

> Things for whose sake the one side was ready to persecute, and for which the other side was ready to suffer persecution, are fundamentally important—even if they lie only on the periphery of systematic orthodoxy, they can become the center point of the test of obedience and witness.[40]

Dualism and Monism

One of the issues that divided the Reformed and Anabaptist positions, according to Yoder, was Zwingli's penchant toward a platonic, spiritual dualism, which the Anabaptists rejected. Zwingli's dualism allowed him to make a distinction between divine justice (which is ordained for heaven) and its implementation in sinful human society. Because of the reality of sin, divine justice can never be transferred to human society. Correspondingly, one cannot talk about Christian social ethics. In the *corpus Christianum,* a Christian social ethic would mean applying those ethics to the whole society in a way that makes no distinction between church and society.[41]

Yoder noted that the general assumption is that it was the Lutherans, with their interest in justification for the individual, who left out social ethics, while the Reformed tradition drew political consequences from their striving for a holy community. He argued, however, that in the disputations he studied, it was the Reformed side that drew distinctions between the inner and the outer, while it was the Anabaptists who insisted that obedience to God's commandments and Christ's work was relevant for social ethics.[42]

The other side of Zwingli's spiritual dualism, according to Yoder, was a covenantal monism which identified Christian baptism with Old Testament circumcision. The discussion soon went far beyond that of covenantal signs and raised the issue of the relationship between the Old Testament and the New Testament. Zwingli understood the unity of the two testaments as related to God's covenant formation of the people of God. In this way, he could appropriate those parts of the Old Testament in which the community of faith was identified with a national community that had political backing.[43]

For Yoder, Zwingli's approach brought out a basic issue in Anabaptist biblical hermeneutics. The Anabaptists obviously could not agree with the way the Reformers associated Old Testament covenantal signs with baptism. As a consequence Anabaptists had to endure the charge that they had rejected the authority of the Old Testament. They denied that charge, arguing instead that they understood the relationship between the two testaments differently—as a relationship of promise and fulfillment. The Old Testament had to be interpreted through Christ, who was the fulfillment of God's promise.[44] Yoder appropriated this hermeneutic for his own interpretation of the Bible.

Yoder noted that the Reformed leaders wanted to interpret Christ through God's covenant with Abraham. In contrast, the Anabaptists insisted on interpreting Abraham through the new covenant with Christ. From a Reformed perspective, everything was essentially the same because God's inclination toward humanity always remained the same. For the Anabaptists, everything has become new because it is only in obedience to Christ that humanity can be in right relationship with God.[45]

In their relationship with Christ, from an Anabaptist perspective, the people of God are distinguished from the national society. According to Yoder, the Anabaptist distinction between church and state became a source of misunderstanding with their Reformed interlocutors who assumed either that they wanted to impose a radical communitarian ethic on all of society or were anarchists. Instead, the Anabaptists were developing a free-church ecclesiology. That ecclesiology is another core Anabaptist conviction that became central to Yoder's theology.[46]

The formal expression of the Anabaptist distinction between church and state is best seen in the Schleitheim Confession. It reads, "The sword is an ordering of God outside the perfection of Christ. . . . but within the perfection of Christ only the ban is used."[47] Accordingly, the ordering of God has two levels, but only the church is within the completeness of Christ, which is a new social and ethical reality for those who confess Christian faith.[48]

In summary, Yoder argued that both Zwingli and the Anabaptists attempted to grasp the duality of human existence. For Zwingli, this duality is platonic-ontological. It encompasses both an inner spiritual reality, in which Christ reigns, and the outer world, characterized by sin and compromise, in which we live. In this outer world no distinction exists between the national society and the people of God or between God's elect and the non-elect. Christians are asked to live responsibly as members of this society, according to their best judgment of what makes for peace.[49]

The Anabaptist dualism, on the other hand, is historical-eschatological. The present age is embodied not only in individual sinfulness but also in authoritarian and violent social structures and the shortcomings of the old covenant with Abraham. The coming age is already being realized in the church through the new covenant with Christ. Baptism is the sign of entering into this community that was formed at Pentecost. It indicates our entrance into a new life described as the "completeness of Christ."[50]

Such Anabaptist theological understandings of biblical hermeneutics and of the church in relation to Christ, the world, and eschatology became the driving force in Yoder's theology. Recognizing such Anabaptist motifs in his theological ethics underscores the importance of study-

ing his historical research on the Anabaptists for an adequate understanding of the development of his thought.

Authority and Tradition

Another aspect of Yoder's thought is the careful way he worked with
the authority of the whole Christian tradition from an Anabaptist perspective.[51] Such attention to tradition is evident in his Anabaptist historical research. He noted that, in their break with Catholicism, the Reformers had argued for the primacy of Scripture over that of church tradition. But almost immediately they found themselves in the position of
protecting their young tradition from challenges by the Anabaptists on
the same grounds of biblical authority. The Reformers were in the uncomfortable position of arguing that the re-baptizers were schismatic
and prone to cause uprisings because they did not respect the authority
of church traditions.[52]

The irony of the situation was not lost on some of their Catholic opponents, who said that the heretics knew how to protect themselves
against other heretics only by resorting to the authority of the church.
One Protestant answer to this charge was that the "errors" that had
caused their break with Catholicism (i.e., celibacy, papal authority, and
monasticism) could be rejected because they were not part of the universal teaching of the church. Infant baptism, on the other hand, had
been accepted by the whole church. The Anabaptists, in turn, argued
that not even infant baptism had been universally accepted in church
history.[53]

A complicating factor, according to Yoder, was that the three parties
to these discussions had different perspectives on the church. Each
claimed to be the one true church on the basis of their respective claims
about the nature of the gathered community. The issues included episcopal hierarchy, historical continuity, biblical authority, and the work of
the Holy Spirit. The Catholics emphasized historical continuity and
episcopal authority. The Anabaptists emphasized biblical authority and
the gathered community as a manifestation of the work of the Holy
Spirit. The Protestant Reformers ended up in the uncomfortable position of arguing the one side of this debate against the Catholics and the
other side against the Anabaptists.[54]

Yoder said that the Protestant Reformers did not necessarily represent a middle position between the Catholics and the Anabaptists. In

some respects, such as an emphasis on concrete expressions of discipleship and on the role of government authorities in church matters, Catholics and Anabaptists were more in agreement with each other than with the Protestants. For example, Protestants were more radical in their theological argument that justification is by faith alone. It was not an accident that the Reformers sometimes accused the Anabaptists of developing a new monasticism.[55]

The Anabaptists also made historical arguments. Yoder insisted that they were not merely biblicists who could not think historically. Their whole position actually depended on their historical argument about the development of the church. Like the Reformers, Anabaptists insisted that historically the church had gone terribly wrong and needed to be restored. The Reformers had located the place of deviation and error with the papacy and medieval developments. The Anabaptists located the problem much earlier, with the developments symbolized by Constantine that had made Christianity the religion of the Roman Empire. It was not only a question of reforming the medieval church, but of reestablishing the community of the New Testament before it had taken on the trappings of empire.[56]

The Anabaptist argument against the Constantinian shift that had taken place in church history became central to Yoder's theology. He discovered that the new postwar era (which many had begun to label the post-Christendom era of the church) had produced a new audience for the argument against Constantianism. It was not only a sectarian argument, but a matter that concerned the whole church. It could even serve as the basis of interfaith dialogue about the nature of the church.[57]

The Church as a Community of Discernment

A crucial question for Yoder was why the Reformation failed in its central mission. It was not only the loss of the deepest views of the Reformation, which had become a wooden orthodoxy by the second generation, nor was it the splintering of the different Reformation groups. It was not even that the Reformers felt compelled to persecute dissidents. Nor was it that the Reformation churches became subservient to the national state. These all constituted secondary problems. Yoder wrote:

> The deepest tragedy of the Reformation, from which all other problems arose, lies in the fact that what everyone believed did not show itself to be true. This was the belief that Scripture alone

was sufficient to clearly decide *all* questions that arose concerning Christian teaching and Christian life.[58]

Yoder said it was not only that Zwingli could not talk with the Anabaptists or that Luther could not talk with Carlstadt; Luther and Zwingli were also unable to talk with each other. The basic problem was the heroic simplicity and the unquestioned and unquestionable trust they placed in the divine Word, believed to be authored and interpreted by the Holy Spirit, which they used to reject the teaching office of the Catholic Church. They failed to consider the further problems of theological knowledge; consequently they identified the Word as they understood it with the Word itself. In the practical application of the principle of *sola scriptura,* the place of theological knowledge was not the church but rather the thought of the individual theologian. Thus a theological opponent could not be seen as a brother or sister but only as an enemy of God.[59]

Yoder asked if *sola scriptura* inevitably leads to hopeless subjectivity. What would have been necessary for mutual understanding and a common confession? The answer, which he saw in the Anabaptist communities, was that the local church is a community of discernment. The community stands under Scripture and over the theologian.[60]

According to this model, the gathered congregation listens to the various arguments and decides which is in accordance with the teaching of Christ. Everyone, including the unordained, should have the right to speak. The community acts with the confidence that God's Spirit is guiding them in the discernment process. Consensus is reached when the silence of the community indicates that all objections have been answered. One need not be overly concerned that the many local communities, acting independently, will bring confusion, because the Word of God, interpreted through Christ, serves as an objective standard. It is the freedom of the local community that is a precondition to unity.[61]

This Anabaptist understanding was an extension of Zwingli's early teaching. The first disputations in Zurich followed such a congregational model of decision-making. When Zwingli began to refer decisions to the city council, the Anabaptists used the historical precedent of the first disputation in their arguments against Zwingli. Such an understanding of what a correct process of discernment included helps one understand why the Anabaptists complained that they had not been heard in the disputations. Being heard was more than being allowed to speak. It meant that their concerns should be recognized in the decision-making process. If the Word and the Spirit agreed, there should be consensus. Instead, the Reformers forced agreement through coercion. According to Yoder, it was the inability of the Reformers to discuss differences that led to a theologically and historically distinct Anabaptist community.[62]

These congregational and ecumenical discernment processes, which Yoder discovered in his historical research, became central to his constructive theology. He was deeply committed to a discernment process in which consensus arises uncoerced out of open conversation. He called such a process the "rule of Paul" (1 Cor. 14:26-33). Closely related was his commitment to "ecumenical patience" and a willingness to be in conversation with one's theological opponents.[63]

Intolerance and Secularization

A central argument of Yoder's dissertation was that Zwingli's earlier emphasis on following Christ, human powerlessness, the omnipotence of God, and a suffering church gave way to an emphasis on the power of the preached Word, the doctrine of predestination, the invisibility of the church, and a reevaluation of the role of the state. At each step of the way, in the process of reform, the challenge was to initiate reforms without creating a backlash from those who had Catholic sympathies while pacifying those who wanted to move more rapidly. Grebel remained in basic agreement with Zwingli, as long as the Reformation proceeded on the basis of tolerance.[64]

The momentum of events in Zürich made Zwingli change his reform strategy. He had great faith in the power of the preached Word and confidence in his rhetorical gifts as a preacher. His confidence that this strategy alone would weaken resistance gradually appeared unrealistic. During the same time, his political clout was growing. This combination of factors made Zwingli decide not to move ahead with his reforms until he had secured the backing of the city council and he had the political power to make them mandatory for all the citizens of Zürich. This meant that the Reformation had to become more authoritarian and would proceed on the basis of religious intolerance. That decision, according to Yoder, was the breaking point between Zwingli and Grebel.[65]

Grebel advocated proceeding on the basis of tolerance and beginning to implement reforms in those churches that were ready for them.

According to Yoder, this approach made it impossible for Zwingli to understand the Anabaptists. Zwingli always considered the problems of the Reformation in terms of their implementation in the whole society. When the Anabaptists advocated a more rapid implementation, he thought they wanted to force reform on the Catholics. When they talked about more economic sharing, he thought they wanted to abolish private property in the civil arena. When they talked about nonviolence, he thought they wanted to abolish the state. Even though the Anabaptists kept insisting that they had no such intentions, he was convinced that they wanted to take civil power into their own hands.[66]

Zwingli's decision to turn the implementation of the Reformation over to the Zürich City Council, according to Yoder, made intolerance a matter of belief. Using the civil authorities to force a unitary expression of the Christian faith had the added consequence of making the civil authorities the custodians of religious faith. Their role in suppressing Catholic and Anabaptist dissidents made this role inevitable, because it was so closely tied to the implementation of the Reformation. Zwingli may have wished that the authorities had used less violence in their suppression of Catholic and Anabaptist nonconformists, but he, nevertheless, approved of suppression in principle. When there was tolerance in the course of the Reformation, it was often lenient statesmen who defended freedom of belief against the theologians.[67]

As a consequence of using civil authorities to enforce unity of faith within the Reformation territories, Yoder argued, the church as an independent sociological entity was removed and transferred to the state. The official churches became a branch of the organizational apparatus of the absolutist state to a degree not seen in medieval Europe. Even when a separate church administration existed within the Reformation, it was still a part of the state and not an independent entity. Church discipline became a state function.[68]

The further consequence of this policy was the secularization of the *corpus Christianum.* The Anabaptists have sometimes been hailed as the forerunners of democracy and modern religious pluralism. Yoder insisted that this is only true with reference to issues such as religious tolerance and the separation of church and state. It was the Reformers and not the Anabaptists who delivered the fatal blow to the medieval *corpus Christianum.* The Reformers had tied their project integrally into the various municipalities and city states that were called on to defend the

Reformation. Consequently, only one choice remained. Either one waged religious war until the enemy was unconditionally defeated, or one made an agreement in which the matter of truth was put to the side. The latter is what happened in the peace of Westphalia, where it was agreed that each ruler would decide the religion in his territory. With that agreement, the state had become secular to put an end to the religious wars.[69]

Consequently, according to Yoder, the medieval religious and social synthesis collapsed. The state had become autonomous along with the economy and the professions. The autonomous state had replaced the sacred realm of the *corpus Christianum*. The guidelines for Christian social conduct became patriotic and pragmatic. The concept of human justice now served the concerns of the nation-state and the emerging modern economic order, even when it was justified in the name of God.[70]

CONSTRUCTING AN ANABAPTIST THEOLOGY

The last section of John Howard Yoder's dissertation began to sketch the outline of a constructive theology from an Anabaptist perspective. It could not be a complete picture, but it could show the uniqueness of the answer the Anabaptists gave to the question of creating Christian communities in the sixteenth century. Yoder wrote that various factors make this a risky endeavor:

> It includes the working hypothesis that Anabaptism, as a form of justified theological thought, can be taken seriously, and that trains of thought can be developed further, for which the Anabaptists had neither the time, the freedom, or even the necessary conceptual material at their disposal. But if one is aware of how little reason or opportunity the Anabaptists had for thinking dogmatically, then the astonishing thing is not the lack of dogmatic material in the sources preserved for us, but rather the clarity and unity of the starting points that these sources offer for carrying these trains of thought further.[71]

According to Yoder, these Anabaptist avenues of thought raise two central issues for contemporary theology. The first is the relationship between the church and the world or the structures of human society. The second is the need to ground Christian ethics in a Christology that takes discipleship seriously. He began to draw out more fully some of the implications of these issues.

Church and Society

It is imperative, according to Yoder, to make some kind of distinction between the church and other social entities such as the state. National structures are a part of the world and cannot be integrated into the church. Yoder argued that it was only in the cultural world of Europe in late Roman history that one could conceive of fusing church, state, and civil order. Even there, it was ambiguous and temporary. People who find the Anabaptist way of formulating the relationship between church and society absurd stand in this European arena. When the state is expressly non-Christian, there is logically no other way of thinking about the relationship than the way the Anabaptists did. That is true for the New Testament churches in their world as well as for the vast majority of Christians in our world.[72]

For the Anabaptists, it was not just a matter of turning back the clock to the pre-Constantinian world of the early church. They perceived that combining church and state was dysfunctional in their century. When the Reformers brought church and state together in a way that had not even been true in medieval Europe, it became destructive. They lost any sense of a world in relation to the church. In doing that, they lost the church as a viable theological and sociological entity.[73]

Yoder argued that the refusal of contemporary Christian social ethicists to consider the Anabaptist conception of church and society made it difficult to renew the church in the twentieth century. The twentieth-century world was much closer to the pre-Constantinian social world than to the sixteenth century. Those who agree with the Reformers that we need to do things differently because the world has become Christian must explain how this is true in modern secular societies. The problem is that modern people are still caught up in such Reformation ways of thinking, even when the result has been so disastrous and has contributed to a post-Christian atheism. Yoder wrote:

> The church community did not want to separate itself from the world, so the world had to separate itself from the church community. The state had to establish itself against the church that

had wanted to dominate it, by taking the form of *nation* and *reason*.[74]

Yoder argued that whoever approves of the alliance between the Reformation and government authorities, with the pragmatic reasoning that it was a matter of survival, must also take account of what actually came of such an alliance. It tied the church to anti-church forces such as rationalism and nationalism, which led to the defensive situation of the church in later centuries. It is this situation that has made faith in Christ unbelievable for many people.[75]

To understand the outlines of the church, Yoder claimed we need to understand the world as a sociological fact. In the language of the New Testament, the world is understood as the fallen, disobedient, social entities of this age. Such disobedience is embodied in the state, in civil religion, in class economics, and in the demonic aspects of autonomous human culture. When the world, as such, became invisible to the Reformers, the church also became invisible.[76]

In contrast, Yoder noticed that the "world" and the "church" were very pregnant concepts for the Anabaptists. The tension between these two realms does not necessarily imply unrelenting animosity or public persecution. The world can decide that it is in its own best interest to have the church in its midst. It may even favor the church if this appears to be useful. But, such recognition and freedom does not give the church reason to baptize the world in a way that has happened since the fourth and fifth centuries.[77]

This refusal to baptize the world, Yoder claimed, does not mean that the Anabaptists were unconcerned about social and cultural matters. They saw the church as having an educational effect on the world, but this impact can be accomplished only with the kind of patience that God displays. Such patience allows the world to be the world and respects its prerogative not to accept the Christian message. It also refuses to equate society and culture with the state and its coercive power, as many interpretations of human history do.[78]

Yoder said that many are inclined to see the Anabaptist position as only dualism and withdrawal from the world. He argued, however, that nobody can get around such dualism. On the one hand, there is the Anabaptist model of a visible church living in tension with a visible world. On the other hand, there is the Zwinglian model of divine justice withdrawing into an inner spiritual realm, to make room for the state, allied with the church. Furthermore, the true church is understood to be invisible. One needs to ask which model has the greater tendency to withdraw from history.[79]

Stated positively, the Anabaptist model, according to Yoder, sees worth in the world. It does not leave it to its own devices. The world, even in its non-belief, still stands under the lordship of Christ and the Christian can testify to the world about what that lordship means.[80] It means rejecting theocracy. The Anabaptists insisted that we should not impose our beliefs on others. The outlines of this Christian witness to the social order maintain a distinction between the church and the world, which contains an inherent dualism. Christian social ethics begin with the Christian community, but they have relevance for the rest of society.[81] Yoder would spend the rest of his life explicating the concrete implications of the Anabaptist model of church and society in the many different situations that arise out of the church's life in the world.[82]

Christian Social Ethics and the "Earthly Way of Jesus."

Yoder's study of the Swiss Anabaptists may appear to be a circuitous way to come to his notion of the "politics of Jesus." But there is logic to it. In a broad sense, one can even argue that his historical study of the Anabaptists prompted Yoder to research the social and political ethics of Jesus. In his sixteenth-century historical research, Yoder was impressed by the extent to which the Anabaptists insisted that "the earthly way of Jesus the person should be a guide for the obedience of all Christians." He noticed that this conviction had been lost for the normal person in the medieval era but showed up again in the humanism of Erasmus.[83] Early in his career, Zwingli was drawn to Erasmus and consequently made following the way of the human Jesus central to his understanding of Christian faith. Grebel and other followers of Zwingli, who later became Anabaptists, brought this conviction to the Anabaptist movement.[84] Yoder found their emphasis on the earthly way of the human Jesus in his Anabaptist research. Using modern biblical research methods, he brought that same emphasis to his "politics of Jesus."

Yoder argued that such discipleship only achieves its full radicalism when it goes beyond personal ethics. Following Jesus in personal ethics would not upset the status quo. It only becomes controversial when the Christian community chooses between the historically lived incarnation of Jesus and other criteria in social ethics. Such ultimate clarification is required in the relationship between the church and the state. Here, typically the appeal is to other standards such as human justice, natural law, or the order of creation. Consequently, it becomes imperative to demonstrate the difference between such ethical systems and Christ's revealed divine justice.[85]

For the Anabaptists it was not a simple matter of imitating Christ's actions but of being socially present in the world in the same way Christ was. For the state church, this option was excluded and discipleship became a secondary motive. That is why Zwingli, arguing against the Anabaptists, insisted that Christians should only follow Christ's example of humility and that the Old Testament kings should serve as the model for social ethics. Picking up the Anabaptist side of the argument, Yoder insisted that Zwingli's perspective undercut the ultimate ethical relevance of Jesus' earthly life, as well as the cross and the resurrection. In contrast, Yoder's notion of the "politics of Jesus" sought to demonstrate the relationship between Christ's incarnation and Christian discipleship.[86]

The meaning of suffering became especially poignant for the Anabaptists. For baptism candidates, this very act included a readiness to face certain persecution. In the most evident way possible, they recognized that following Christ meant taking up one's cross. Yoder claimed that the cross did not mean enduring natural calamities, nor did it refer to suffering that God brought to them to purify them. Instead, it had a hard ethical meaning. It was the result of their battle with the evil social structures of the world.[87]

This ethical commitment to "following Jesus" and the "way of the cross" powerfully shaped Yoder's thought. He committed his academic career to retrieving this Anabaptist social ethic and making that same argument again in the last half of the twentieth century, when the close synthesis between church and state was increasingly being questioned.[88] Church leaders and scholars, Yoder believed, were now more ready to critique the legacy of the *corpus Christianum* that was inherited from the medieval world. Perhaps the Anabaptist argument for a consistent Christian social ethic, following the example of the human Jesus, would have a new opportunity to be heard.

Though that is still true, it has to be recognized that the motivation to use religion in the service of national politics is ever present. Politicians are always tempted to use religion for their own ends and religious leaders are always tempted by the perks that come from the cozy association with national political power. At the beginning of the twenty-first century, we had witnessed the emergence of a prevailing coalition between a major political party and a religious base in America. The so-called global "war against terror" had raised the specter of a "Christian nation" fighting its enemies in the name of God.[89]

Hermeneutical and Historiograpical Questions

Several hermeneutical and historiographical questions emerge in Yoder's Anabaptist research. One that has been alluded to several times is the relationship between his sixteenth-century historical research and the questions from his twentieth-century, post-World War II context, which he brought to that research. It is the familiar problem of the hermeneutical circle and the way our own lives and interests shape the way we read any historical text.[90] A related problem is the role of Yoder's own writing, which stands between his sixteenth-century material and the reader.[91]

The questions Yoder brought to the material created fresh and challenging new possibilities for reading. That was his genius. He was certainly aware that every reading, including his own, is an interpretation, but he was not overtly reflective about the way he read, what such a reading brought to the text, or the way his writing stood between the original sources and the reader. Nevertheless he was exceptionally confident of his ability to read texts sympathetically and to read history with an objective eye.

Like all of us, Yoder did not read history straight. His reading of the Swiss Anabaptists was especially indebted to the previous work of Harold Bender and Fritz Blanke, who stressed the Protestant character of Swiss Anabaptism through its association with Ulrich Zwingli.[92] Such a reading reflects their desire to make the Anabaptists (and their Mennonite progeny) acceptable in the Protestant world of the 1950s.

More recent Anabaptist historiography has questioned the thesis of Bender, Blanke, and Yoder about the exclusively Zwinglian beginning of Swiss Anabaptism. Instead, it argues for a "polygenesis" of Anabaptist origins and emphasizes a plurality of influences, including medieval mystics and Peasants' War revolutionaries.[93] Another lacuna in Yoder's Anabaptist research is that it ignores or downplays the influence of mysticism and the economic and social struggles of the peasants.[94]

This difference is readily evident in Yoder's efforts to distinguish his prototypical Anabaptists, associated with the Zurich circle and Schleitheim, from others who did not measure up to this ideal type.[95] The weakness of his approach was that it failed to appreciate the rich diversity of influences that shaped the Anabaptists. His penchant to categorize served the useful purpose of defining the emerging theological convictions of his prototypical Swiss Anabaptism, which could be used as the materials for his theological *Vergegenwärtigung* or contemporary, updated theology from an Anabaptist perspective. In that sense, he was more of a theologian than a historian, and it is not surprising that he eventually decided to focus primarily on theology and theological ethics. He had an uncanny ability to articulate such Anabaptist distinctives in a way that had ecumenical saliency.

Conclusion

To summarize, it was out of a combination of both interest (a desire to work on a contemporary theology from an Anabaptist perspective) and necessity (the fact that European Protestants were unwilling to approve such a doctoral project) that John Howard Yoder decided to do his doctoral work in historical theology by focusing his dissertation on the disputations between the Swiss Anabaptists and Protestant reformers. That allowed him to do both historical and theological research. A central purpose of his historical work was to discern the avenues of Anabaptist thought the disputations helped develop. With such concepts he built the theological structure of his "politics of Jesus."

The two key concepts of Anabaptism, according to Yoder, were *community* and *discipleship*. Ethical commitments, such as nonviolence, truth telling, servant leadership, and economic justice are integrally related as aspects of these two key concepts. If one views this from the perspective of the breaking point between the Anabaptists and the Reformers, the concern for a visible community becomes dominant. But if one asks why such a community is necessary, it is because of the central commitment to follow Jesus Christ. It is more than an individual ethic of imitation. It is the work of the body of Christ as a distinct community in the world.[96]

This distinct community in the world was the core of the "usable past" Yoder found in his sixteenth-century historical research. That work, in relation to his biblical scholarship, informed his theological articulation of "the politics of Jesus." There is no question about the quality of his historical scholarship and the contribution he made to sixteenth-century historical research on the Anabaptists. Even those who question some of his conclusions recognize the contribution he made. But his biggest contribution would come in theology.

No one can doubt the efficacy of the way Yoder developed the avenues of thought he found in sixteenth-century Anabaptism. His work had a far-reaching impact in academic circles as well as in the church and in various initiatives for social transformation. It spoke to concerns in the last half of the twentieth century in ways that he could not have imagined. He taught many people how to think theologically. The task of the next chapter will be to better understand his theology and the way he worked at the theological task.

NOTES

1. The standard work that had become sacrosanct was by Daniel Kauffman, ed., *Doctrines of the Bible: A Brief Discussion of the Teachings of God's Word* (Scottdale, Pa.: Mennonite Publishing House, 1929). During the first half of the twentieth century, the *Doctrines of the Bible* served a similar anti-modernist catechetical function in Mennonite communities that the *Baltimore Catechism* served in American Catholic communities. For an excellent account of the doctrinal orientation of North American Mennonite communities in the first half of the twentieth century, see Juhnke, *Vision, Doctrine, War,* 112-119.

2. John C. Wenger, *Introduction to Theology: A Brief Introduction to the Doctrinal Content of Scripture Written in the Anabaptist-Mennonite Tradition* (Scottdale, Pa.: Herald Press, 1954).

3. John Howard Yoder, letter to Harold Bender, January 12, 1951, Bender papers, box 42, AMC.

4. John Howard Yoder, letter to Paul Peachey, April 8, 1954, JHY papers, box 11, AMC. An added question was that, according to Paul Peachey, Fritz Blanke had a reputation of being a *Sammler* (a collector), rather than a systematic thinker. That appears to be a somewhat derogatory assessment. Peachey wondered if working with a more systematic dissertation advisor would be better. See Paul Peachey, letter to John Howard Yoder, April 4, 1954, JHY papers, AMC.

5. Ibid. Some scholars have asked why Yoder almost completely disengaged from the world of sixteenth-century Anabaptist studies after the early 1970s. See Mark Thiessen Nation, *The Ecumenical Patience and Vocation of John Howard Yoder: A Study in Theological Ethics* (Ph. D. dissertation, Fuller Theological Seminary, 2000), 60-62. Yoder's personal letters, referred to above, help answer that question. They demonstrate that he was always more interested in theology than in Anabaptist his-

torical research.

6. Both sections of Yoder's work were published in German. The historical section was published as *Täufertum und Reformation in der Schweiz: I. Die Gespräche zwischen Täufern und Reformatoren 1523-1538* (Karlsruhe: Buchdruckerei und Verlag H. Schneider, 1962). The second section, which he called a dogmatic-historical examination, was later published as *Täufertum und Reformation im Gespräch: Dogmengeschichtliche Untersuchung der Frühen Gespräche zwischen Schweizerischen Täufern and Reformatoren* (Zurich: EVZ-Verlag, 1968). Both volumes have recently been published in English as *Anabaptism and Reformation in Switzerland: An Historical and Theological Analysis of the Dialogues Between Anabaptists and Reformers*, ed. C. Arnold Snyder, trans. David Carl Stassen and C. Arnold Snyder (Kitchener, Ontario: Pandora Press, 2004). For the information about Yoder's dissertation defense, see *Täufertum und Reformation im Gespräch*, vii-viii or *Anabaptism and Reformation in Switzerland*, 139-140.

7. Toews, *Mennonites in American Society*, 86-87. Stanley Hauerwas and Alex Sider note that Yoder was a beneficiary and participant in a Mennonite *ressourcement* movement similar to the one in Catholicism associated with Yves Congar and Henri de Lubac before Vatican II. See "Introduction" in Yoder, *Preface to Theology*, 14.

8. The fact that Yoder was not even able to have someone like Barth serve as a reader for his dissertation indicates that there was considerable theological distance between them.

9. See Craig Carter's discussion of this in "Classical Orthodoxy and Social Ethics," in *The Politics of the Cross*, ed. Stanley Hauerwas et al, 113-136. Carter argues that Yoder had a deep commitment to creedal orthodoxy. He is responding to the criticism of people like A. James Reimer, who claim that Yoder's theology is incompatible with the trinitarian and christological affirmations of the ecumenical creeds.

10. There is an interesting collaboration of the relationship between Yoder's Anabaptist research and his "politics of Jesus" in a comment he once made to Ray Gingerich, a Mennonite theologian and one of Yoder's former students. Gingerich talked to Yoder about the need for a contemporary work on Anabaptist theology. Yoder's response was that he had already written it in his book *The Politics of Jesus*. Interview with Ray Gingerich, October 8, 2003.

11. Michael G. Cartwright, "Sorting the Wheat from the Tares," in Hauerwas, et al., *The Wisdom of the Cross*, 351.

12. As noted above, the recent English publication by Pandora Press is John Howard Yoder, *Anabaptism and Reformation in Switzerland*.

13. Nation, *The Ecumenical Patience and Vocation of John Howard Yoder*, 50.

14. Stanley Hauerwas said that Yoder did not provide new answers to old questions; instead, he changed the questions. See Hauerwas, et al., *The Wisdom of the Cross*, x.

15. Yoder, *Anabaptism and Reformation in Switzerland*, 118-121.

16. Leonhard von Muralt and Walter Schmidt, *Quellen zu Geschichte der Täufer in der Schweiz*, vol. 1 (Zürich: Hirzel Verlag, 1952), 89.

17. Yoder recognized that they had some conversations with Carlstadt, but they

did not work together in any kind of partnership. See Yoder, *Anabaptism and Reformation in Switzerland,* 121-126.

18. Beside Ulrich Zwingli, the other Swiss reformers included Wolfgang Capito, and Martin Bucer in Strassbourg. The two most prominent Anabaptist leaders were Conrad Grebel, the son of a patrician Zürich family and a close confidant to Zwingli, and Michael Sattler, the former prior of the Benedictine monastery in the Black Forest. Yoder produced a separate book in which he translated and edited materials related to Michael Sattler and the formative Anabaptist council at Schleitheim in 1527. See *The Legacy of Michael Sattler* (Scottdale, Pa.: Herald Press, 1973).

19. Yoder, *Anabaptism and Reformation in Switzerland,* 114-118.

20. Ibid.

21. Ibid., 121.

22. Yoder, *Anabaptism and Reformation in Switzerland,* 5-25.

23. Ibid., 114-134.

24. John Howard Yoder, "The Turning Point of the Zwinglian Reformation," *The Mennonite Quarterly Review* 32 (April 1958): 140. This article, taken from his dissertation, demonstrates how much significance he placed on his argument about the basic difference between Zwingli and the Anabaptists. Hans Hillerbrand and Robert Walton later debated some of the details of his argument. See Hans Hillerbrand, "The 'Turning Point' of the Zwinglian Reformation: Review and Discussion," *The Mennonite Quarterly Review* 39 (October 1965): 309. See also Robert C. Walton, "Was There a Turning Point of the Zwinglian Reformation?" *The Mennonite Quarterly Review* 42 (January 1968): 45-46. Yoder responded to Hillerbrand and Walton in the article "The Evolution of the Zwinglian Reformation," *The Mennonite Quarterly Review* 43 (January 1969): 92-122.

25. Yoder, *Anabaptism and Reformation in Switzerland,* 130. See also John Howard Yoder, "Anabaptist Origins in Switzerland," *An Introduction to Mennonite History,* ed. Cornelius J. Dyck (Scottdale, Pa.: Herald Press, 1967), 32.

26. This Zwinglian development actually tied the church to the authority of the rising national governments in a way that it had not been in the medieval era. Making the state sovereign in matters of church discipline later became known as Erastianism. See Justo L. González, *A History of Christian Thought,* vol. 3 (Nashville: Abingdon Press, 1975), 254.

27. The *Brüderliche Veringung* or Brotherly Union is not a full confession of faith because its purpose was more limited in scope. It defined the critical areas of agreement in the fledgling Anabaptist movement. For Yoder's historical overview of this period in Anabaptist history, see "Persecution and Consolidation" in *An Introduction to Mennonite History,* 36-43.

28. Yoder, *Anabaptism and Reformation in Switzerland,* 130.

29. Yoder, *The Legacy of Michael Sattler,* 29.

30. Ibid., 21, 25, n.18, 19. An intriguing question, which goes beyond the scope of my inquiry, is the extent to which Sattler's thought represented a radical laicization of Benedictine theology and practice.

31. Historians debate Sattler's position in Strasbourg during that time. There is

little historical evidence. It is known that he was not expelled along with Ludwig Hätzer and Hans Denk, two other Anabaptist leaders, in December 1526. The primary historical resources are his letter to Bucer and Capito, stating his reasons for leaving Strasbourg and the letters of Bucer and Capito which refer to him. See Yoder, *The Legacy of Michael Sattler,* 18-26; 86-99. Yoder postulates that Sattler went to Strasbourg with the hope of collaboration and discussion rather than with a "settled sectarian assumption that he belonged to a different group." See Yoder, *The Legacy of Michael Sattler,* 26, n. 48. In opposition to Yoder, Arnold Snyder postulates that Sattler arrived in Strasbourg "with a separatist program in hand." See Arnold Snyder, *The Life and Thought of Michael Sattler* (Scottdale, Pa.: Herald Press, 1984): 94.

32. Michael Sattler, "Letter to Bucer and Capito," in Yoder, *The Legacy of Michael Sattler,* 23.

33. Yoder, *The Legacy of Michael Sattler,* 19.

34. Wolfgang Capito, "Letter to Bürgmeister and Council at Horb," in Yoder, *The Legacy of Michael Sattler,* 87.

35. Ibid., 92.

36. John Howard Yoder, letter to Harold Bender, January 12, 1951, Bender papers, box 42, AMC.

37. Yoder, *Anabaptism and Reformation in Switzerland,* 142.

38. Ibid., 142-143.

39. Ibid., 148-149.

40. Ibid., 150.

41. Ibid., 152. Like liberation theologians, Yoder was allergic to such theological dualisms.

42. Ibid., 162-163. An insight from Abraham Friesen's historical work on Erasmus and the Anabaptists supports Yoder's contention that such dualism undercuts Christian practice and social ethics. Erasmus, the sixteenth-century humanist and biblical scholar, noted in the *Annotations* to his Greek New Testament that the command to teach and make disciples precedes baptism (Matt. 28:19). Friesen claims that the Anabaptists were the only Reformation-era group to put that insight into practice because they read Erasmus' work without the customary platonic overlay that separates ideas and ideals from particular expressions in the world. See Abraham Friesen, *Erasmus, the Anabaptists, and the Great Commission* (Grand Rapids: Eerdmans, 1998), 38, 44-48. The issue of abstract platonic thought reemerges in Yoder's dispute with contemporary Protestant ethicists, such as Reinhold Niebuhr. For an example of such platonic idealism in Niebuhr's thought, see Niebuhr, *Moral Man and Immoral Society,* 82.

43. Yoder, *Anabaptism and Reformation in Switzerland,* 166-168.

44. Ibid., 168-172.

45. Ibid.

46. Ibid.,172-173.

47. Yoder, *The Legacy of Michael Sattler,* 39. In this sixteenth-century Anabaptist parlance the word *sword* refers to coercive state power and the word *ban* refers to the simple avoidance of someone who has not responded to a process of church discipline and initiatives for dialogue. It was understood as a more humane approach to

church order, in contrast to the Protestant and Catholic use of coercive government measures, including torture and execution, to discipline people charged with heresy.

48. Yoder, *Anabaptism and Reformation in Switzerland,* 172-173.

49. Ibid., 174-175.

50. Ibid.

51. In the introduction to a seminary course on systematic theology that Yoder taught from the early 1960s to 1981, he wrote that theological method is a somewhat simple procedure of studying the historical tradition and asking probing questions. Such an inquiry attempts carefully to read history forward from Jesus Christ and the early Christian communities. It then studies the postbiblical material and the way Christians have read the Bible through the centuries. The approach is inductive and historical, characterized by patience and empathetic reading of the various texts. See John Howard Yoder, *Preface to Theology,* 37-42.

52. Ibid., 56-58.

53. Ibid.

54. Ibid., 65.

55. Ibid., 65-70.

56. Ibid.

57. John Howard Yoder, "The Disavowal of Constantine: An Alternative Perspective on Interfaith Dialogue," *The Royal Priesthood,* 243-261.

58. Yoder, *Täufertum und Reformation im Gespräch,* 99-100 (my translation). The translation in Yoder, *Anabaptism and Reformation in Switzerland,* 218, is combersome and confusing. The original German text reads as follows: "Das tiefste Verhängnis der Reformation, aus dem all andere hervorging, leigt darin, dass das sich nicht als wahr erwies, was alle glaubten, nämlich, dass die Heilige Schrift genüge, *alle* auftretenden Fragen christlicher Lehre und christlichen Lebens eindeutig zu entscheiden."

59. Yoder, *Anabaptism and Reformation in Switzerland,* 219.

60. Ibid.

61. Ibid., 220-224. I do not believe that Yoder's articulation of the Anabaptist answer to this dilemma is adequate. One must at least expand the hermeneutical community beyond the local congregation. I discuss this argument more fully in the following chapter.

62. Ibid.

63. Yoder kept developing this Anabaptist hermeneutic and applying it to contemporary processes of discernment. He attributes the moniker, "The Rule of Paul," to Zwingli, from whom the Anabaptists learned this process of discernment. See his article "The Hermeneutics of the Anabaptists," *The Mennonite Quarterly Review* 41 (October 1967): 291-308. Also see his chapters, "Binding and Loosing" and "The Rule of Paul," *Body Politics,* 1-13, 61-70.

64. Yoder, *Anabaptism and Reformation in Switzerland,* 228-229.

65. Ibid., 241-247. Yoder postulated that this change of direction involved an inner crisis for Zwingli. Zwingli later wrote that the Lord had revealed to him the necessity of waiting to abolish the Mass until he had the unequivocal support of the state to abolish it in all parishes. Otherwise, he would run the risk of having uncon-

trolled conventicles functioning independently. Yoder thought such an appeal to direct divine revelation indicated Zwingli's awareness of the fundamental shift in strategy he was making. It also indicates the personal struggle involved in making such a decision. See Yoder, "The Turning Point of the Zwinglian Reformation," *The Mennonite Quarterly Review* 32 (April 1958): 139.

66. Yoder, *Anabaptism and Reformation in Switzerland,* 246-247.

67. Ibid., 247-250.

68. Ibid., 252-253. For a sociological analysis of this phenomenon within the Protestant Reformation, see José Casanova, *Public Religions in the Modern World* (Chicago: The University of Chicago Press, 1994), 20-25.

69. Yoder, *Anabaptism and Reformation in Switzerland,* 252-253.

70. Ibid., 254-255.

71. Ibid., 260.

72. Ibid., 259-264.

73. Ibid.

74. Ibid., 264.

75. Ibid.

76. Ibid., 265.

77. Ibid., 264-267.

78. Ibid., 268.

79. Ibid., 270-71.

80. Ibid., 281. Stating that the world is "under the lordship of Christ" indicates Yoder's indebtedness to Oscar Cullman's New Testament studies more than to his sixteenth-century historical research. While the difference is not necessarily contradictory, the Anabaptists did not formulate the relationship between church and world in this way. One way to see this difference is to compare it with the Schleitheim statement that "the sword is an ordering of God outside the perfection of Christ."

81. Yoder, *Anabaptism and Reformation in Switzerland,* 281-285.

82. Some of Yoder's books in which this is most evident are *The Christian Witness to the State, The Priestly Kingdom,* and *Body Politics.*

83. Yoder, *Anabaptism and Reformation in Switzerland,* 285-286.

84. Ibid. As has been seen, this focus was also indebted to the influence of the Benedictine tradition that Michael Sattler brought to the Anabaptist movement.

85. Ibid.

86. Ibid., 287.

87. Ibid., 289-292.

88. This statement does not ignore the formal separation of church and state in the United States since its founding. Instead it recognizes the cultural establishment of Protestantism that exists in the United States even in the twenty-first century. For an in-depth sociological study of this phenomenon in a New England city, read N. J. Demerath III and Rhys H. Williams, *A Bridging of Faiths: Religion and Politics in a New England City* (Princeton, N.J.: Princeton University Press, 1992).

89. Kevin Phillips, former Republican strategist and political commentator, argues that the coalition between the Republican Party and the Religious Right has become the

first American religious party in the history of the nation. See Kevin Phillips, *American Theocracy: The Peril and Politics of Radical Religion, Oil, and Borrowed Money in the Twenty-First Century* (New York: Viking Penguin, 2006), 182-217.

90. Nobody reads a text straight as a dispassionate, objective reader. We all bring our perspectives, interests, and biases to the reading of any text. The challenge is not to overcome our subjectivity but to become more aware of how it shapes our reading. For a discussion of how our personal interests invariably shape our interpretation of texts, for good or for ill, see Hans-Georg Gadamer, *Truth and Method,* 2nd. rev. ed. (New York: Continuum, 1994), 265 ff.

91. For a discussion of this hermeneutical phenomenon, see Edward W. Said, *The World, the Text, and the Critic* (Cambridge, Mass.: Harvard University Press, 1983), 50-53.

92. Fritz Blanke, *Brüder in Christo* (Zürich: Zwingli-Verlag, 1955); Harold Bender, *Conrad Grebel, c. 1498-1526: The Founder of the Swiss Brethren* (Scottdale, Pa.: Herald Press, 1971, c. 1950).

93. Ibid., 161-162. Yoder's argument that the Swiss Anabaptists were originally followers of Zwingli is historically beyond dispute. However, the broader claim, made by Harold Bender and Fritz Blanke, that early Swiss Anabaptists represent the beginning core and normative center of Anabaptism has been challenged on historical grounds. At question is the extent to which Yoder is making this broader more dubious claim. See James Stayer, Werner Packull, and Klas Deppermann, "From Monogenesis to Polygenesis: The Historical Discussion of Anabaptist Origins," *The Mennonite Quarterly Review* 49 (June 1975): 83-121. Without denying the separate development of Anabaptism in various parts of Europe, recent scholarship has made an effort to move beyond polygenesis by identifying links between the various Anabaptist movements. The second, revised edition of *Becoming Anabaptist,* by J. Denny Weaver, is a narrative Anabaptist history that incorporates this new scholarship. For a description of the efforts of identifying links between the various Anabaptist movements, see *Becoming Anabaptist,* 168-69.

94. Stayer, Packull, and Deppermann, "From Monogenesis to Polygenesis, *The Mennonite Quarterly Review,* 83-121. For a historical treatise on the influence of medieval mysticism and mystics, such as Meister Eckhardt on the Anabaptists see Werner O. Packull, *Mysticism and the Early South German-Austrian Anabaptist Movement, 1525-1531* (Scottdale, Pa.: Herald Press, 1977). For a historical treatise on the influence of the Peasant's War and revolutionaries, such as Thomas Müntzer see James M. Stayer, *Anabaptists and the Sword* (Lawrence, Kan.: Coronado Press, 1973). For an excellent discussion of the social and economic aspects of the conflict between the Swiss Reformers and the Anabaptists see James M. Stayer, *The German Peasants' War and Anabaptist Community of Goods* (Montreal & Kingston: McGill-Queen's University Press. 1991), 61-92. Stayer's work demonstrates that Yoder did not pay enough attention to such matters.

95. Yoder even went so far as to argue that the Schleitheim Confession gave "Anabaptism" (*Täufertum*) the basis on which to finally get rid of "fanatics" (*das Schwärmertum*) and allowed them to separate themselves "from the right and from the left, from above and below." What is ironic is that *Schwärmer* or fanatics is the

same derogatory term that the Protestants used against the Anabaptists. See Yoder, *Täufertum und Reformation in der Schweiz,* 169, or Yoder, *Anabaptism and Reformation in Switzerland,* 130.

96. Yoder, *Anabaptism and Reformation in Switzerland,* 299.

SIX

UNDERSTANDING
THE "POLITICS OF JESUS"

T he effect of John Howard Yoder's "politics of Jesus" was like a wedge driven into the academic discussion about theological ethics during the last half of the twentieth century. This dialectical move both challenged and disturbed mainline Protestant ethics, a not surprising result when one remembers that Yoder consciously constructed his work as a response to mainstream Protestant theological ethics in the twentieth century. Beyond that, he brought into question the way the discussion had been framed ever since the sixteenth century. That is why James Gustafson says that all constructive Christian theology needs to be defined over against Yoder's radical option.[1]

Many welcomed the new paradigm Yoder brought. Baptist theologian James McClendon said that reading *The Politics of Jesus* changed his life because it reintroduced him to his Anabaptist roots.[2] Stanley Hauerwas has said that Yoder taught us how to think theologically. He did not provide new answers to old questions; he changed the questions. Hauerwas believes we are only beginning to learn the lessons that Yoder's work represents.[3]

Perhaps more than any other contemporary theologian, J. Denny Weaver consciously recognizes his indebtedness to Yoder for the formulation of his distinctively Anabaptist and nonviolent theology.[4] Others, such as Duane Friesen, John Langan, S. J., and Glen Stassen, have said that Yoder taught them the relevance of New Testament practices for analogous secular social processes.[5] Lisa Sowle Cahill has called Yoder the most renowned Christian pacifist writer in the United States during his time and commends him for the unusual expertise in biblical exegesis he brought to the field of social ethics.[6] People who recognized Yoder's contribution were not shy about expressing their appreciation.

The purpose of this chapter is to understand and evaluate Yoder's constructive theology. To that end, the chapter uses a typology formulated by David Tracy to characterize Yoder's theology in relation to other theological languages. I then look more carefully at Yoder's theological language in relation to the methodological steps he took. A central following task is to identify the ordered pattern of relationships in his constructive theology. Finally, I raise a few critical questions about the limitations and lacunae in Yoder's work.

One should keep in mind that the various experiences and mentors studied in earlier chapters have powerfully shaped Yoder's constructive thought, even though that influence is not always explicit. Once one is familiar with that experience and those voices, one can see their imprint on his thought again and again. Making those voices visible is a primary contribution to the process of understanding and evaluating his thought.

A final note is that Yoder was more than an academic. As seen in previous chapters, he was also a social activist and a churchperson. One cannot adequately understand him without taking those lived dimensions into account. Thus the chapter includes a brief section on how lived praxis continued to shape his "politics of Jesus."

CHARACTERIZING THEOLOGIES

Yoder completed his coursework at the University of Basel in 1957[7] and published his dissertation on the Swiss Anabaptists in 1962.[8] By that time, as described in previous chapters, he had developed his basic theological commitments. The mature version of this theology is best seen in three books that he wrote in the next ten years: *The Christian Witness to the State,* published in 1964; *The Original Revolution,* published in 1971; and *The Politics of Jesus,* published in 1972.[9] These books draw on the work Yoder was already doing in the 1950s. They represent a flowering of his earlier work and will be the primary resources for the discussion of his constructive theology. As will be seen, Yoder never changed the basic theological commitments formed during those years, even as he kept shaping his theology in various ways to respond to new challenges.

My work in this chapter engages Yoder's thought at this foundational stage in his theological development. As a first step, it will be helpful to compare Yoder's thought to other theological languages. Philosopher and theologian Bernard Lonergan speaks of this task of comparing and evaluating as a basic exegetical operation in hermeneutics.[10]

I begin the task of evaluating Yoder's theology by using theologian David Tracy's characterization of theological languages as analogical and dialectical.[11] Analogical language focuses on discovering continuities and parallels from God to the world, while dialectical language emphasizes contrasts between God and the world as we know it. Tracy argues that these two major conceptual languages have served and continue to function as the "classic *theological* languages." For analogical theologies, the unifying reality of God lends a single focus to the set of ordered relationships of God-self-world. The overwhelming reality is the disclosure of God's grace in the event of Jesus Christ. Various dialectical theologies focus either on the sovereignty of God as Other, or on the in-breaking reign of God in history. They resist taking God's grace for granted. Their point of departure is God's judgment on human sinfulness and unjust social relationships.[12]

Tracy notices that, by concentrating on the focal meaning of the Christ event, theologians develop ordered relationships for the whole of reality. In the way these relationships are developed, he distinguishes between theologies of manifestation, theologies of proclamation, and theologies of historic prophetic action. Theologies of manifestation are more universal and analogical, concentrating on similarities-in-difference. They focus on the always-already reality of God as love and grace in all of life.

Theologies of proclamation emphasize God's naked majesty and sovereignty as Other. They are radically dialectical in their emphasis on the discontinuity between the Other and the self.

Theologies of historic prophetic action are also dialectic in the sense that they emphasize God's liberating action. They turn to history as the surest sign of God's gracious always-already reality.

These various characteristics are not mutually exclusive. Instead, they identify the points of departure and the internal coherence of the various theologies. Tracy says that each theology must maintain fidelity to its own paradigm, while allowing for the full reality of the world.[13]

It is possible to identify representative twentieth-century theologians who fit Tracy's categories. Karl Rahner, with his starting point in human existence and his emphasis on a world of grace, fits the category of manifestation. Karl Barth, with his starting point in God as Other and his emphasis on the limitations and sinfulness of all human construction, fits the category of proclamation. Gustavo Gutiérrez, with his starting point in the reality of oppression and his emphasis on God's liberating action in history, fits the category of historical prophetic action.[14]

When one analyses Yoder's theological language by using Tracy's categories, it becomes obvious that Yoder has impeccable dialectical credentials. He took the revelatory significance of Jesus' life and ministry, as seen in the gospel narratives, and insisted that it be taken seriously in social ethics. He used his doctoral research on the Swiss Anabaptists as the basis of his radical critique of Christendom and the Protestant Reformation. He used his New Testament studies under Oscar Cullmann to construct the first-century politics of Jesus in relation to the oppression of the Roman Empire. Finally, he studied under Karl Barth, the dialectical theologian who pronounced a resounding "no" to the final adequacy of all human constructions and their propensity to overreach their rightful limitations. All these aspects of Yoder's dialectical theology are rooted in the reality of Christ crucified by the rulers of his age. Consequently, there is an ever-present no to an easy identification of Christian faith with prevailing cultural norms and social structures at or near the surface of his constructive theology.

It is too simple, however, to focus only on the dialectical nature of Yoder's theology. When that powerful dialectic has done its work, it creates new analogies.[15] While his early thought, up to and including *The Politics of Jesus,* was strongly dialectical, it was centered (as will be seen) on his prime analogue about the relevance of Jesus Christ for Christian social ethics. Especially later in his career, he kept finding such analogues to his theological project in disparate places. One analogue was his insistence that his own pacifist ethic and the just war ethic both involved a moral judgment against war even though he emphatically rejected the historical just war association with established social structures. Consequently, he said that he had a stake in helping to formulate a more credible just war ethic.[16]

Another analogue was the way he sought to tease out parallels between his own disestablished understanding of the church in society and the social stance of diaspora Judaism. He even made the claim that Jesus was much closer to later rabbinic Judaism than to later anti-Judaic Christianity.[17] Again, it was Yoder' underlying dialectical no to oppressive forms of social establishment that teased out this different kind of analogy. It was his combination of a dialectical and analogical imagination that gave Yoder's thought its disclosive power, making it troubling to standard theological discourse.

When Tracy provides an expanded treatment of the character of theologies of prophetic action, it becomes evident that Yoder's theology most readily fits within that mode of theological discourse. Tracy writes:

> For those theologians whose major focus for understanding the self is historical prophetic action, the ideal for the self is the futural, eschatological ideal of the future reign of God affecting and commanding every self to enter the struggle for justice now. That ideal, interpreted as radically historical and global, discloses the future reality of a kingdom of love and justice—the kingdom present in history through God's acts and promises to the people Israel and the cross-resurrection of Jesus Christ.[18]

There are obvious family resemblances between Yoder's theological ethics and Latin American liberation theology, even though they come from different social and church backgrounds. These family resemblances include a commitment to the prophetic biblical tradition and the praxis of the historical Jesus. They share a commitment to doing theology from below in response to the existential challenges of their particular historical situation. Yoder and Gutiérrez share indebtedness to Oscar Cullmann's exegetical work on Jesus and the first-century political world of Palestine.[19] Yoder spent considerable time in Latin America, including a year of teaching in Argentina (1971-72). He soon became fluent in Spanish.[20] He wrote various articles on liberation theology and had a deep respect for the work of Gutiérrez and Juan-Luis Segundo.[21]

Despite these developments in Yoder's thought, one looks in vain for a major shift in his theology, or even a clear repudiation of an earlier position. One reason for this is the way he took the motifs he found in Swiss Anabaptism and kept applying them to whatever topic he was asked to address. Such social ethics and historical theology followed in the steps of Guy Hershberger and Harold Bender, his early Mennonite mentors. This contributed a deeply rooted and ongoing consistency to his thought.

One of his critics characterizes him as someone who never substantially changed his mind on anything and was sure that he had thought of all the relevant arguments.[22] That seems unfair. Admittedly, Yoder could be frustratingly sure of his arguments and doggedly consistent in the way he kept building on them. It is even possible to take one of his later books, such as *Body Politics,* and recognize it as a further explication of themes already central in his doctoral dissertation. However, he does keep formulating such themes in new ways and, as has been seen, there is an ongoing development to his thought.[23]

YODER'S THEOLOGICAL LANGUAGE

There is no explicit, detailed explanation of Yoder's theological method in any of his writings. In his later writings he discussed the issue in the form of a critique of what he called "methodologism." He saw some value in isolating and defining the processes and conceptual tools used in practical moral reasoning but was skeptical of the pursuit of first principles thought to lay a foundation for subsequent moral discourse. He disputed that laying such a groundwork is somehow before our capacity to do ethics. He wrote:

> The life of the community is before all possible mythological distillations. The role of the distillation process, which lifts up this or that dimension for this or that purpose internal to the community's identity, cannot be to short-circuit the appeal to all of the community's resources.[24]

One cannot find such epistemological reflection in Yoder's earlier work. His epistemology is, however, indebted to his historical work on the congregational process of discernment among the Swiss Anabaptists, where the silence of the community indicated that all objections had been met.[25] For Yoder, the hermeneutical community was always before, the setting for, and the final arbiter of any system of argumentation. The process of discernment includes what he called the "walk" or socially engaged praxis of the community. Such knowing, as a basis for theology, is rooted in the way of Jesus as witnessed to by the gospel narratives and the conviction that we can have confidence in the leading of God's Spirit in the congregationally based hermeneutical process. No argumentation can do an *a priori* end run around this process by making foundational epistemological claims.

Identifying Methodological Steps

Having said that, one can certainly identify certain consistent methodological steps which Yoder's thought took throughout his career. There have been various attempts to identify the components of his thought in more systematic or methodical ways.[26] Nancey Murphy attempts to do this in a way sympathetic to Yoder's thought. She applies the model of a research program developed by philosopher of science Imre Lakatos. It includes a core theory which provides a general view of the entities being investigated. The core is surrounded by auxiliary hypotheses, which further define and support it. The program involves a positive heuristic or plan for development, which takes into account the emergence of new data.[27] Murphy defines the core theory of Yoder's program as follows:

> The moral character of God is revealed in Jesus' vulnerable enemy love and renunciation of domination. Imitation of Jesus in this regard constitutes a *social* ethic.[28]

To this is added an auxiliary methodological hypothesis on favoring the sociopolitical analysis of Scripture over other sources, as well as various auxiliary doctrinal hypotheses related to Yoder's Christology and ecclesiology. The program, as Murphy develops it, reflects the substance of Yoder's thought and is useful in that respect. Arne Rasmusson, however, argues that Murphy misunderstands Yoder in that the substance of his thought is not something that can be condensed into a theoretical core. It is, rather, an engagement with the life of Jesus as seen in the gospel narratives and the social embodiment of the way of Jesus in the life of the church. Rasmusson says this includes its own form of reasoning:

> Yoder defends a form of practical reason that includes a finally unformalizable discernment formed by an ecclesial discourse-practice. He thus does not defend some blind obedience to rules, nor the idea that ethics and politics can be directly derived from Scripture. But the church thinks and lives inside this Christian discourse-practice (or so it should), although she employs knowl-

edge derived from many different sources. Even if the Christian understanding of reality does not give him the means to calculate, it still gives an empirically meaningful perspective from which to think. Yoder thus reads reality theologically.[29]

Yoder himself had difficulty putting his theological method into words or communicating how he worked. It may be like asking an artist to explain her or his work. Perhaps that task is done better by critics who are intimately familiar with the work of a given artist. Later in Yoder's life, Mark Thiessen Nation asked him to write a short description of his theological method. Yoder's response was far from a systematic articulation of his method. Instead, he talked about a few central characteristics and convictions that informed his work.[30]

One needs to be aware that this statement to Nation is Yoder's self-understanding near the end of his life. It is fair to say that there was a more combative dialectic in his earlier work than in his later writings and his later self-understanding. Nevertheless, this later statement is still helpful in understanding his notion of the "politics of Jesus," and it does fairly represent the way he worked throughout his life—any differences are a matter of degree. The first thing Yoder wrote to Nation was that he was willing to take on issues in the categories of others, unfolding the critique of the other's view from their own structure rather than beginning with his own "correct" position. He understood this as being consistent with his rejection of any foundationalism, which would impose on others the right language or the right place to start.[31]

Yoder developed this skill early in his life, when he needed to figure out how to work from an Anabaptist theological perspective in a European environment that placed real limitations on his ability to do so. It is instructive to recognize that the very fact that he had to do his dissertation in history means that he could not easily work as a colleague with a theological mentor such as Karl Barth. He had to figure out how to work in such a world while remaining true to his own convictions.

Consequently, Yoder learned how to engage people on their own turf. He discovered that this approach was actually an advantage. He wrote, "My position is stronger if/as/because it is not my own, not stated on the grounds of a basis I first lay out. A foundationalist beginning is by definition sectarian."[32] Such insight reflects his ability to work in foreign settings such as Europe, South America, and other places. He had an extraordinary ability to learn languages and to communicate in various idioms. One way to understand this ability at communication is that he was missional in the sense that he learned how to engage people in their own context and learn from them before offering his own evaluation and critique. A little known fact about him is that he worked with and related to mission agencies during much of his life.[33] Practically speaking, he was a missionary.

The next thing Yoder emphasized in his memo was his way of reading the Bible. He said that he neither feared nor worshiped the historical-critical method. He did not accept the polarity between scholastic orthodoxy and liberalism that was part of the American scene in the 1950s. He talked about his commitment to a "biblical realism" perspective that accepted and used the historical-critical method, but he did not consider it to be an autonomous discipline or put it in service of an unbelieving ontology. Accordingly, it became thinkable that there might be something about the biblical perspective of reality that refused to be pushed into the mold of a given worldview but stood in creative tension with the culture of any age.[34] He wrote:

> To take a text seriously is to enable the text to dictate the terms of a fair reading of it. "The message of the Bible in its own terms" is never a simple possibility, but neither is it simply impossible in a way that would justify any other goal. Of course every reading is biased and finite; but some biases are more congenial with the intent of a text than others.[35]

It is informative that the proper way to read biblical texts was so central to Yoder's understanding of the way he worked. One can see the influence of various biblical scholars that he knew and worked with, as well as Barth's notion of thinking along with a biblical text (*nachdenken*). This way of working goes beyond interpreting biblical texts. It is how Yoder worked in his historical research on the Swiss Anabaptists. Beyond that, it was the way he engaged his contemporary interlocutors by using the categories of their own thought.[36]

Next, Yoder said that it matters that his style has been ecumenical, polyglot, and gentle. (Not everyone would agree that his style was gentle.)[37] Nevertheless, Yoder said that it is about more than style. It is about meeting people on their own terms. He wrote:

> I eschew foundationalism because it is a power move which seeks to win the game by decreeing the rules before the game, begin-

ning somewhere else than amid the story/web. Meeting people in their own terms rather than mine means locating, classifying, hearing before evaluating and refuting.[38]

Yoder resented being pressed into an "against culture" position by his theological interlocutors. He complained that James Gustafson and Jeffrey Stout "politely" and "respectfully" say that he is negating this or that worldly norm. Instead Yoder insisted, "I am claiming the real-world relevance of Jesus as Lord which they deny."[39] He affirms Christ transforming culture but is ready to be countercultural and unpopular if that is required. However, he is not willing to accept as much negation as others ascribe to him because they need it to fit him into their own grid.[40]

The Agenda of the "Politics of Jesus"

Even if he was misunderstood, such misunderstanding gave Yoder an opportunity for further clarification. He saw some utility in that. In an article that was published posthumously, he attempted to clarify what he wrote in *The Politics of Jesus*. He said that the particular challenge he addressed in his book was internal to the discipline of Christian ethics. He understood it as reappropriating the relevance of Jesus for Christian political and social ethics, which he believed had been lost to the majority theological positions in Christianity for a millennium and a half. It makes no difference if these ethicists have understood themselves as orthodox or liberal. They all believed that the part of the scriptural tradition which speaks to Christian social ethics is a general anthropology of sin and grace and a general doctrine of the proper role of civil order in the world. Once that has been established, one needs to go to other sources for one's social ethics. The teaching and example of Jesus cannot be taken as normative. The role of Jesus as liberator and Lord, which is present in the New Testament, has no immediate relevance.[41]

It was on this basis that Yoder insisted he was claiming the real-world relevance of Jesus as Lord denied by ethicists like James Gustafson. Yoder kept making that argument all his life. *The Politics of Jesus* was designed as a sympathetic ordinary reading (*nachdenken*) of the narrative and ethical texts which would suffice for making the claim that the New Testament sustains a political reading of Jesus and the early Christian movement. Yoder read with a stated readiness to question whether the majority positions on social ethics were adequate. Such reading earned him the label of being "radical." However, he did not assume that the majority positions were wrong—but neither did he give them the benefit of the doubt.[42]

The question at stake, according to Yoder, was not the normative authority of Scripture in the Christian community, but the narrower question of how that authority should function. The reason Jesus is not normative for ethics is not rooted in doubts about the authority of the New Testament canon. Instead, it is the result of broader systemic considerations, such as the doctrines of creation or the atonement, which set Jesus aside in favor of other sources for moral guidance. Reinhold Niebuhr's understanding of "social responsibility" serves the same function. Among such presuppositions is what Gustavo Gutiérrez calls a "distinction of planes," in which the dualistic distinction between the natural and the supernatural undermines the relevance of Jesus for social ethics.[43]

Thinking with Yoder

One way to understand Yoder's thought is to think along with him as he addresses real-world issues from the perspective of the Christian tradition. Such a method is actually appropriating the way he worked and using it to understand his thought. Yoder understood this as teaching and testing the tradition for coherence and faithfulness to the revelation of God in Jesus Christ. Such theology continues through time by restating the problems in relation to present exigencies without thinking that one always has to return to the beginning to be sufficiently guided by the texts one finds there.[44] Bernard Lonergan speaks of it as the basic exegetical tasks of understanding, judging, and stating what one judges to be the correct understanding of the text. He writes:

> To judge the correctness of one's understanding of a text raises the problem of context, of the hermeneutical circle, of the relativity of the totality of relevant data, of the possible relevance of more remote inquiries, of the limitations to be placed on the scope of one's interpretation.[45]

Accordingly, a central task is understanding how Yoder's theological ethics were shaped by various influences, including the twentieth-century North American Mennonite experience, his work in postwar Europe, his doctoral studies with Oscar Cullmann and Karl Barth, and his dissertation on the Swiss Anabaptists. Having done this, it is possible to identify various premises in his theological ethics that became the frame he used to construct his thought. Such identification involves an exegetical process of evaluating and judging.

Nancey Murphy's work is helpful in that respect. She has made a real contribution by laying out what she calls Yoder's core theory and his supporting hypotheses. However, I elected not to use her scientific research model for my own work, preferring rather to use David Tracy's explication of theological languages and the way they work because it lends itself more naturally to the elucidation of Yoder's project in theological ethics.

Tracy recognizes that all theologies that adequately convey the power and grace of God disclosed in Jesus Christ have both analogical and dialectical characteristics. An analogical theology which loses its sense of the negative does not produce a beautiful harmony but rather a "cheap grace" characterized by boredom and sterility.[46] Conversely, a dialectical theology will lead us into the whirlwind unless it discovers that its own radical, liberating power is rooted in the same reality as its analogical counterparts. Tracy calls this reality "the always-already, not-yet event of the yes disclosed in the grace of Jesus Christ."[47]

Consequently, one should expect to find a constructive, analogical core to Yoder's theology related to a primary focal meaning of the Christ event. Tracy defines such analogical language as "a language of ordered relationships articulating similarity-in-difference." He writes:

> The order among the relationships is constituted by the distinct but similar relationships of each analogue to some primary focal meaning, some prime analogue. A principal aim of all properly analogical languages is the production of some order, at the limit, some harmony to the several analogues, the similarities-in-difference, constituting the whole of reality.[48]

A Primary Focal Meaning

There is indeed such a primary focal meaning (to use Tracy's nomenclature) in Yoder's theological language. This focal meaning functions as a core which grounds the ordered relationships in Yoder's discourse. In the following pages I will explain how that functions in

Yoder's constructive theology. I begin by identifying the focal meaning as it is articulated in *The Politics of Jesus*. The second chapter of *The Politics of Jesus* is Yoder's exercise in reading along with the Gospel of Luke to identify the socio-political stance of Jesus in first-century Palestine. At the end of the chapter he articulated what he discovered:

> Jesus was not just a moralist whose teachings had some political implications; he was not primarily a teacher of spirituality whose public ministry unfortunately was seen in a political light; he was not just a sacrificial lamb preparing for his immolation, or a God-Man whose divine status calls us to disregard his humanity. Jesus was, in his divinely mandated (i.e. promised, anointed, messianic) prophethood, priesthood, and kingship, the bearer of a new possibility of human, social, and therefore political relationships.[49]

Notice how this focal meaning begins with the negative dialectical move of defining who Jesus is not. Each one of these negations is aimed at a common theological understanding of the work of Jesus. Next, Yoder turned to his prime analogue or constructive heuristic with the claim that *Jesus is the bearer of a new possibility for human, social, and political relationships.* His claim serves a double function. First, it separates Yoder's political interpretation of Jesus from other common theological interpretations of Jesus. More significantly, it serves as the core of a pattern of ordered relationships that develop and give coherence to his thought. After the major work of identifying the ordered relationships of his theological language below, I will lay them out more explicitly as the basic principles of "the politics of Jesus" in the next chapter.

YODER'S CONSTRUCTIVE THEOLOGY

To identify the ordered pattern of relationships which give coherence to Yoder's constructive theology, I now turn to his thought in his seminal work *The Politics of Jesus* as well as two other early constructive efforts, *The Christian Witness to the State* and *The Original Revolution*.[50] Central to Yoder's project in theological ethics is the historical argument that Jesus had a social and political agenda that was normative for his original disciples, which raises the question of why it is no longer normative for most Christians.

The Historical Argument

Yoder addressed the historical question of why Jesus is no longer normative for Christian ethics in chapter six of *The Politics of Jesus*. Here he explores the extent to which Jesus' social ethic reached into the other parts of the New Testament. Did it even survive the translation from the cultural idiom of the early Jewish churches to the Hellenistic churches? Drawing extensively on the epistles of the apostle Paul, Yoder argued that it did. He claimed that Pauline themes such as "serving others as Christ served" (Rom. 15:1-7) and "dying with Christ" (2 Cor. 4:10) represent more than mystical or psychological identification with Christ.[51] He wrote:

> As long as readers could stay unaware of the political/social dimension of Jesus' ministry (which most of Christendom seems to have done quite successfully), then it was also possible to perceive the "in Christ" language of the epistles as mystical or the "dying with Christ" as psychologically morbid. But if we may posit—as after the preceding pages we must—that the apostles had and taught at least a core memory of their Lord's earthly ministry in its blunt historicity, then this centering of the apostolic ethic upon the disciple's cross evidences a substantial, binding, costly social stance.[52]

If Yoder was correct in his insistence that there was no fundamental shift between the "politics of Jesus" and those of the early church, the corresponding task is to identify where the shift occurred. To do that, Yoder turned to the Anabaptist historiography found in his dissertation on the Swiss Anabaptists. That historiography identified the shift with the gradual but critical changes that took place when Christianity became the religion of the Roman Empire—roughly synonymous with the era of Constantine.[53] The very notion of a "Constantinian shift" became a distinguishing mark of Yoder's theological ethics. He made this argument with varying degrees of sophistication throughout his writings.

According to Yoder, it was the identification of the church with the dominant political structures in society that undercut the relevance of the social and political ethics of Jesus. He insisted that it is not the task of the church to religiously sanctify such power structures but to call them to use constraint in the ways in which they exercise their power. He made the argument that throughout history churches have increasingly identified with ever more particular and regional political entities. That identification was the scandal of the Protestant Reformation. Referring to the breakup of the medieval church into various national churches, he wrote:

> Perhaps we should identify this situation as "neo-Constantian-ism." It is a new phase of unity or a new kind of unity between church and world. This unity has lost the worldwide character of the epoch of Constantine, yet the fusion of church and society is maintained. We can even say it is tightened, since the wars of religion linked particular churches with particular national governments in a way which had not obtained in the Middle Ages. Now the church is servant, not of mankind at large but, of a particular society; not the entire society, but of a particular dominating class.[54]

Consequently, Yoder identified the theological task as to challenge the various churches to recover the social and political ethics of Jesus, to embody these ethics in their internal life, and to witness to the way of Jesus to their particular national societies and the political powers within those societies.

Christology

Yoder's Christology is deliberately set over against both orthodox and liberal systematic theological traditions because he accused them of avoiding the social and ethical normativeness of Jesus Christ. For this reason, he appreciated the approach, taken by the World Council of Churches during the 1950s, of working toward Christian unity through refocusing on the person of Jesus Christ rather than the traditional creeds. He saw this move as complementary to Karl Barth's renewal of the theological disciplines through concentrating on the truth claims of Christ. Yoder wrote:

> But the figure of Christ is crucial not only in the context of unity, as a more promising basis of common confession than the comparison of traditional creeds would be, and not only for mission, as one whose human ministry is explicable and can be communicated to man in every culture. Beyond this, the appeal to Christ represents a particular type of confession of truth, a criterion

whereby to evaluate faithfulness (and unfaithfulness) within the Christian community.[55]

As an example, Yoder drew on the experience of the Confessing Church in Nazi Germany. He said that their feeble but real resistance to Hitler centered on the confession of the authority of Jesus over against fixed doctrinal statements. Their opponents, instead, took the traditional Lutheran confession, that there is revelation in the orders of creation and in the course of history, to an extreme by using it as the basis of their support for Hitler.[56]

Liberal and orthodox theologies alike, according to Yoder, have limited the relevance of Jesus for social ethics. Jesus' public career and his death on the cross are not understood as morally relevant. Such theologies often make majestic, orthodox sounding statements about the cosmic significance of Christ, but the effect of such language actually undercuts the social significance of the human Jesus. One example is the way H. Richard Niebuhr used a trinitarian scheme to posit an ethic of the Father and an ethic of the Holy Spirit, related respectively to the structures of creation and history, which led away from an ethic of the Son. In contrast, Yoder claimed that recent developments in New Testament studies have given us a new awareness of the social humanity of Jesus as a normative source for ethics.[57]

Some might argue that Yoder, in turn, is more christocentric than trinitarian. Arne Rasmussen defends Yoder on this point:

> Yoder would rightly answer that this objection builds on a misunderstanding of the doctrine of the Trinity. What this doctrine says is that we must talk about God so that God the Creator is none other than God as we meet God in the life and destiny of Jesus Christ and in the continuation of Christ's life through the Spirit in the existence of the church. There is no other God behind this God.[58]

Yoder traced the problem in the theological tradition back to the Nicene and Chalcedonian creeds. The creeds understand the incarnation as a metaphysical transaction through which Jesus saved humanity by entering into it. At the same time, they ignore his public career by leaping from his birth to the cross.[59] The overriding question for the creeds is that of substance—how the human nature and the divine nature can be together in one person. Yoder claimed that New Testament theology reframes the question:

> But when, in the New Testament, we find the affirmation of the unity of Jesus with the Father, this is not discussed in terms of substance, but of will and deed. It is visible in Jesus' perfect *obedience* to the *will* of the Father. It is evident in Jesus that God takes the side of the poor. It is evident in Jesus that when God comes to be King He rejects the sword and the throne, taking up instead the whip of cords and the cross. The gospel is that God does this for His enemies. Then if this is what God reveals Himself to be doing, this is by the same token a revealed moral imperative for those who would belong to and obey Him.[60]

Having challenged the creeds on such issues, Yoder nevertheless argued that his position was more radically Nicene and Chalcedonian than other purportedly orthodox theologies. He recognized the historic task of dealing with the many ways, ebionitic and docetic, of avoiding the normativeness of Jesus. He was not advocating some new, unheard of understanding of Jesus. Instead, he was insisting that "what the church has always said about Jesus as Word of the Father, as true God and true Man be taken more seriously, as relevant to our social problems, than ever before."[61] But, that relevance needs to be redefined.

Discipleship

Various interpreters of Yoder's theological ethics have recognized how central the cross is to his understanding of Christian discipleship. For Yoder, the cross had a very specific meaning. In his typical dialectical style, he began by defining what it is not. It is not any kind of sickness or suffering that we need to bear as human beings. It is also not the inner struggling of the sensitive soul with self and sin. Instead, it is the consequence of the disciple's imitation of Jesus. Again, it is not any kind of imitation, such as a romantic attachment to Jesus' poverty or his life as a village artisan. Instead, Jesus is our example in his cross, which is the social consequence of representing God's coming reign in an unwilling world.[62]

Nancey Murphy characterizes Yoder's discipleship ethic of the cross as the core of his theology. This ethic asserts that the moral character of God is revealed in Jesus' renunciation of domination, vulnerable enemy love, and ultimate self-sacrifice on the cross.[63] For Yoder, this ethic has concrete social manifestations. The renunciation of domination has two foci: one is economic sharing, the other is servant leadership. First, Jesus' program of economic sharing was built on his proclamation of the year of Jubilee (Luke 4:18-19). It involved the remission of debts, the liberation of slaves, and the redistribution of capital. The phrase in the Lord's Prayer about the forgiveness of debts (Mat. 6:12) is a summary of this Jubilee ethic, which Yoder claimed was at the center of Jesus' proclamation of the reign of God.[64]

Second, Yoder recognized an anti-Roman and anti-Zealot thrust to Jesus' ethic of servant leadership. This directive was provoked by the desire of two of his disciples to have places of privilege in his kingdom. Jesus did not simply tell his disciples to be servants; rather, he was contrasting that command with commonly recognized forms of lording it over others (Matt. 20:25-28). The account in Luke 22:25 adds the detail that those in power love to be called "benefactors," indicating the desire for moral legitimation of their privileged status.[65]

Much of Yoder's theological writing was devoted to nonviolence and the problem of war—a concern that emerged out of his Mennonite background and his European postwar experience. Nonviolence, however, did not have an independent status in his theological ethics. It was one aspect of discipleship—a form of imitating Jesus' vulnerable enemy love. Yoder's nonviolence has often been misunderstood because it is neither a withdrawal from social responsibility (a form of religious separatism), nor is it primarily a calculated use of nonviolent tactics to achieve specific social goals or to gain political power.[66]

Yoder said that imitation of Jesus is actually a participation in God's inexplicably nonresistant patience with humanity. It is sharing in the divine condescension (Phil. 2:3-14).[67] Consequently, he could talk about such vulnerable enemy love as "nonresistance"—understood as the renunciation of retaliation in kind.[68] In an often misunderstood chapter, he referred to such self-giving love as "revolutionary subordination" in contrast to either violent revolution or passive acquiescence to social evil.[69]

Church and World

Yoder's social stance cannot be adequately understood apart from his distinction between church and world. Drawing on the Anabaptist tradition, he insisted that the church is not the world. It is a voluntary, serving, witnessing body with an existence sociologically distinct from the surrounding society. He saw a new ecumenical appreciation for such an understanding of the church after World War II. There had been various stimuli for such a recovery of the significance of the church. One was the foreign missions movement, which led to a different conception of the church than that of medieval Europe. Another was the attention given to historical-critical biblical studies, which recognized that the New Testament church embodied a distinct social reality in the ancient world. Yet another was the disciplines of psychology and sociology, which enable us to see the church as a distinct community more clearly than before.[70]

All human efforts to understand their experience, according to Yoder, are prone to various polarizations or dualisms. Among those that Christians have traditionally used are distinctions between the visible church and the invisible church, between spirit and body, between love and justice, and between clergy and laity. He said that a more biblical distinction would not attempt to distinguish between realms of reality, but between those who confess Jesus Christ as Lord and those who do not. Drawing on his historical research on Anabaptist ecclesiology, Yoder defined it as the distinction between church and world.[71] It is not a prior metaphysical distinction, nor is it a distinction that timid Christians have built up around themselves. Instead, it is the result of the freedom of humans to not believe in the God revealed in Jesus Christ.[72]

The distinction between church and world has profound implications for Yoder's social ethics. It implies that the church functions as a minority in society. Yoder wrote:

> To recognize that the church is a minority is not a statistical but a theological observation. It means our convinced acceptance of the fact that we cannot oblige the world to hold the faith which is the basis of our obedience, and therefore should not expect of the world that kind of moral performance which would appropriately be the fruit of our faith. *Therefore* our vision of obedience cannot be tested by whether we can ask it of everyone.[73]

Yoder contended that recognizing the minority status of the church should not lead to social cynicism or withdrawal but to a profound intellectual reorientation. A problem is that old habits of thought still persist even though the church has lost its social status in the secular world.

The church still thinks of herself as the moral teacher and the soul of the existing society. She still thinks she needs to provide religious resources for the morality of everyone in society. Because of the accommodations needed to meet such a standard, she has felt the need to provide religious legitimation for war and violence. He maintained that the Constantinian synthesis of church and society eventually collapsed because of such internal contradictions.[74]

In a post-Christian age, the church recognizes that she is no longer fully in charge; often the church is not even a majority in a given society. Yoder asked, "Now that the church has become weak, may we not recognize with joy that her calling is to be weak?"[75] He made the claim that the church is the only community whose social hope does not depend on being in charge of society. Christians have a different hope because they believe that Christ, the lamb who was slain, is Lord. This social vision is rooted in the global church as the body of Christ with a transformed vision and community, rather than the conviction that we need to take control of the political process to accomplish some yet unachieved restructuring of society.[76] Consequently, Yoder contended:

> What we have to discern for the church is not a new way to establish a much more promising alliance with the most constructive powers that we can see at work in society, as much as to discern the shape of the moral independence that is demanded to exercise over against these powers the ministry which only the church can exercise, her constant call to sobriety and to respect for human dignity.[77]

Eschatology

Two chapters in Yoder's early constructive theology address social ethics in relation to eschatology. One is "If Christ is Truly Lord" in *The Original Revolution*.[78] The other is the "The War of the Lamb" in *The Politics of Jesus*. Yoder's eschatology is built on Oscar Cullman's distinction between the "old age" and the "new age," as seen in New Testament eschatology. The "new age" is the age of the church inaugurated in Christ's victory over death and the evil powers in his resurrection.[79]

In the "new age," evil is potentially subdued. Its submission is already a reality in the reign of Christ, but the final victory of God awaits the consummation at the end of the age. The consummation will be a vindication of the way of the cross and a revelation that the ultimate meaning of history is in the work of the church. Vulnerable enemy love will be shown to be right, in its deepest sense, because it anticipates the victory of Christ.[80] It was on this basis that Yoder claimed:

> The cross and not the sword, suffering and not brute power determines the meaning of history. The key to the obedience of God's people is not their effectiveness but their patience. . . . The triumph of the right is assured not by the might that comes to the aid of the right, which is of course the justification of the use of violence and other kinds of power in every human conflict; the triumph of the right, although it is assured, is sure because of the power of the resurrection and not because of any calculation of causes and effects, nor because of the inherently greater strength of the good guys. The relationship between the obedience of God's people and the triumph of God's cause is not a relationship of cause and effect but one of cross and resurrection.[81]

Because Christ renounced the claim to govern history, Yoder argued that Christians should emulate the "impotence" and "powerlessness" of Christ's refusal to control events. This renunciation was not only made by the second person of the Trinity but by a poor, tired rabbi who traveled from Galilee to Jerusalem to be rejected. What Jesus renounced, according to Yoder, was not first of all violence, but rather the compulsiveness of purpose that leads us to violate the dignity of others. By the same token, he insisted that the cross is not a recipe for resurrection, nor is suffering a good in itself. Instead, it is the willingness to accept apparent defeat rather than complicity with evil because of our confidence in the ultimate victory of Christ. The way of Christ, culminating in the cross and resurrection, is the model of Christian social efficacy and transformation—the power of God for those who believe.[82]

Witness to the State

Yoder's understanding of how Christians relate to their national governments assumes that the church is the center of God's purposes in history. He argues for the corresponding priority of the church in Christian social strategy. Consequently, an authentic relationship depends on recognizing the church as an independent sociological entity. Furthermore, his understanding of the relationship between church and state is

deeply indebted to Hendrikus Berkhof's theological argument about social structures in relation to the notion of the "powers" in the epistles of
the apostle Paul.[83]

The events surrounding World War II led theologians to reexamine
Paul's language about the "powers" in relation to contemporary social
institutions and ideologies. Yoder applied such language to the state, understood as an outward expression of the "powers" that have their origin
in God's creative purpose. As such, they are part of the divine gift of ordered relationships. Even in their present fallen condition, with their
propensity toward evil and idolatry, they continue to exercise an ordering function that reflects the providence of God. These "powers" crucified Christ (1 Cor. 2:8) and God triumphed over them in Christ's death
and resurrection (Col. 2:13-15). Consequently, the church participates
in both Christ's revolutionary subordination to the "powers" and in his
triumph over them.[84]

Yoder constructed his argument about the Christian witness to the
state on such theological premises concerning the place of the church
and the state in God's economy in relation to the work of Christ. Drawing practical implications from this, he wrote:

> Thus the church's prophetic witness to the state rests on firmly
> fixed criteria; every act of the state may be tested according to
> them and God's estimation pronounced with all proper humility.
> The good are to be protected, the evildoers are to be restrained,
> and the fabric of society is to be preserved, both from revolution
> and war. Thus, to be precise, the church can condemn methods
> of warfare which are indiscriminate in their victims and goals of
> warfare which go further than the localized readjustment of ten-
> sion. These things are wrong for the state, not only for the Chris-
> tian. On the other hand, a police action within a society or under
> the United Nations cannot on the same basis be condemned on
> principle; the question is whether the safeguards are there to in-
> sure that it become nothing more.[85]

Such witness assumes a distinction between church and state. It is
not a pragmatic realism that collapses the church into the national society under the premise of "social responsibility" in a way that denies
Christ's rule over the "powers." It is skeptical of all national ideologies,
including the appeal to democracy as a fundamentally new kind of social

order, and it resists uncritically aligning the church's social agenda with such ideological commitments. It is also careful about taking kingdom ethics, which belong to the church, and insisting on applying them to a society which does not claim to know Christ. For example, it does not directly apply an ethic of vulnerable enemy love, in imitation of Christ, to state actions.[86]

The Christian witness to the state should not be guided by an imagined pattern of the ideal society. Yoder claimed that such an ideal society is impossible in a fallen world. The Christian does not seek to create an ideal society but asks how the state can best fulfill its responsibilities in a fallen world. That is best done through specific proposals in relation to concrete social problems. It does not mean that Christians will be satisfied when such proposals are implemented. Instead, they will appeal to a new level of attainment for the state in keeping with their understanding of God's purposes.[87]

To that end, Yoder proposed the use of middle axioms, which can mediate between the general principles of Christian ethics and the concrete problems of social application. Such middle axioms do not claim a metaphysical status, but they go beyond a pragmatic articulation of common sense. They serve as tools for the meaningful communication of Christian social thought, which recognizes the distinction between church and world.[88] Accordingly, a Christian social critique will speak to available or at least conceivable alternatives related to the elimination of specific abuses rather than demand a perfect society. For example, it will never completely accept government violence but does not just insist that a government be completely nonviolent. Taking a middle axiom approach will be to ask the government to take the most just and least violent action deemed possible.[89]

Social Action

As can be expected, Yoder's agenda for Christian social action maintains his distinction between church and world. He takes issue with common ways of approaching social issues. One common assumption is that social leadership is the business of the state, which solves problems by creating and changing institutions. If something is morally wrong, we think the solution is to put pressure on the state to outlaw it. An example of such a mentality is church leaders pressuring local authorities to enact non-discriminatory policies in real estate transactions when most of the people involved in such transactions are church members.[90]

Yoder questioned the reliance on such government processes while ignoring the character of the church as a community with its own internal resources and procedures for implementing Christian ethics. He challenged the propensity to think that using top-down societal power is the best way to address social problems. (Such reluctance to rely on coercive government action reflects his indebtedness to Mennonite sensibilities and to the social ethics of Guy Hershberger).[91] Yoder said that our inability to think beyond using government actions to address social problems leads to the preposterous assumption that Christians need to manage society if they want to be socially responsible.[92]

What will Christian social action look like if it has given up the compulsion to be in control? Yoder spoke of it as the relevance of a sign, as the unmasking of idols, as the work of pioneering, and as the transcendence of hope. Such social action serves as an analogy of the work of Christ who was crucified and raised again. Yoder related the relevance of a sign to the civil-rights movement in the United States:

> Much of the achievement of the civil rights movement in the United States must be understood by means of this category of symbolic evaluation. A sit-in or march is not instrumental but it is *significant*. Even when no immediate change in the social order can be measured, even when persons and organizations have not yet been moved to take a different position, the efficacy of the deed is first of all its efficacy as sign.[93]

There are times, according to Yoder, when a society is so controlled by a destructive ideology that the only recourse is to say no in the name of a higher authority. Such denunciation is not predicated on the ability to propose an alternative social strategy. Drawing on the experiences of both Mennonite conscientious objectors and resistance to the Nazis by Christian pacifists like Andre Trocmé, Yoder argued that it is often the nonconformist or the conscientious objector who will discover new and creative solutions, but the right to say no does not depend on the ability to offer such solutions. The courage to say no, by itself, unmasks the idolatrous pretensions of such ideologies.[94]

Yoder emphasized the pioneering aspect of grassroots Christian social initiatives throughout history. He noted that social commentators have often recognized that American democracy can be traced to the pattern of congregational meetings in nonconformist and evangelical churches. Churches first experimented with and developed schools and hospitals, creating institutional models, which were later adopted by the society and supported by the state. More recently, churches developed the concept of voluntary service for young people, which is now increasingly adopted by universities and governments as various forms of community service.[95]

Furthermore, all Christian social action is an expression of our transcendent hope in the God of history. Yoder wrote:

> This is the hope which our efforts seek to proclaim. It would be best if our "demonstrations" and "manifestations" were concerned to demonstrate or manifest something rather than to wield power as instruments of coercion and pressure, obliging an adversary to yield unconvinced.[96]

Such hope includes aspects of wonder, of seeing subterranean springs of water bubbling up in unexpected places, and of getting a foretaste of distant goals. A full historical accounting of social change needs to include the inexplicable (providential) coincidences at decisive points, which go beyond the brilliant solutions, heroic struggles, and careful organizing of the people involved. Those involved in social action often experience a foretaste of their goals in their own community of struggle. An example is marchers singing "Freedomland" during the civil rights movement. Such action involves the sense that we will not get to the Promised Land by our own momentum, but we want to be the kind of people who will not feel like strangers when we get there. Yoder wrote:

> In such ways there is a link between our obedience and the accomplishments of God's purposes. We see it when we find life by way of the cross, power by means of weakness, wisdom by means of foolishness. We see it when we find wealth by throwing our bread on the waters, when we find brothers and sisters and houses and lands by giving them up, when we save our life by losing it.[97]

CRITICAL ISSUES

If, as Stanley Hauerwas has said, we are only beginning to learn the lessons that Yoder's work represents, part of that learning will be more than an appreciative inquiry about his theological ethics. It will also raise some critical questions that are germane to the development of his thought. It is not so much a question of refuting him as the challenge of recognizing the limitations and lacunae in his work.

As seen in Tracy's characterization of different theological languages, each has its own unique contributions and limitations. One can learn from the inherent limitations as well as the contributions of a particular theology. Furthermore, the work of any one person has various lacunae. No one can do it all, not even a prolific genius like Yoder. This is not the place extensively to explore these questions. I merely identify some of the issues that will require further work by people who have learned from Yoder and want to continue developing his approach to theology and theological ethics.

One critical issue already raised in this chapter is theological method. Yoder legitimately rejected what he called "methodologism." The flip side, however, is his refusal or inability to be explicit about the outline of his constructive theology. One can recognize that systematizing his thought (as Nancey Murphy and Craig Carter have done in different ways) always loses something in the translation. That is to be expected, but it does not invalidate the effort. One can learn from it.

Arne Rasmussen is correct when he says that Yoder's form of practical reasoning finally cannot be formalized.[98] However, this does not invalidate the fact that Yoder could have been more explicit about the characteristic elements of his constructive work. To claim otherwise is a form of mystification. As seen in the previous section, the kinds of constructive arguments he made are quite obvious and methodical. Bringing more clarity to the methods he used can help elucidate his thought. Such work will be integral to the task of understanding Yoder's theological ethics.

A second issue that merits attention is Yoder's historical argument about the so-called "Constantinian shift." There needs to be more historical research regarding the effects on Christian social ethics of making Christianity the Roman Empire's official religion. Yoder has not done that work. He basically depended on Roland Bainton's historical survey of Christian attitudes toward war and peace for his historical scheme.[99]

Such research will seek more informed answers to some of the following questions. How definitive was the so-called "Constantinian shift" throughout the church? Is such language too categorical? How deep was the capitulation to imperial designs? Conversely, in what ways, if any, did Christian social ethics mitigate the excesses of imperial Rome? There may well be a deeper Christian commitment to nonviolence in the following centuries than has often been acknowledged. To what extent was there continued Christian resistance to an easy identification with imperial Rome? Who were the groups and where were the places that such resistance might be seen?

Yoder's own historical research on the legacy of Michael Sattler indicates that there was some resistance in the Benedictine devotional heritage.[100] What about medieval communities of women, such as the Beguines who practiced a very non-established form of Christian faith?[101] What about medieval mystical traditions? For example, Gustavo Gutiérrez states:

> We usually find the theology of the poor emanating from spiritual movements of the poor, which are frequently social movements as well. Certain streams of medieval piety would be a good example of this tendency. This is significant, for the life and reflection of the poor always have a contemplative and mystical dimension—and at the same time a dimension of protest and social transformation.[102]

What are the medieval points of departure for the Anabaptist historiography Yoder used? Surely, it did not emerge out of nowhere in the sixteenth century. To be sustained and developed, Yoder's historical argument needs more research.

A third issue is Yoder's use of the Bible. One of his contributions to Christian social ethics was the biblical exegesis he brought to the discussion. However, one also needs to ask about the limitations of his so-called "biblical realism." Was his commitment to read along with the Bible (*nachdenken*) always adequate? This way of reading served his purposes well, but it also had a tendency to ignore some basic hermeneutical issues.

One example is Yoder's penchant to read Old Testament stories of holy war as literal historical accounts rather than theological interpretations written centuries later. He said he wanted to read those stories as believing Jews would have read them, rather than with modern questions in mind.[103] To what extent is that even possible, let alone desirable? It suggests an inordinate confidence in his ability to read the Bible straight, without paying too much attention to historical and hermeneutical issues.[104]

Another aspect of this hermeneutical issue is Yoder's response to the Reformation problem of *sola scriptura* as the basis of authority. His answer, taken from the Swiss Anabaptists, was that the congregation is a community of discernment which stands under Scripture and over the individual theologian.[105] This is an improvement on the often unstated premise that the individual reader is her or his own interpreter. However, it begs the question of how adequately the congregation can discern the will of God through the corporate reading of Scripture. And it hardly begins to tackle the problem of discernment when Scripture does not directly address a given issue.

Pastors and theologians who have been questioned about their beliefs by a congregation or other local church body know that such groups often do not have the necessary critical tools for adequate discernment. Such pastors and teachers know the tension between being faithful to their vocations and relating to congregations and even denominations with an inadequate understanding of Scripture and theology. At the least, one needs an expanded understanding of the hermeneutical community to which one is responsible, a community that includes all the resources of the ecumenical church. In a real sense, it was such an ecumenical community of discernment that Yoder was responsible to throughout his life. His understanding of the church as a community of discernment could better reflect that reality.

A final issue is Yoder's image of God. There is considerable tension (if not a contradiction) between his portrayal of God as a God of vulnerable enemy love revealed in Jesus and his portrayal of God as one who actively channels vengeance and violence as seen in various Old Testament and Pauline texts. Yoder claimed that God harnesses vengeance through the state as a way to preserve order. It is not made good through this process but is made subservient to God's purposes.[106] At the same time, Yoder said that we are called to vulnerable love for our enemies because the God we know in Jesus is like that.[107]

The way Yoder sought to resolve this contradiction was by using some rather strained logical gymnastics to claim that God does not take moral responsibility for the domination and violence of such powers. He wrote:

> The sergeant does not produce the soldiers he drills, the librarian does not create nor approve of the book he catalogs and shelves. Likewise God does not take the responsibility for the existence of the rebellious "powers that be" or for their shape or identity; they already are.[108]

There are several reasons for this bifurcation in Yoder's image of God. One is his argument that the roots of Jesus' nonviolence can be traced to faith in Yahweh, the Hebrew warrior God, and the belief that God's people do not need to fight because "God will fight for us."[109] Another was his commitment to "biblical realism," which included tendencies to harmonize divergent texts and to read them objectively as God's word.[110] Such tendencies kept him from reading biblical passages about God's purported vengeance and violence more critically, as reflecting the understanding of a fallible people of God, or more dialogically in light of what we know of God through Jesus Christ.

This is a serious issue for Christians committed to nonviolent social ethics. Ultimately one's praxis reflects one's image of God and vice versa. It is not that Yoder necessarily had a violent image of God. It was rather that he struggled to reconcile the nonviolent image of God revealed in Jesus and the Hebrew prophets with the many violent images of God in the Bible. He was not willing to dismiss or easily dissolve that tension.[111]

A LIVED PRAXIS

Before concluding this discussion, it is important to note that John Howard Yoder was not only a scholar or a theoretician. His theology and social ethics were rooted in a lived praxis. A good example is that, as someone from a peace church tradition who had been involved in the reconstruction effort in Europe following World War II, much of his thought engaged the problem of war. He did not only think and write passionately about this problem—he was also an antiwar activist.

Antiwar Activism

One example of his antiwar activism was his refusal to pay the portion of his income taxes which supported the United States military budget. He said he did this not to keep his own hands clean but as a Christian witness to the way of peace. Relating it to his years of service in Europe, he wrote:

> The governments under which I lived, including the one whose passport I carried when I went overseas, were making a major contribution to the terror which threatens all the nations of the world. They were taking the greatest initiative in poisoning the outer atmosphere of the globe and the inmost springs of heredity with nuclear tests. Statesmen were making their bids for election primarily on the basis of how "firm" they were prepared to be in threatening the other half of the world with nuclear destruction.[112]

Yoder could be intransigent. For years he fought with the Internal Revenue Service, making them confiscate the portion of his taxes that went for military purposes. He became a goad to the institutions he worked for by asking them to not automatically deduct that portion of his tax bill. He worked to create a military tax resistance movement in Peace Church and Fellowship of Reconciliation circles. He doggedly kept working at this project, along with a small circle of other committed people, even though they could not claim any great success.[113]

At the same time, Yoder encouraged religious pacifists to serve as chaplains in the military. He schemed to incorporate nonviolent principles in policing tactics and even dreamed about how they could be applied to the administration of penal institutions.[114] He positively engaged just war ethicists as persons who, like him, were opposed to the *realpolitik* nature of modern warfare and international relations, encouraging them to be honest in their own thinking. He had an activist's heart and wanted nothing less than to change the way governments used military power.

Church as Politics

Another significant part of Yoder's activism involved the church. He was deeply committed to a congregational ecclesiology and the renewal of the local church. He had a very different idea of the church than the normal Sunday morning worship service or American denominational structures. For him, the church was political. It embodied a new kind of social reality. He wrote:

This . . . demands for the church an existence, a structure, a sociology of her own, independent of the other structures of society. She can no longer be simply what "church" has so long meant in Europe, the administrative division of civil government which arranges to have preachers in the pulpits, nor can she be what is so often true in America, one more service club which, even though it has many members registered, still needs to compete with other loyalties for their time and attention.[115]

As seen in chapter two, Yoder was intimately involved in the renewal of the Mennonite churches in France during the time he was in Europe. He had a passion for the creation and nurture of churches that would embody the ethics of Jesus within their communal life and witness to the way of Jesus in their national society. When he returned from Europe in 1957, he was soon deeply involved with individuals and groups working to renew American churches along similar lines. They were interested in experimental activist church models, organized around an intentional community core, which reached out to disadvantaged urban neighborhoods. One congregation built on this model, which he related to, was the Reba Place Fellowship in Evanston, Illinois.[116]

Yoder kept relating to various radical experiments in church life. He wrote for *Sojourners,* a radical evangelical magazine, and worked closely with its editor Jim Wallis and the Sojourners Community in Washington D.C. In the 1970s there was a whole network of such radical church groups.[117] Yoder called the creation of such intentional and activist Christian communities the "original revolution" because they have an alternative set of values derived from the example of Jesus, and they embody a coherent way of incarnating these values.[118] Their lived praxis, which he personally participated in, informed and shaped his theology.

Lest we fall into the trap of hagiography, we need to also recognize Yoder's relational failures and transgressions. He was an extreme introvert who existed in his own world. That made him difficult to live with. Furthermore, he occasionally used his powerful intellect as a weapon in ways that could devastate other people. Such failures in interpersonal relationships caused great pain to himself, his family, his students, and his colleagues. He found it difficult to relate to ordinary people in healthy ways. These personal limitations hindered his ability to develop meaningful and sustained relationships in a local congregation. Later in his life, various women accused him of transgressing healthy sexual boundaries. Most problematic was the way he used his powerful intellect to create a logic that excused such behavior. More positively, when the allegations of sexual impropriety led to a church disciplinary process he submitted to the drawn-out and painful conversations which eventually led to personal restoration in the church and a degree of reconciliation with those he had injured.[119]

CONCLUSION

The purpose of this chapter was to better understand and to evaluate Yoder's theological ethics. It began by briefly reiterating the steps Yoder took as he worked at his project in the post-World War II era. It used David Tracy's depiction of different theological languages to help define where Yoder's theological language fits within the field of theology. It included a study of Yoder's theological language, beginning with his focal meaning or core claim that *Jesus is the bearer of a new possibility for human social and political relationships.* It identified and discussed the components of his constructive theology which supported that claim. It identified some critical issues in Yoder's thought that need further work by people committed to Yoder's theological agenda and a nonviolent social ethic. Finally, it briefly noted the ways in which Yoder's lived praxis of antiwar activism and commitment to radical Christian community were related to his thought.

The work of understanding Yoder's thought in this chapter serves as the basis for the task of assessing the impact of his notion of the "politics of Jesus" on religious thinking and initiatives in social justice and peacebuilding. Yoder made his own applications to various social justice initiatives. Others have picked up were he left off and further developed his ideas. Identifying what they are and assessing them in relation to Yoder's thought will be the task in the following chapter.

NOTES

1. James Gustafson, *Ethics from a Theocentric Perspective,* vol. 1 (Chicago: University of Chicago Press, 1981), 75.

2. James McClendon, *Ethics: Systematic Theology,* vol. 1 (Nashville: Abingdon Press, 1986), 7.

3. Stanley Hauerwas, in Hauerwas, et. al., *The Wisdom of the Cross,* x, xi.

4. J. Denny Weaver, *The Nonviolent Atonement* (Grand Rapids: Eerdmans, 2001), 4, 12-13. See also his *Anabaptist Theology in the Face of Postmodernity* (Telford, Pa.: Pandora Press U.S., 2000). Weaver attributes his project of rethinking theology from a peace church perspective to his reading of Yoder.

5. Glen Stassen, ed. *Just Peacemaking: Ten Practices for Abolishing War* (Cleveland: The Pilgrim Press, 1998), 19.

6. Lisa Sowle Cahill, *Love Your Enemies: Discipleship, Pacifism, and Just War Theory* (Minneapolis: Fortress Press, 1994), 223.

7. John Howard Yoder, "Courses Taken by John H. Yoder in the Theological Faculty of the University of Basel, Switzerland," Mark Thiessen Nation, Yoder Collection at Eastern Mennonite Seminary, Harrisonburg, Virginia.

8. John Howard Yoder, *Täufertum und Reformation in der Schweiz: I. Die Gespräche zwischen Täufern und Reformatoren 1523–1538* (Karlsruhe: Buchdruckerei und Verlag H. Schneider, 1962). As noted in a prior chapter, it has recently been translated and published in English as *Anabaptism and Reformation in Switzerland: An Historical and Theological Analysis of the Dialogues between Anabaptists and Reformers,* ed. C. Arnold Snyder; trans. David Carl Stassen and C. Arnold Snyder. Kitchener, Ontario: Pandora Press, 2004.

9. Yoder also had *Karl Barth and the Problem of War* published in 1971. This book, as the title suggests, is a critique of how Barth understands of the problem of war. In that respect, it is not as helpful as the other three titles in understanding Yoder's own constructive theology.

10. Lonergan calls the supposition that one should simply attend to the text the "principle of the empty head." The truth of such an understanding is the well known problem of not listening carefully and sympathetically to the text. Nevertheless, it is mistaken in believing that all the interpreter has to do is look at the text without reference to his or her own subjectivity and other frames of reference. See Lonergan, *Method in Theology,* 156-158.

11. The word *dialectic* is used in the Socratic sense of exposing false beliefs, rather than a Hegelian sense of change through a process of thesis, antithesis, and synthesis.

12. David Tracy, *The Analogical Imagination: Christian Theology and the Culture of Pluralism* (New York: Crossroad, 1991), 405-408.

13. Ibid., 429-438.

14. Daniel Migliore also uses Tracy's typology to characterize different methods of asking theological questions. See Daniel Migliore *Faith Seeking Understanding: An Introduction to Christian Theology* (Grand Rapids: Eerdmans, 1991), 14-18.

15. For a fuller treatment of the way dialectical theologies create new analogies, see Tracy, *The Analogical Imagination,* 415-421.

16. John Howard Yoder, *When War is Unjust: Being Honest in Just-War Thinking,* rev. ed. (Maryknoll, N.Y.: Orbis Books, 1996), 6.

17. Yoder, works at that analogy in *For the Nations: Essays Public and Evangelical,* (Grand Rapids: Eerdmans, 1997), 51-78. It is further developed in his comparison of the free-church vision and the Jewish tradition in his book *The Jewish-Christian Schism Revisited,* ed. Michel Cartwright and Peter Ochs (Grand Rapids: Eerdmans, 2003), 103-144.

18. Tracy, *The Analogical Imagination*, 434.

19. See Gustavo Gutiérrez, *A Theology of Liberation: History, Politics, and Salvation* (Maryknoll, N.Y.: Orbis Books, 1988), 130-135.

20. JHY papers, box 13, AMC. See also Mark Thiessen Nation, "John H. Yoder, Ecumenical Neo-Anabaptist: A Biographical Sketch," in *The Wisdom of the Cross*, ed. Stanley Hauerwas et al, 19.

21. Yoder could also be critical of liberation theologians, especially when he thought they too quickly legitimated the resort to violence. For a helpful reflection on Liberation Theology, see John Howard Yoder, "Biblical Roots of Liberation Theology," *Grail* (September 1985): 55-74.

22. A. James Reimer, "Theological Orthodoxy and Jewish Christianity: A Personal Tribute to John Howard Yoder," in *The Wisdom of the Cross*, ed. Stanley Hauerwas et al, 431, 432.

23. Another development, which Lisa Sowle Cahill notices, is that, in the decades following the publication of *The Politics of Jesus*, Yoder makes a stronger and more certain case for Christian social involvement. See Cahill, *Love Your Enemies*, 225.

24. John Howard Yoder, "Walk and Word: The Alternatives to Methodologism," in *Theology Without Foundations: Religious Practice and the Future of Theological Truth*, ed. Stanley Hauerwas et al (Nashville: Abingdon Press, 1994), 82.

25. Yoder, *Anabaptism and Reformation in Switzerland*, 220.

26. Among these efforts are Michael Cartwright's introductory chapter, "Radical Reform, Radical Catholicity: John Howard Yoder's Vision of the Faithful Church," in John Howard Yoder, *The Royal Priesthood: Essays Ecclesiological and Ecumenical* (Grand Rapids: Eerdmans, 1994). Another effort, which has already been referred to, is Craig Carter's work of fitting Yoder's thought into the outline of a systematic theology. See Carter, *The Politics of the Cross*.

27. Nancey Murphy and George F.R. Ellis, *On the Moral Nature of the Universe: Theology, Cosmology, and Ethics* (Minneapolis: Fortress Press, 1996), 178.

28. Nancey Murphy, "John Howard Yoder's Systematic Defense of Christian Pacifism," in *The Wisdom of the Cross*, ed. Stanley Hauerwas et al, 48.

29. Arne Rasmusson, "Historicizing the Historicist," in Hauerwas et al., *The Wisdom of the Cross*, 243.

30. John Howard Yoder, memo to Mark Thiessen Nation, December 17, 1991, Mark Thiessen Nation, Yoder Collection at Eastern Mennonite Seminary, Harrisonburg, Virginia.

31. Ibid.

32. Ibid.

33. He worked as an administrative assistant at the Mennonite Board of Missions from 1959 to 1965. During that time he related to church groups around the world. He worked with the World Council of Churches for more than twenty years, including being a member of the Study Commission on the Theology of Mission. He also initiated contacts with evangelical leaders and the National Association of evangelicals. See Mark Thiessen Nation, "John H. Yoder, Ecumenical Neo-Anabaptist: A Biographical Sketch," in *The Wisdom of the Cross*, ed. Stanley Hauerwas et al, 18.

34. Ibid. One can find references to "biblical realism" throughout the corpus of

Yoder's work. He relates it to the biblical scholarship of people such as Hendrik Kraemer, Otto Piper, Paul Minear, Markus Barth, and Claude Tresmontant. See Yoder, *The Politics of Jesus* (1972), 5.

35. John Howard Yoder, memo to Mark Thiessen Nation, December 17, 1991, Mark Thiessen Nation, Yoder Collection at Eastern Mennonite Seminary, Harrisonburg, Virginia.

36. One of the best examples of this is the way he engaged Karl Barth's thought in *Karl Barth and the Problem of War.*

37. In the correspondence I read and the people I interviewed, a common perception is that Yoder was a formidable debater with an enigmatic personality. One early example is a comment from Paul Peachey in a letter to Yoder, "I'm not trying to be critical. As you know, I have the highest appreciation for your crystal clear logic and hope that by all means you will continue your work. It is simply to repeat something that I mentioned to you already in Europe, namely that for most of the rest of us common mortals for whom insights come more slowly and foggily, there must be ample charity. Even truth must be stated in love that will be understood as love." See Paul Peachey, letter to John Howard Yoder, June 19, 1954, Yoder papers, box 11, AMC. Others, however, experienced him as someone who was patient, kind, and not given to self-reflection. Stanley Hauerwas writes, "He viewed his own life with a godly indifference. Such indifference could be mistaken as a kind of arrogance, but it was anything but that, Yoder, born with extraordinary mental powers, had those powers shaped by a people for whom all power is a gift of service. . . . Among Mennonites John not only could be but was combative. But he approached those outside the Mennonite world, Christian and non-Christian alike, first as a listener." See Stanley Hauerwas, "Remembering John Howard Yoder," *First Things* (April 1998): 15.

38. John Howard Yoder, memo to Mark Thiessen Nation, December 17, 1991, Mark Thiessen Nation, Yoder Collection at Eastern Mennonite Seminary, Harrisonburg, Virginia.

39. Notice how such negative dialectics slips into his language, even when he talks about meeting his interlocutors on their own turf. It is instructive to compare this with liberation theologian José Miranda's dismissal of Karl Rahner's entire theology as nonbiblical. The family resemblances between Yoder's and Miranda's theology are striking. See José Miranda, *Marx and the Bible: A Critique of the Philosophy of Oppression* (Maryknoll, N.Y.: Orbis Press, 1974), 249.

40. John Howard Yoder, memo to Mark Thiessen Nation, December 17, 1991. The grid that Gustafson and Stout were using was the classic typology of H. Richard Niebuhr in *Christ and Culture* (New York: Harper & Row, 1951). Yoder was a strong critic of that typology. See his chapter, "How H. Richard Niebuhr Reasoned: A Critique of *Christ and Culture,"* in *Authentic Transformation: A New Vision of Christ and Culture,* ed. Glen Stassen et al (Nashville: Abingdon Press, 1996), 31-89.

41. Yoder, *To Hear the Word,* 52-53.

42. Ibid., 54.

43. Ibid., See Gutiérrez, *A Theology of Liberation,* 36-46.

44. Yoder, *Preface to Theology,* 381-382.

45. Bernard Lonergan, *Method in Theology* (Toronto: University of Toronto Press, 1994), 155.

46. Tracy, *The Analogical Imagination,* 413.

47. Ibid., 421.

48. Ibid., 408.

49. Yoder, *The Politics of Jesus* (1972), 62-63.

50. I do not attempt a comprehensive review of Yoder's thought within the categories of systematic theology. Instead, I focus on those elements of his thought that help to elucidate his contribution to theological ethics as seen in his early constructive endeavors up to and including *The Politics of Jesus.*

51. Ibid., 94 ff.

52. Ibid., 130-131.

53. Yoder, *Anabaptism and Reformation in Switzerland,* 193-197.

54. Yoder, *The Original Revolution* (1971), 150-151.

55. Ibid., 133.

56. Ibid., 134.

57. Ibid., Yoder, *The Politics of Jesus* (1972), 103. This use of trinitarian dogma by H. Richard Niebuhr can be seen in *Christ and Culture* (New York: Harper & Row, 1951), 80-82.

58. Arne Rasmusson, "Historicizing the Historicist," in *The Wisdom of the Cross,* ed. Stanley Hauerwas et al, 241-242.

59. Yoder, *The Politics of Jesus* (1972), 106.

60. Yoder, *The Original Revolution* (1971), 136.

61. Yoder, *The Politics of Jesus* (1972), 105.

62. Yoder, *The Politics of Jesus* (1972), 97.

63. Murphy and Ellis, *On the Moral Nature of the Universe,* 178-181.

64. Yoder, *The Politics of Jesus* (1972), 64-77.

65. Ibid., 126-127.

66. Ibid., 93.

67. Ibid., 124-125.

68. Ibid., 204.

69. Ibid., 163-192.

70. Yoder, *The Original Revolution* (1971), 114-115.

71. Yoder, *Anabaptism and Reformation in Switzerland,* 259-277.

72. Yoder, *The Original Revolution* (1971),116.

73. Ibid., 122-123.

74. Ibid., 122-131.

75. Ibid., 122-123.

76. Ibid., 127-131.

77. Ibid., 159.

78. This chapter was originally presented as a paper with the title "Peace Without Eschatology?" at a Theological Study conference in the Netherlands in 1954.

79. Cullmann's exposition of New Testament eschatology and the concept of stages of redemptive history can be especially seen in Oscar Cullmann, *Christ and Time: The Primitive Christian Conception of Time and History,* trans. Floyd Filson

(Philadelphia: The Westminster Press, 1954).

80. Yoder, *The Original Revolution* (1971), 62-64.

81. Yoder, *The Politics of Jesus* (1972), 238.

82. Ibid., 243.

83. Hendrikus Berkhof, *Christ and the Powers*, trans. John H. Yoder (Scottdale, Pa.: Herald Press, 1962).

84. Yoder, *The Politics of Jesus* (1972), 142-149.

85. John Howard Yoder, *The Christian Witness to the State* (1964), 5.

86. Ibid., 26.

87. Ibid., 32.

88. Ibid., 32-33. Yoder took the concept of middle axioms from the social ethics discussion at the World Council of Churches' Amsterdam General Assembly in 1948. Michael Cartwright attributes the notion of middle axioms to J. H. Oldham. See Yoder, *The Royal Priesthood*, 17. While Yoder stopped using the terminology of middle axioms after the 1960s, he continues to work with the concept of translation between the social ethics of the community of faith and their applicability to other social bodies such as national governments. An excellent example of that is his small book *Body Politics*, published in 1992. For a more extended discussion of Yoder's use of the concept of middle axioms and of the problem of the translation of social ethics between different kinds of communities, see Craig R. Hovey, "The Public Ethics of John Howard Yoder and Stanley Hauerwas: Difference or Disagreement," in *A Mind Patient and Untamed: Assessing John Howard Yoder's Contributions to Theology, Ethics, and Peacemaking,* ed. Ben C. Ollenburger and Gayle Gerber Koontz (Telford, Pa.: Cascadia, 2004), 205-220.

89. For a application of such middle axioms to specific social problems, see Yoder, *The Christian Witness to the State* (1964), 35-44.

90. Ibid., 86.

91. Hershberger, *The Way of the Cross in Human Relationships,* 174-180.

92. Yoder, *The Politics of Jesus* (1972), 248.

93. Yoder, *The Original Revolution* (1971), 161.

94. Ibid., 163.

95. Ibid.

96. Ibid., 161-162.

97. Ibid., 165.

98. Rasmusson, in *The Wisdom of the Cross*, ed. Stanley Hauerwas et al, 243.

99. Bainton, *Christian Attitudes Toward War and Peace.* One of Yoder's more nuanced discussions of what he called the Constantinian sources of Western social ethics is in his book *The Priestly Kingdom,* 135-147. His argument is more theological than historical, even though it involves his interpretation of the sweep of Western Christian history in relation to this issue.

100. Yoder recognized, but did not explore, the possible Benedictine contribution to Anabaptist thought. See Yoder, *The Legacy of Michael Sattler,* 21. As has been seen, his historical research focused on the relationship between Anabaptism and the Protestant reformer Ulrich Zwingli.

101. Michael Sattler's wife Margaretta was a former Beguine. See Yoder, *The*

Legacy of Michael Sattler, 80.

102. Gustavo Gutiérrez, *Essential Writings,* ed. James B. Nickoloff (Maryknoll, N.Y.: Orbis Books, 1996), 104.

103. Yoder, *The Politics of Jesus* (1972), 78-79.

104. For a more extened discussion of the problematic way Yoder interpreted Old Testament holy war texts, see David Jantzen, "The God of the Bible and the Nonviolence of Jesus," in *Teaching Peace: Nonviolence and the Liberal Arts,* ed. J. Denny Weaver and Gerald Biesecker-Mast (New York: Rowman & Littlefield, 2003), 58-63. Jansen claims that Yoder's reading is problematic because it ultimately imputes violence to God. In contrast, Janzen argues for a Christocentric reading of holy war texts.

105. Yoder, *Anabaptism and Reformation in Switzerland,* 220. Yoder's understanding of discernment was that God's will is known through consensus that arises out of the open, uncoerced conversation of the gathered congregation. He drew an analogy between this congregational discernment process and enlightenment precepts of democracy and freedom of assembly as well as Gandhi's truth finding process that includes hearing one's adversaries. See Yoder, *Body Politics,* 67-69.

106. Yoder, *The Original Revolution* (1971), 62.

107. Ibid., 52.

108. Yoder, *The Politics of Jesus* (1972), 203.

109. Yoder, "God Will Fight for Us," *The Politics of Jesus.*, 78-89. I am indebted to Ray Gingerich for this insight. Gingerich has carefully analyzed the warrior God motif in Yoder's theology in his article "Theological Foundations for an Ethics of Nonviolence: Was Yoder's God a Warrior?" *Mennonite Quarterly Review* 77 (July 2003), 417-435.

110. Such a tendency to harmonize Scripture can also be seen in his effort to harmonize Romans 13 with other New Testament passages concerning Christian relationships with the state. See Yoder, *The Politics of Jesus* (1972), 193-214. This tendency is most likely a product of the kind of biblical studies he was trained in during the 1950s. For example, one can see these same tendencies in Oscar Cullmann's exposition of Romans 13. See Cullmann, *The State in the New Testament,* 95-114.

111. In contrast, the U.S. Catholic bishops, speaking directly of the nonviolent image of God in the New Testament, write, "There is no notion of a warrior God who will lead the people in an historical victory over its enemies in the New Testament." As quoted in John Dear, S. J., *The God of Peace: Toward a Theology of Nonviolence* Maryknoll, N.Y.: Orbis Books, 1994), 37.

112. John Howard Yoder, "Why I Don't Pay All My Income Tax," *Gospel Herald* (January 22, 1963): 81, 92.

113. The correspondence about war tax resistance is in the Yoder papers, box 31, AMC.

114. Interview with Howard Zehr, November 28, 1998. Zehr is an internationally known authority on restorative justice who occasionally talked with Yoder about such matters.

115. Yoder, *The Original Revolution* (1971), 114-115.

116. Various documents concerning this relationship can be found in the JHY

papers, box 7, AMC.

117. Jim Wallis, letter to John Howard Yoder, November 14, 1975, Yoder papers, box 18, AMC.

118. Yoder, *The Original Revolution* (1971), 28.

119. Calvin Redekop, an early colleague, talked about John Howard Yoder's relational problems throughout his life (personal interview with author, August 10, 2001). Such problems frequently became a topic of discussion when I talked about my research with people who knew Yoder. Those who knew him best said he cared deeply and was genuinely sorry when he hurt others. For more information about the allegations about Yoder's sexual indiscretions and the church disciplinary process, see the series of news articles by Tom Price, *The Elkhart Truth* (July 12-16, 1992).

CHAPTER SEVEN

THE "POLITICS OF JESUS" AS SOCIAL PRACTICE

Gustavo Gutiérrez, the Peruvian liberation theologian, instructs us that theology is a reflection on practice.[1] Accordingly, as seen in previous chapters, Yoder's "politics of Jesus" engages contemporary social issues in light of the revelation of God in the life and ministry of Jesus, the man from Galilee. Yoder had a keen personal interest in relating his thought to concrete social problems. This task involves a fundamental hermeneutical principle. Theological understanding is not as straightforward as objectively grasping the historical meaning of a text and then *applying* it to a given situation. Instead, interpretation and application comprise one unified process. As Hans-Georg Gadamer states:

> A law does not exist to be understood historically, but to be concretized in its legal validity by being interpreted. Similarly, the gospel does not exist to be understood as a merely historical document, but to be taken in such a way that it exercises its saving effect. This implies that the text, whether law or gospel, if it is to be understood properly—i.e., according to the claim it makes—must be understood at every moment, in every concrete situation, in a new and different way. Understanding here is always application.[2]

My purpose in this chapter is better to comprehend the saving effect of the gospel as seen in Yoder's notion of the "politics of Jesus." I do that by examining several case studies in which people attempt to live out its implications. The task is not as straightforward as distilling the historical essence of the gospel as understood by Yoder and then applying it to concrete situations. The process is at once more messy and more unified. The very process of social application helps bring clarity to the meaning of "the politics of Jesus." In that respect this chapter is a fitting conclusion to this book.

Such an understanding of the hermeneutical task does not mean that one does not have to pay close attention to the reading of texts in relation to their historical contexts. To the contrary, much of Yoder's project involved a careful and sympathetic reading of the gospel narratives, using the tools of biblical criticism. Much of my study of Yoder's "politics of Jesus" involved a similar reading of his work. Nevertheless, the task is not complete until that reading of Yoder is put into conversation with contemporary efforts in just peacebuilding that seek to embody such an understanding of the "politics of Jesus." Such social application throws new light on the meaning of historical texts and, as Gutiérrez has said, theology becomes a reflection on practice.

THE CHALLENGE OF JUST PEACEBUILDING

Peace is often defined as a state of tranquility, as harmony in personal relationships, and as freedom from civil unrest. A more wholistic way to define peace is found in the Hebrew concept of *shalom,* which expresses God's basic intension or vision for creation, including physical well-being, right social relationships, and moral integrity.[3] In this respect, one can define peace as human flourishing and sustaining the integrity of creation. Peace then is much more than outward tranquility or the absence of overt conflict. It is an achievement that takes courage, ingenuity, and effort and is often attained at great cost.

Christian peacebuilding involves analysis, strategies, and basic principles. It is waged in the same way that any monumental human effort, such as war, is waged.[4] It is a multifaceted praxis (reflective practice) with layers of tradition and continued development in various arenas of human endeavor. First, the praxis of peace is intimately personal, involving a continual journey of personal development and spiritual direction throughout the various stages of one's life. Second, it involves the praxis of the Christian community as the body of Christ—what John

Howard Yoder called "body politics." Finally, its ultimate concern is the well-being of the whole human race and all creation, reflecting God's love for the world.

The twentieth century witnessed violence and warfare on a scale not seen before in human history, including an unprecedented expenditure of social and material resources for the development and manufacture of conventional armaments and weapons of mass destruction. Yoder was deeply concerned about the role of the United States in the creation and deployment of such weapons in the 1950s and 1960s. That concern is even more urgent today. The resources that the United States pours into military expenditures, in comparison to other countries, have grown exponentially since that time.[5] Massive and unrelenting global economic inequality and poverty is integrally related to war and military spending.[6] The agenda that peacebuilders have inherited from the twentieth century is daunting.

However, the inheritance from the twentieth century is not completely bleak. There has also been real progress in developing both the theory and the practice of peacebuilding in the past century. Though its resources are miniscule compared to those poured into national military establishments, nonviolence as a social practice has grown and can increasingly offer alternative strategies for resolving conflict. These strategies range from working at domestic violence to mediating international conflicts. Various universities now offer programs in peacebuilding and conflict mediation. Their graduates bring these skills to various government and non-government agencies around the world, working in many different venues.

Peacebuilding initiatives have deep religious roots. Mahatma Gandhi is perhaps the most well-known twentieth-century nonviolent strategist who worked from a religious perspective. Other well-known religious peacebuilders are the Dalai Lama and Thich Nhat Hanh. Working from a more secular perspective, Gene Sharp has done significant research into the nature of political power and the theory of nonviolent political action. From within the Christian tradition, major contributions have come from theologians, biblical scholars, and practitioners such as Martin Luther King Jr., Dorothy Day, Thomas Merton, John Howard Yoder, Elise Boulding, Walter Wink, Jean and Hildegard Goss-Mayr, Ched Meyers, Daniel Berrigan, and Dorothee Soelle. Many others, too numerous to name, have contributed to the praxis of peace.

Some have even pioneered new peacebuilding disciplines such as restorative justice.

Basic Principles of the "Politics of Jesus"

For the purpose of social application, I formulate some basic principles of Yoder's "politics of Jesus" as seen in earlier chapters. These principles focus the central characteristics of Yoder's theological ethics in relation to various just-peacebuilding initiatives. That in itself is an interpretative effort. Those principles are not a straight reading of Yoder's thought. They are my attempt to formulate Yoder's thought in a way that can be a useful tool for reflecting on social action and the formation of Christian community.

In what follows, I engage some of Yoder's own applications of his "politics of Jesus" to concrete social issues. At the time of his death in 1997, he was in the middle of a book project focused on active nonviolence. Parts of the book were already completed or near completion, and other parts were in various stages of being written.[7] These materials served as a resource for my study of Yoder's personal application of his theological ethics to nonviolent social initiatives.

Yoder's commitment to just-peacebuilding processes within society are sometimes overlooked or misunderstood because of his theological focus on the church as the primary locus of Christian social ethics. Nevertheless, for him the "politics of Jesus," as understood and practiced in Christian communities, was always *for the nations,* as indicated by his book with that title. In this regard, he sought to distinguish his position from that of his colleague Stanley Hauerwas, who provocatively refers to the Christian stance as *against the nations* or as *resident aliens* within society.[8] Yoder, on the other hand, was always trying to figure out how his unapologetically Christian social ethics could be translated into analogous social practices within the wider society.

To that end, I will relate Yoder's "politics of Jesus" to three just-peacebuilding arenas: (1) Yoder's dialogue with the just war tradition; (2) the social challenge of churches in the global South and in affluent societies; and (3) the emerging just-peacebuilding disciplines including restorative justice and conflict mediation or conflict transformation. Restorative justice applies nonviolent principles to the field of criminal justice. Conflict transformation studies and responds to social conflict by creating constructive change processes that reduce violence and increase justice.[9]

The correlation between Yoder's "politics of Jesus" and the three just-peacebuilding arenas will be on the basis of ten basic principles drawn from Yoder's theological ethics listed below. The goal is not to establish direct causal links between Yoder's theology and other peacebuilding theologies and practices. (That would be difficult and hardly fruitful, even if it were possible). Instead, it is to place Yoder's contributions within a broad and continuing peacebuilding tradition that is a growing stream with many tributaries. Yoder himself was most creative when he was in conversation with all kinds of people on their own turf. It is most encouraging and hopeful to recognize such congruence and interdependence within a tradition fed by many different sources. Yoder's "politics of Jesus" was fed by and contributed to that tradition.

The following ten basic principles come largely from Yoder's early work. They would, however, be incomplete if they did not include some principles taken from his later work on the process of discernment, his thought on how to relate in a pluralistic world, and his work on the Jewish experience of exile as a paradigm for the people of God in society.[10] These principles serve as a kind of frame or "grid" (the word Yoder occasionally used) to inform religious initiatives in social justice and peacebuilding. They begin with what David Tracy calls the prime analogue or focal meaning of a given theological language:

Jesus is the bearer of a new possibility for human social and political relationships, and provides the focal meaning or primary analogue for Christian social ethics. Other sources of moral guidance should not set aside or negate the claims of Jesus.[11]

The ten following principles reflect the natural development of Yoder's theological ethics in relation to this focal statement.

(1) The Galilean Jesus—who proclaimed the reign of God, sided with the poor, chose the way of nonviolence, healed the sick, served those in need, and revealed the nature of God—is our exemplar for Christian social ethics.[12]

- Jesus' life and ministry represent God's coming reign in a world that is threatened by that reality. His vulnerable enemy love and the renunciation of domination resist every violent and hegemonic will to power that sets itself up against the reign of God.
- Jesus' death on the cross is the social consequence of his struggle

against the powers that oppose the reign of God. Those who follow
Jesus' example can expect to face the same kind of opposition from
such powers.

- The social and political ethics of Jesus, as seen in the gospel narratives, serve as a standard of morality directly applicable to those who
follow Jesus. It is also indirectly applicable to other people and social
entities, including the state. This morality is never forced. Instead, it
models God's patient and suffering love, which respects people's
freedom to not believe in God and the way of Jesus.

(2) The Bible is to be interpreted through the nonviolent life and
teaching of Jesus, as seen in the gospel narratives. Likewise, the Old Testament is read through the Hebrew prophets and their condemnation of
ancient imperial aspirations.[13]

- A faithful reading of Scripture uses historical-critical tools but does
not allow them to become ends in themselves. Ancient texts should
be read empathetically with regard to their original settings.
- A faithful reading of Scripture values all the different segments of
the Bible (avoiding proof-texting), while reading it through the lens
of the life and teaching of Jesus.
- Such an empathetic and elicitive reading should also be applied to
all historical texts, as well as the positions of our contemporary interlocutors.

(3) The "politics of Jesus" distinguishes between those who are committed to the way of Jesus and those who are not. It makes a basic distinction between the community of those who follow Jesus (the church)
and those who do not claim to follow Jesus (the world).[14]

- The church is a voluntary, serving, witnessing community with an
existence that is sociologically distinct from the surrounding society.
- Recognizing the church as a minority community is a theological
observation which recognizes that we cannot oblige the world to
live by the faith that informs the life of the church.
- The Jewish experience of exile can serve as a paradigm for the social
existence of the church as the people of God identified with the
common life of the community, the praxis of community members,
and the shared remembering of the story through the development
and ritual reading of Scripture.
- The religious community in exile seeks the welfare of the society in
which God has placed it (Jer. 29:7) and is a channel of God's grace
to the nations.

- Identifying the church with the dominant political structures in society undercuts the relevance of the social and political ethics of Jesus. The religious community should not sacralize or give ultimate religious sanction to any given social order.

(4) The "politics of Jesus" works from the premise that, while the state is part of God's ordering function in the world, it is not at the center of God's purposes in history; instead, the community of those who follow the way of Jesus resides at the center.[15]

- The state is an expression of the ordering "powers" that have their origin in God's creative purpose. As such, the state is part of the divine gift of ordered relationships. Even with its self-serving propensity toward violence and domination, the state reflects something of this providential ordering function in the world.
- The Roman Empire, as an expression of these "powers," crucified Jesus, and God triumphed over them in the resurrection. The church participates in Jesus' revolutionary subordination to the "powers" and in his triumph over them.

(5) The "politics of Jesus" does not assume that social leadership necessarily involves the state and its functions. Consequently, one does not need to manage society through the coercive power of the state to be socially responsible.[16]

- Christian social action that has given up the compulsion to be in control serves as an analogy of the work of Christ. It takes on the relevance and efficacy of a sign, pointing to the reign of God and the possibilities of social life, even if it is not immediately effective in changing the social order.
- Sometimes a society is so controlled by a destructive ideology that the only recourse is to say no in the name of a higher authority. The right to say no does not depend on the ability to offer better solutions. Instead, the simple courage to say no can unmask ideological pretensions and create a space in which new possibilities can emerge.
- Christian social action is characterized by a pioneering spirit of grassroots initiatives, which embody the political and social ethics of Jesus in diverse social arenas such as participatory democracy, healthcare, education, conflict transformation, sustainable living, and restorative justice initiatives.

(6) The "politics of Jesus" includes a prophetic witness to the state based on the way of Jesus and the experience of the community of those who follow him in life.[17]

- The community of those who follow Jesus (the church) serves as a sign of God's purposes for humanity and all of creation.
- A prophetic social witness recognizes the state's legitimate tasks of protecting the good, restraining evil, and preserving the fabric of society. On this basis it critiques state actions that are indiscriminate or do not fulfill the state's legitimate role in society.
- The social stance of the church resists both a nationally oriented political realism that collapses the church into the national society, and an idealism which insists on applying gospel ethics, which belong to the church, directly to society.
- The social experience and life in community of those who follow Jesus can inform analogous social processes in society, such as government policies. This is best done in relation to concrete social problems. To that end, their social witness can use middle axioms that mediate between the general principles of Christian social ethics and concrete problems of social application.

(7) The theological process of discernment is so committed to the conversation that it is willing to take on issues in the categories of others, rather than beginning with one's own "correct" position, which is by definition sectarian. It learns how to work in the strange worlds of other people while remaining true to its core commitments.[18]

- The person engaged in such a process of discernment is willing to be countercultural and unpopular, if that is required, but does not seek to be contrarian. One does not just assume that majority positions are wrong, but one does not give them the benefit of the doubt either.
- Such a theological discernment process is organically linked to the praxis of the community that follows Jesus. The socially engaged community is before, the setting for, and the final arbiter of any system of argumentation.

(8) The "politics of Jesus" engages our pluralistic social reality with the moral claims of Jesus in a way that respects that pluralism and the relativism that accompanies it.[19]

- The attempt to construct a meta-language or an epistemological solid ground above the waves of pluralism and relativism is futile and self-defeating. Instead, the challenge is to ride those waves without being dissolved into them or allowing them to push us where they will.[20]
- Pluralism and relativism are not new phenomena. History demonstrates that reality was always pluralistic and relativistic. The exam-

ple of the early Christian communities can teach us how to respond to that reality.

(9) The "politics of Jesus" engages social problems with the conviction that Jesus' social stance of nonviolent, suffering love goes with the grain of the universe, and that is why nothing else will ultimately be successful in creating just and peaceful communities.[21]

- Christians committed to Jesus' way of peace live in the tension between the "old age" controlled by death and oppressive powers and the "new age" inaugurated in Christ's victory over those powers. Evil is already potentially subdued, but Christians live in anticipation of the final victory of God at the end of the age.
- As seen in Christ's death and resurrection, it is suffering love and not brute power that determines the meaning of history. Vulnerable enemy love will be shown to be right because it participates in Jesus' victory over the forces of death and evil.
- Christian peacebuilders should emulate the "impotence" and "powerlessness" of Jesus' refusal to control events. What he rejected was not first of all violence, but the compulsiveness of purpose, which leads us to violate the dignity of others.[22]

(10) The "politics of Jesus" is characterized by a transcendent hope in the God of history. This hopeful praxis includes the joy and wonder of transformative events that go beyond the brilliance, heroic struggle, and careful organizing of the people involved in social struggle.[23]

- People involved in social action often experience a foretaste of their goals in the community of struggle. This involves a recognition that we will not usher in the reign of God through our own efforts, but that we want to be the kind of people who will not feel like strangers when it arrives.

A Conversation with Catholic Peace Traditions

One place where social action that embodies the "politics of Jesus" is readily seen is in John Howard Yoder's dialogue with Catholic peace traditions, especially the just war tradition. Various principles of his "politics of Jesus," including his passion for nonviolence as well as his ability to take on issues in the categories of others, are demonstrated by this conversation. He especially engaged the just war tradition because he wanted to dispel the notion that the just war tradition and the pacifist tradition are necessarily opposed to each other. He argued that the belief that they were in opposition originated in sixteenth- and seventeenth-century Protestant creeds that made the just war theory a dogma and pacifism a heresy. In reality, in most cases these traditions agree with each other about the morality of war and lethal violence, as compared to other common positions. Consequently, Yoder said he had a stake in the moral integrity of the just war position.[24]

The possibility of a constructive dialogue owes much to the development of Catholic thought on war and lethal violence in the twentieth century. Activists like Dorothy Day and contemplatives like Thomas Merton demonstrated the possibilities of nonviolence as a viable Catholic moral option. In a related development, the Second Vatican Council gave official recognition to active nonviolence as a means of overcoming injustice. The Council wrote:

> We cannot but express our admiration for all who forgo the use of violence to vindicate their rights and resort to those other means of defense which are available to weaker parties, provided it can be done without harm to the rights and duties of others and of the community.[25]

It needs to be recognized that the Council statement expresses an appreciation of nonviolent methods but does not necessarily affirm the pacifist tradition. Its overriding concern is the common good of the whole community. The U.S. Catholic Bishops' 1983 pastoral letter, *The Challenge of Peace,* moved the conversation a step further by recognizing the worldwide impact of the nonviolent witness of people like Mahatma Gandhi, Dorothy Day, and Martin Luther King. It encouraged "the development of a theology of peace and the growth of the Christian pacifist position among Catholics."[26] The letter stated:

> While the just war teaching has clearly been in possession for the past 1,500 years of Catholic thought, the "new movement" in which we find ourselves sees the just war teaching and nonviolence as distinct but interdependent methods of evaluating warfare. They diverge on some specific conclusions, but they share a common presumption against the use of force as a means of settling disputes. Both find their roots in the Christian theological tradition; each contributes to the full moral vision we need in pursuit of a human peace.[27]

Yoder believed the pastoral letter was breaking new ground that had both theological and political significance. Even though pacifists were only a tiny minority within Catholicism, their position was now being recognized as legitimate. Despite their small numbers, their witness had been such that in the atmosphere of the 1980s the bishops included them in the story. Moreover, it was a logic that was shared by Brian Hehir, the principal drafter of the letter, as well as other Catholic moral theologians such as David Hollenbach.[28]

It was out of this context that Yoder wrote his small book *When War is Unjust* as a friendly critique of the Catholic just war tradition. The book included a response from Drew Christiansen, a Catholic moral theologian who taught with Yoder at the University of Notre Dame. Christiansen described their relationship as one of the most nourishing intellectual dialogues in his life. He said that Yoder's influence on Catholic moral theologians was profound. He attributed the Catholic acceptance of Yoder's thinking to developments that began at the Second Vatican Council, which accelerated both ecumenical relationships and a reexamination of Catholic peace theology. He also attributed it to the integrity of Yoder's own theological vision and his willingness to engage just war thinkers in honest dialogue.[29]

A fascinating twist to the dialogue developed when Orbis Books invited Gordon Zahn, a prominent Catholic pacifist and conscientious objector, to write a blurb for the book. Zahn refused because he questioned the wisdom of giving such recognition to the just war tradition. He said that a doctrine under which generations of Christians found it possible to kill each other while thinking they were serving Jesus Christ should not receive even that much scholarly legitimation. Yoder was taken aback. He said that Zahn was right, and that he also did not want to imply that kind of legitimacy to the just war tradition.[30] Yet it was an issue that went to the very core of Yoder's pacifism as well as his commitment to ecumenical dialogue. He wrote:

> The dialectical challenge of "seeming to imply" the respectability of the convictions of the Other is always at the heart of the ecumenical challenge. I do not take this position on pragmatic grounds because I have any confidence that it will convert people. My position is itself a form of the love of the enemy, turning the other cheek, affirming the dignity of the adversary, which also underlies my refusal of war.[31]

Yoder recognized that dialoguing on the interlocutor's terms might appear to grant legitimacy to a position with which one disagrees. Furthermore, he worried that majority positions could appear to be inclusive by listening to, and even honoring, the minority position, but still refuse to take it seriously. In the end, he thought that Gordon Zahn had more freedom to be a prophetic rebel because he was Catholic. Yoder, on the other hand, needed to begin with the ecumenist's benefit of the doubt.[32]

The self-doubt and unease Yoder revealed in this reflection fails to appreciate the impact that he had on Catholic social teaching. For example, Kenneth Hallahan sees Yoder's influence reflected in the U.S. Catholic Bishops' position in *The Challenge of Peace.* Hallahan notes that Yoder's position is solidly grounded in every aspect of his thought, while the Catholic social teaching on war is in transition.[33] In any case, no matter how one assesses Yoder's influence on Catholic social teaching, it does demonstrate the value of the ecumenical discussion to which he was committed.

The conversation was reframed by the U.S. Catholic Bishops' argument that both the just war tradition and the pacifist tradition are rooted in the Christian theological tradition and share a common presumption against the use of force. Yoder's willingness to dialogue with them from that premise opened the way for broader collaboration in just-peacebuilding efforts. One way to recognize what the just war and pacifist traditions have in common is to compare them with various commonly held positions on war and the use of lethal force. It is possible to identify various positions that have little compunction about the use of lethal force for particular ends.[34] Among them are these:

- *A Warrior Ethos:* This position glorifies war and the use of violence. It is seen as a way of building character in individuals, making them and their nation strong and self-reliant. It honors war heroes and the exploits of a nation's armed forces as noble and honorable with little concern for other people or the justice of the cause for which they are fighting. War itself is good and violence is redemptive.
- *The Crusade:* This position legitimates the use of violence for a just or noble cause. This was the position of the Christian crusades in the Middle Ages. It can also take more secular forms, as when secular nations fight for freedom and democracy or when revolutionary liberation movements use lethal violence to free people from various kinds of oppression.

- *Realpolitik:* This position sees the self-interest of a particular nation as the ultimate good. Any means is justified to further or protect that self-interest, including the use of war or various forms of lethal force. It has its roots in nationalism and the writings of Machiavelli (d. 1527). It is the position of many contemporary political science experts and government leaders who see national interests as the ultimate good in an anarchic world characterized by the use of raw power.

- *Self-Defense:* This position legitimates the use of lethal force for the self-defense of oneself or one's family (occasionally it is used to legitimate protecting one's property). It is a common American position in relation to the use of lethal force within our society. American foreign wars are characterized as wars of self-defense and seek religious and moral legitimation on such grounds.

Other moral positions are ambivalent or reject the use of war or lethal force for any ends. War must always be understood as a lesser evil or moral failure. Among such positions are these:

- *The Just War Tradition:* This position is grounded in an ethic of creating communities characterized by peace and justice. The use of lethal force is legitimated only as a last resort to protect the common good. It must be used only within strict constraints such as proportionality and protecting the lives of innocent civilians. The just war position has been the dominant Christian stance since Ambrose and Augustine adopted it from Roman just war arguments in the late fourth century.[35] (Although all twentieth- and twenty-first-century American wars claimed to have met just war criteria, their primary impulses have been the warrior ethos, crusade, and *realpolitik* positions listed earlier).[36]

- *The Pacifist Tradition:* This position argues that any deliberate use of lethal force is always wrong. Christian pacifists base this conviction on their commitment to follow the example of Jesus Christ. This was the position of the early Christians, of various monastic orders, and of the sixteenth-century Anabaptists. It is the position of present-day churches within the peace church tradition and has recently been recognized as a legitimate Roman Catholic moral position.[37]

- *Active Nonviolence:* This position finds its inspiration in the life and teaching of Jesus and owes much of its strategies to activists such as Mahatma Gandhi and Martin Luther King. It condemns the use of physical violence and seeks to raise public awareness of situations of oppression or injustice. It advocates the use of just-peacebuilding practices to create communities of peace and justice. Both persons from the just war and the pacifist traditions may advocate active nonviolence as the normal Christian just-peacebuilding praxis.

It would be a mistake to consider only the influence that Yoder had on Catholic social teaching about war. Catholics also shaped the debate in a way that positively influenced the pacifist tradition. For people from the peace church tradition it was a breath of fresh air to relate to a communion that had not given the just war doctrine the status of dogma. This gave the peace churches recognition and a place at the table.

Without ignoring the fact that there were still fundamental differences, the conversation could develop with the recognition that both positions find their home in a common theological tradition. It was also empowering to recognize that they would generally agree with each other (in an honest evaluation of moral options) when it came to concrete choices related to warfare. Now the conversation could turn to ways in which people from the just war and the pacifist traditions could challenge each other to be faithful to the way of Jesus.

Within this frame, the Catholic just war tradition can challenge pacifists that their peace position should not be an end in itself. It has to be rooted in a social praxis committed to the common good. It cannot be a separatist ethic primarily concerned with the purity of the faith community while ignoring the needs associated with governing an entire society. It can raise the question of what effect pacifism has had in preventing a given war or constraining its excesses.

On the other hand, the pacifist tradition can challenge just war proponents that Christian moral responsibility begins with the church and the coming reign of God rather than the life and aspirations of a given nation-state or society. Furthermore, throughout history just war criteria have hardly served to prevent participation in an unjust war when it involved one's own nation. The just war perspective has never answered the question of who decides or how Christians should respond to such a decision. Too often, what passes for a just cause for war is actually an argument defined as self-defense but based on *realpolitik* considerations.[38]

JUST-PEACEBUILDING COLLABORATION

Even though people from the just war and pacifist traditions will hardly resolve the basic differences between their traditions, they can agree to work together to foster peace and justice. A set of problems that confront peace activists is how to define violence and the alternatives to violence. John Howard Yoder worked at this in a lecture he presented at the South Africa Council of Churches in 1979. He noted that violence is a verbal noun that does not refer to a thing or a condition but to a deed. It is a cognate of "violate," which is a transitive verb that has an object, which it harms or destroys. With reference to human life and dignity, Yoder defined "violence" as "intentional harm done to the physical or psychic integrity of anyone."[39]

In that respect "nonviolence" can be defined as "the intentional renunciation of intent to harm." This creates a strange semantic situation, because "renunciation" and "nonviolence" sound like negative terms yet what they signify is positive. It is as if the only word we had for sexual fidelity in marriage was "non-adultery." He wrote:

> Most Christians are, by custom and by conviction, nonviolent most of the time. What therefore matters is a still narrower definition. We are interested in actions directed nonviolently toward those ends toward which others would justify violence. For this, the standard term has come to be "Nonviolent Direct Action." When we say "direct," we often mean that the action bypasses ordinary indirect procedures of working for change such as the ballot, parliamentary action, or education. We further mean that a precise, attainable goal calls for specified, aimed action.[40]

In the immediate context, Yoder was encouraging South African Christians to eschew violence and to employ the strategies of Gandhi and King in their struggle against apartheid.[41] More broadly, nonviolent direct action can be understood as part of a praxis of peace with various components, all working together toward attainable goals in human relations. Part of that task is to overcome the nomenclature and perception of passivity that is often associated with nonresistance and pacifism. A more extensive and ongoing task is to keep developing the practice and theory of nonviolence.

For these reasons, I prefer referring to that task as "just peacebuilding," which signifies that there can be no peace without justice and that it is a continuing endeavor that takes great effort on many different fronts.[42] The dialogue between the pacifist and just war traditions is one aspect of that effort, which can lead to new creative possibilities.

Faith and Order Dialogues

A just-peacebuilding initiative that held the promise of more collaborative effort was a series of three ecumenical dialogues about the nature and unity of the church and its mission of peacebuilding, under the auspices of the Faith and Order Commission of the National Council of Churches in the United States. A specific agenda was to work at the confessional divisions between the pacifist and just war traditions. John Howard Yoder did not directly participate in the dialogues, but his theological work and his spirit of ecumenism shaped the discussions.[43]

The last of the two books to emerge from the dialogue, *The Fragmentation of the Church and Its Unity in Peacemaking,* was dedicated to Yoder, honoring his insistence that theology and ethics cannot be separated. In their introduction, Lauree Hersch Meyer and Jeffery Gros write:

> John Howard Yoder admonished us, saying that for the Church to achieve unity in matters of faith and order, other churches must adjust to the Historic Peace Churches' "alien idiom" of peacemaking. This is an invitation to conversation. The invitation is a two-way street, however, for the Historic Peace Churches must also adjust to the "alien idiom" of churches which are genuinely concerned for and committed to peace but which have rarely expressed this commitment in terms of nonresistance or understood peacemaking to mean pacifism.[44]

In a summary statement following the second dialogue, the participants agreed that differences among churches on Christian participation in violence and war stands in the way of confessing a common faith in the same way that sacramental and creedal differences do. Consequently, a movement toward Christian unity requires serious ecumenical work related to the church's peace witness. There was broad agreement that peace is a central theme in the Bible, that it is rooted in the reign of God, and that Jesus did not resort to violence. They differed in their understanding of what this meant for contemporary churches.[45] They found hope in the fact that

Peacemaking is beginning to inform the churches' appropriation of Scripture in ways that relativize the traditional interpretations that have undergirded confessional divisions along just war and pacifist lines. The fact that all these statements have recently been produced by these groups does seem to indicate that concern for peace witness, which had earlier been left largely to the historic peace churches, has now become important for virtually all Christian groups.[46]

Participants in the series of dialogues recognized that substantial differences remained between the churches, but that the movement toward unity was itself a sign and a model of their peacemaking vocation. It endorsed the importance of spiritual formation in peacemaking and the emulation of Jesus' creative way of nonviolence. It noted that Christian unity and peacemaking needs to be rooted in the apostolic faith, recommended programs of faith formation that developed skills of nonviolent Christian living, and called for prayer for peace and ecumenical unity.[47]

These dialogues did some ecumenical spadework that led to deeper understanding of the various confessional positions on the church's peace witness and held the promise of further collaborative just-peacebuilding initiatives. Others were already hard at work, developing and implementing such transforming initiatives.

Transforming Initiatives

Glen Stassen, professor of Christian Ethics at Fuller Theological Seminary, has worked tirelessly at implementing Yoder's social ethics in the form of specific just-peacebuilding initiatives.[48] Relating that quest to the Gulf War, Stassen developed an alternative model to the options of going to war or acquiescing to Saddam Hussein's occupation of Kuwait. The cause was clearly just. Nevertheless, in our increasingly interdependent world, we need to find alternatives to actions such as the Gulf War in which the American military and its allies killed more than 200,000 Iraqis. Such actions can only fuel rage and escalate the cycle of violence that engulfs our world.[49] They are hardly just, let alone informed by Christian social ethics. Even more basic, the future of the human race depends on finding new models for resolving conflict.

The alternative model Stassen developed incorporates many of the principles of the "politics of Jesus" I drew from Yoder's social ethics.

Stassen worked closely with Yoder and was deeply indebted to him. His model also demonstrates familiarity with and competence in the world of politics and international relations, relying on the work of people like Harold Saunders, a Middle East expert and advisor in the Camp David talks.[50] It also demonstrates the applicability of just-peacebuilding initiatives to international relations.

Stassen lamented the intransigence, hubris, and missed opportunities on both sides of the Gulf War conflict. According to him, various just-peacebuilding steps could have been taken. Among them are (1) affirm one another's valid interests; (2) take independent initiatives to reduce threat; (3) enter into serious negotiations using methods of conflict resolution; (4) seek democracy and human rights; (5) acknowledge the vicious cycles of violence both sides are captive to; (6) be sensitive to the animosities and prejudices stirred up by judgmental statements; (7) listen empathetically and learn to know each other; and (8) work with grassroots and religious peacebuilding groups.

These recommendations do not assume that government and military leaders will adopt national policies modeled after the "politics of Jesus."[51] That is not the purpose for making such recommendations. Just-peacebuilding initiatives cannot ignore the *realpolitik* nature of the way economic interests, governments, and militaries have functioned for centuries. Nor can they ignore the brutal megalomania of certain persons who hold such power. There can be no easy assumption that a just-peacebuilding ethic, committed to the way of Jesus, is directly applicable to such social entities, which tend to regard it as ineffective at best and political suicide at the worst.[52]

Nevertheless, a just-peacebuilding ethic is built on both practical experience and principled commitments.[53] If one believes it is the only kind of ethic that will ultimately work—because, as Yoder says, "it goes with the grain of the universe"—one will feel compelled to make it a viable option. It can be presented as an ethical model that works in Christian communities and, by analogy, can be appropriated step-by-step by other social entities, including governments. According to Yoder, it can be applied to concrete social problems through the use of middle axioms. That is the crucial task at which Stassen has been working.

It is important to recognize that imaginative and resourceful social alternatives will hardly emerge from top level political and military circles. They are much more likely to oppose such initiatives. Consequently one will find oneself resisting the interests of such "powers," sometimes at great personal cost.

Just-peacebuilding practices will find their natural home in mid-level or grassroots groups in society, including government and non-governmental organizations. Few groups or organizations are mono-lithic. It is sometimes possible to introduce just-peacebuilding initia-tives at one level or one part of an organization while resisting the gen-eral orientation of the organization. Democratic governments are espe-cially pluralistic, representing the interests and objectives of many dif-ferent groups. This offers various venues for engagement from local school boards to different branches of a national government.

With that task in mind, a group of twenty-three scholars, activists, and practitioners met at the annual meetings of the Society of Christian Ethics for five consecutive years to develop a road map for just-peace-building actions. They also met in two major working conferences. One was held at the Abby of Gethsemani in Trappist, Kentucky, and the other was held at the Carter Center in Atlanta. The product of their work was the book *Just Peacemaking: Ten Practices for Abolishing War,* ed-ited by Glen Stassen.

The ten practices that the group worked on were divided into the following categories: (1) peacemaking initiatives; (2) advancing justice for all; and (3) strengthening cooperative forces of love and community. The group worked within the frame of normative practices, as written about by ethicists from different schools, beginning with John Howard Yoder and Michael Walzer.[54] They also worked with Yoder's idea of the analogous relationship between social processes in the Christian com-munity and secular processes in society. In the book's introduction, Duane Friesen, John Langan, S.J., and Glen Stassen write:

> We have learned from John Howard Yoder to notice that New Testament practices such as building inclusive community that includes even enemies are processes that a secular social scientist could observe among the early Christian community and that re-semble analogous secular processes in the world. In fact, some of those secular processes historically were set in motion or strongly supported by Jewish and Christian community.[55]

The book reflects the confidence in democratic processes associated with the time when it was being written, at the end of the Cold War, but it also recognizes that peace does not just happen. It needs to be waged. It is an arduous and long-term project that involves engagement on many different fronts. Recognizing that degree of struggle, the introduction states:

> The ten just peacemaking practices in our consensus model are not merely a wish list. They are empirical practices in our present history that are, in fact, spreading peace. They are engendering positive-feedback loops, so they are growing in strength. They are pushing back the frontiers of war and spreading the zones of peace. We believe that because these emerging empirical practices are changing our world for the better and pushing back the frontiers of war, they are moral as well as empirical guides for all responsible and caring persons.[56]

One of the limitations of this project is that all the participants were American academics and professionals. That creates a perspective which circumscribes its usefulness in an increasingly interdependent global community.[57] Another project, related to the World Council of Churches' Program to Overcome Violence, overcomes some of those limitations by drawing on the wisdom and practical experience of academics, activists, and grassroots practitioners around the world. Judy Zimmerman Herr and Robert Herr, from the Mennonite Central Committee Peace Office, coordinated this joint project of the historic peace churches and the Fellowship of Reconciliation. They also edited the book *Transforming Violence: Linking Local and Global Peacemaking,* which grew out of it.[58]

The book devotes a major section to the religious foundations for a just peace. It studies several grassroots peace initiatives in Africa and Eastern Europe, giving concrete examples of just-peacebuilding practices. It draws on the experience of people working in conflict mediation and nonviolent direct action. It is clearly ecumenical and at least begins to be interreligious. Though it does not explicitly draw on the thought of John Howard Yoder, it is clearly within the peace tradition in which he worked.

The strength of both these efforts is that they draw on the experience of peacebuilding practitioners engaged at various levels of society around the world. In this way they are helping to create a just-peacebuilding praxis which undergirds and lends credibility to both the pacifist and just war traditions. If war is going to be an honest last resort within the just war tradition, there need to be viable alternatives to war. The pacifist tradition also needs an analogous engaged praxis that can translate its convictions into concrete possibilities for social action. The growing just-peacebuilding disciplines provide the resources that both traditions need for a social ethic that has integrity.

THE SOCIAL PRAXIS OF THE CHRISTIAN COMMUNITY

As shown in prior chapters as well as in my formulation of the principles of the "politics of Jesus," a basic conviction in Yoder's theology is that Christian social action is integrally related to the church. If Christian social ethics and actions are built on the premise that the community of those who follow the way of Jesus is at the center of God's purpose in history, they will take the church seriously as a transformative community.

Too often, the unspoken assumption is that real social transformation depends on government initiatives. Christian social initiatives are then primarily oriented toward changing government social policies in a more humane direction. Persuading the state to be more humane is a laudable objective, but it should not be the central focus of a Christian just-peacebuilding ethic. The "politics of Jesus" places the emphasis on the transformative praxis of the church, understood as the body of Christ. It does not discount a Christian social witness to the state, but that witness is always secondary, growing out of the social praxis of the religious community.

In the Global South

In our world today, the cutting edge of a transformative church centered social praxis is often found in the global South. An inspiring and instructive example of such church centered social involvement, which I became familiar with in the Philippines, is the work of Niall O'Brien, an Irish-born Columban priest who has spent more than thirty years in the Philippines. O'Brien tells about his often heart-rending ministry among the sugarcane workers on the island of Negros. As a young priest, O'Brien arrived in the Philippines in 1964, when the Second Vatican Council was in session. His work spanned a period when the Vatican II changes gradually transformed the liturgy and the social consciousness of the parishes in Negros.[59]

O'Brien speaks about the Vatican II inspired liturgical change of moving the altar so that the priest faces the congregation while saying the Mass. For him, this became a symbol of a renewed focus on the empowerment of the local church as the body of Christ. In his pastoral assignment among the sugarcane workers in Negros, O'Brien says he came to understand the celebration of the Mass as nothing less than an act of revolution—a call for personal and social transformation. It asks us to offer our lives in the struggle for freedom and human dignity.[60]

While O'Brien demonstrates familiarity with Yoder's theological ethics, his early inspiration came from the pastoral encyclicals of Pope John XXIII and the documents of the Second Vatican Council. He is also deeply indebted to the peace activism of Jean and Hildegard Goss-Mayer, who led seminars on nonviolent direct action in the Philippines.[61] With the help of such sources, he developed his personal account of living the gospel in the revolutionary situation of Negros. There is a fascinating congruence in the church-based social praxis of O'Brien and Yoder that is undoubtedly linked to their mutual understanding of the life and ministry of Jesus as recorded in the gospel narratives. They both have a political interpretation of Jesus. O'Brien writes:

> For me it was the heart of what Jesus did that mattered. Everything he said must be interpreted in the light of what he did: his walking up to the jaws of death, his struggle at the threshold with himself, his cry of anguish before it swallowed him . . . all spoke to me of nonviolence.[62]

Such convictions, O'Brien says, were tempered by the Catholic social teaching that people have a right to defend themselves with arms as a last resort when confronted with egregious oppression. That was confirmed by what he saw in Negros. There were times when you could not tell people that they did not have the right to defend themselves. "Even so," he said, "in my heart I felt that even justified counter-violence was not the answer."[63] He would follow the path of nonviolence.

Such an ethic can only make sense if it is rooted in the praxis of the church—the community of those who follow the way of Jesus—as Yoder insisted. The real contribution that O'Brien brings to Yoder's theological ethics is his pastoral work in helping to create such Christian communities in Negros and integrating his just-peace activism into the life of those communities.

When O'Brien first arrived in the Philippines, he was overwhelmed by the immensity of the task of serving the enormous parish of Kabankalan, where he was assigned as an assistant priest. Many rural communities in the parish had no worship services except for the infrequent occasions when a priest was able to be there. As a partial answer to that problem, O'Brien began organizing lay led worship services in the villages. After several years he came to realize that a worship service is still not a Christian community.[64]

He then began to work with a group of young Filipino priests to organize small Christian communities (often called Base Christian Communities) throughout the island of Negros. They should be kept small enough to maintain a human touch, no more than thirty families. The heart of these Christian communities is gospel reflection. This involves a daily or a weekly gathering in which the gospel is read prayerfully, followed by a discussion of the values it portrays or the problems it poses in relation to the experience of their own small community. The communities have five basic characteristics:

- sharing their time, resources, and talents as a form of development and crisis intervention in the community;
- participatory decision-making and the empowerment that results from that process;
- working together to eradicate injustice using the principles of nonviolent direct action;
- embodying forgiveness and reconciliation;
- communal worship and praying together.[65]

These Base Christian Communities became the center of Catholic social action in Negros, which included community development, union organizing in the sugar mills, creating zones of peace in war-torn communities, documenting human rights abuses, and nonviolently confronting local oppressors. The books that O'Brien wrote about this struggle are his personal account of the adventure in peacebuilding, drawing out the spiritual and social lessons he learned in the process.[66]

In Affluent Societies

Each social context poses its own challenges for living out the social and political ethics of Jesus. Churches in poor communities in the global South face one set of realities. Churches in more secular and economically advantaged societies that have traditionally considered themselves Christian face another set of challenges. In these societies, powerful business, media, government, and military institutions dominate the public square. In such contexts, the church finds itself at the margins of society, and it becomes increasingly difficult to create a social space in which Christian lives can be formed.

In such secular societies, Yoder's use of the Jewish experience of exile as a paradigm for the social existence of the church becomes especially relevant. The task of forming a people of God identified with the common life of the religious community becomes a priority. Scripture becomes our home in exile. The shared remembering and study of the gospel story creates the social space in which the Christian community can flourish. In a new way, we learn about the power of words to create a world. Religious rituals that define the community take on new meaning. Christian education for all age groups becomes integral to the life of the community.[67]

Such community formation needs to be integrally related to the church's mission in the world. Global economic, governmental, and military institutions have created or ignored vast human populations characterized by overwhelming poverty and destitution. They have wrecked havoc on the world's ecosystems. The gap between rich and poor in the global economy keeps growing at an alarming rate.[68] The life and integrity of churches in affluent communities depends on their ability to find ways to walk with their poor and destitute sisters and brothers. This involves economic decisions that few affluent churches have been willing to make. How we spend our money is no trifling matter. How can we say that we share God's deep concern for the poor when we spend all but a fraction of our resources on ourselves?

Walking with integrity in such a world involves more than finances. It includes building human connections across the economic, social, and racial divides in our world. It is not only that poor people need the compassion and assistance of the affluent. Even more, the affluent need the compassion and the gifts of the poor to lead whole lives. Churches and other religious communities that cross such divides and minister out of deeply held religious convictions are crucial to the just-peacebuilding task.

A significant aspect of such religious communities is the multilingual and relational skills they develop. These skills enable the communities to be cultural brokers in a pluralistic world. They create their native religious idiom and learn how to draw analogies that translate between that idiom and other languages. They have an inner spiritual dynamic that compels them to transcend normal human boundaries of class, ethnicity, race, and nationality because of their commitment to a higher loyalty to the divine. Their communal life serves as a laboratory for authentic and life-giving human relationships. Such characteristics make them ideally suited for the complex and difficult task of just peacebuilding.

My characterization of religious communities engaged in just-peacebuilding practices should not be understood as ignoring or downplaying the historically ambiguous relationship between religion and violence. All religious traditions have been responsible for various forms of violence. Some of the most horrendous human acts, including genocide, have been legitimated in the name of the transcendent. Ignoring that historical reality as well as ignoring the creative peacebuilding potential of religious communities, are both forms of reductionism.

Scott Appleby characterizes two types of religious militants—extremists and peacemakers. The extremist, according to Appleby, "is committed primarily to *victory over the enemy,* whether by gradual means or by the direct and frequent use of violence." In contrast, "the religious peacemaker is committed primarily to the cessation of violence and the resolution of conflict: *reconciliation or peaceful coexistence with the enemy is the ultimate goal.*"[69] Appleby's interest, like mine, is in the peacebuilding potential of religious communities and the constructive function of religious peacebuilding activists. He writes:

> A new form of conflict transformation—"religious peacebuilding"—is taking shape on the ground, in and across local communities plagued by violence. This is a promising development, but it remains inchoate and fragile, uncoordinated and in need of greater numbers of adequately trained practioners, more study and testing, and theoretical elaboration.[70]

A Religious Peacebuilding Program

One example of the kind of religiously oriented peacebuilding program that Scott Appleby is advocating is the Center for Justice and Peacebuilding (CJP) at Eastern Mennonite University in Harrisonburg, Virginia.[71] CJP was founded by people deeply indebted to John Howard

Yoder and his notion of the "politics of Jesus." It seeks to embody his conviction that Jesus is the bearer of a new possibility for human social and political relationships. It attempts to take social processes in the Christian community related to "the politics of Jesus" and translate them into analogous social processes in society. In that respect, it is the ideal case study of the application of Yoder's theology and social ethics.

CJP has grown out of Mennonite Central Committee (MCC) programs in conflict mediation and restorative justice.[72] These programs are oriented toward peacebuilding practice and training in local communities. It was the need for training such practitioners and trainers that initially fed the vision to start an academic program built on the social sciences, with a strong emphasis on mentorship and fieldwork, and undergirded both theologically and ethically by Mennonite perspectives on peace. This distinguishes it from other academic peace studies programs that are more theologically and theoretically oriented.[73]

A confluence of factors made the beginning of such a program possible on the campus of Eastern Mennonite University, a small Christian liberal arts institution, which only a half century earlier had still functioned within a separatist religious ethos that avoided such social activism. The overarching factor making that possible is the rapid social change that has taken place in Mennonite communities since World War II. A related factor is that many of the faculty and staff at Eastern Mennonite University have done mission and service assignments around the world with Mennonite mission agencies. The theology of John Howard Yoder and other Mennonite scholars such as C. Norman Kraus (who himself served overseas) has enabled them to conceptualize such broader social activism from a distinct Mennonite peace orientation. All these factors feed into the stated vision of Eastern Mennonite University as an academic institution built on the values of "Christian discipleship, community, service, and peacebuilding."[74]

With the concerted effort of administrators and various faculty members, CJP was able to enroll its first two students in a master's degree program in 1993. The initial core faculty members had all previously worked in MCC programs in conflict mediation and restorative justice. All of them have been influenced by the work of John Howard Yoder. John Paul Lederach, the founding director of CJP, tells about keeping a supply of *The Politics of Jesus* to give to people who are interested in the basis of his peacebuilding work. Lederach talks about Yoder as both an *idealist,* with a long view of history related to the Messianic community, and as a *pragmatist,* looking for the pregnant possibilities of next steps. He writes:

> I found Yoder to be a pragmatist. Throughout his work, but more particularly in my direct interactions with him, he never avoided the question of what potentials the moment at hand held for doing something specific that made progress toward the far off horizon possible. The key was to have a clear horizon in mind that informed creative action in the immediate while not aspiring to take control of political power or history itself through those actions. This was pragmatism with a divine twist. It was not pragmatism pushed by the immediacy of problem-solving for the purposes of meeting political demands or assuring economic efficacy. This was pragmatism that sought to make known ultimate Truth through the practice of specific and concrete action, a pragmatism of radical dependence on the grace of God whereby faithful but specific and practical action created opportunity for God to be present and enter the everyday.[75]

Lederach recognizes a practical bent in Yoder that has not always been evident to others. Framing Yoder's theological ethics as a combination of pragmatism and idealism can, however, miss the genius of his work. Yoder was, above all, a gifted and imaginative interpreter of the Christian tradition. He had an incredibly logical mind combined with an intellectual grasp of the nuances that such theological work entails. What appears as a kind of pragmatism and idealism was most certainly rooted in his interpretation of some biblical or historical precedent in relation to a contemporary problem or opportunity. His commitment to engaging others on their own turf contributed an added breadth to his interpretative insights.

Such a practical bent, tied to a given faith tradition, has infused CJP from its inception in 1994. To these ends, the program has been structured with three different components. At its center is a two-year master's level curriculum leading to a Master of Arts in Conflict Transformation. Another component is the Summer Peacebuilding Institute, which brings peacebuilders from around the world to the Eastern Mennonite University campus for an intensive six-week block of training each summer. The third component is the Institute for Justice and Peacebuilding, which is the practice and research arm of CJP. A related undergraduate program is the trans-disciplinary major in Justice, Peace, and Conflict Studies.[76]

CJP was made possible by taking advantage of the various opportunities mentioned above and through collaboration with various religious and secular relief, development, and peacebuilding organizations. Religious relief and development organizations, such as Catholic Relief Services, World Vision, Church World Service, and Mennonite Central Committee, have provided scholarships and service opportunities for students. Gifted and respected people lent their expertise by helping to conceptualize the program and agreeing to serve on the Board of Reference. Among them were Harold Saunders, a former Middle East negotiator and director of international affairs at the Kettering Foundation; Elise Boulding, a well known peace activist and professor at Dartmouth College; and Christopher Mitchell, a professor of Conflict Analysis and Resolution at George Mason University. Various organizations, including Pew Charitable Trusts, the Winston Foundation for World Peace, the Hewlett Foundation, the McKnight Foundation, and the United States Institute of Peace provided crucial grants that made starting the program possible.[77]

As of 2006, the program had grown to about one hundred master's level students coming from North America and conflict regions around the world. This included a yearly cohort of from eight to twelve Fulbright Scholars from the Middle East and South Asia. The Summer Peacebuilding Institute (SPI) brings about one hundred and eighty peacebuilders to campus each year. It has spawned other regional summer peacebuilding institutes in the Philippines, Zambia, and Ghana. After the September 11, 2001, destruction of the World Trade Center, the CJP Practice Institute began collaborating with Church World Service in providing Seminars on Trauma Awareness and Recovery (STAR) for religious leaders around the world. In addition to trauma recovery work, the Practice Institute is also involved in defense-based victim liaison work in the United States court system.[78]

The success of CJP as a religiously oriented peacebuilding program has created some unique challenges. Among them is the ongoing question of the theological underpinnings of a program based in the social sciences. There is a distinct difference between a seminary-based peace studies program grounded in theology and biblical studies and CJP— which prepares students for the practical application of strategies of conflict transformation and peacebuilding and assumes that Mennonite perspectives on peace inform the teaching of core faculty members. To provide more explicit religious content, CJP offers one or two courses on theological ethics and the religious dimensions of peacebuilding in its master's degree curriculum. SPI also offers at least two religion-based courses each summer. Some students also elect to take additional seminary courses.

The religious identity issue cuts two ways. CJP students come from many different religious traditions around the world. Such interfaith work and religious inclusivity still troubles many Mennonites. Sometimes that unease involves simple things like the kinds of prayers offered at interreligious program events. There is a concern that CJP not soft-peddle its religious identity to appeal to an increasingly diverse constituency. The other side of the issue is the concern that CJP not be encumbered by a parochial church identity that unnecessarily interferes with its ability to do its work. Students from other faith traditions often express the apprehension they felt when they first discovered that CJP was based on the campus of a small Christian university. Other supporters of the program worry about the possibility that significant tensions will develop between influential church leaders and CJP over the direction of the program.[79]

The challenge is to negotiate the creative tension between the Mennonite religious tradition that gave birth to CJP and its growing relationships in a pluralistic world. That will take both interpersonal skills and an ability to nurture and articulate the core religious values that have been the genius of the program. The basic principles of the "politics of Jesus," which I isolated from the corpus of Yoder's theology, can help serve as a frame of reference for that task. A crucial component of that task will be to implement Yoder's conviction that social processes, informed by the experience of religious communities, can inform analogous processes in other contexts. The challenge is figuring out how to do that without losing one's core religious identity.

Nurturing the faith tradition and lived experience of the CJP community is crucial to the ongoing contribution the program can make to the task of peacebuilding. Responses from graduating students indicate that the program has had some success in doing that. A common refrain from departing graduates has been that they came to learn the theory and practice of dealing with conflict nonviolently but that they have been personally transformed in the process. Among the things learned that contributed to such personal transformation are the gift of humble service, that it is possible to "walk your talk," and how to make people from all religious traditions feel welcome and valued. Devanand Remiah, a graduating Fulbright Scholar from Sri Lanka states:

> CJP is built upon Mennonite values. Nobody should feel apologetic about this. Without these values, CJP wouldn't be what it is. I believe Gandhi said, "Be open to other cultures and let them flow through, but don't let your inner core go," because that is what holds things together. Even though Eastern Mennonite University is a Christian institution, it is open to others. People outside need to know this. The spirituality here is a subtle experience. It is not forced upon you. I embraced it of my own accord. The credit goes to all of you for living it in your daily lives.[80]

The ability to be hospitable and open to others while maintaining one's core identity is a central component for a viable peacebuilding community of learning and practice. One never arrives; it remains an ongoing task that we realize more or less adequately. The community experiments, fails, succeeds, adapts, and grows in a continuous process. It takes courage rooted in a core vision of flourishing, sustainable human communities characterized by just-peace. For CJP that vision is rooted in the Anabaptist tradition and Mennonite values out of which the program has grown. Yoder's formulation of the "politics of Jesus" is central.

CONCLUSION

As seen in the last chapter, religious peacebuilding is a multifaceted task incorporating the practice and reflection of various communities and disciplines. It includes the theological task of inquiring how the will of God is interpreted and lived out in communities of faith. For Christians, a central component of that task is discerning how Jesus informs the practice and witness of their communities. As demonstrated in chapters four, five, and six, that is the groundbreaking contribution made by John Howard Yoder in his insightful articulation of the "politics of Jesus."

The just-peacebuilding task involves the ecumenical dialogue about the nature and unity of the church and its mission of peacebuilding. As discussed in chapter three, Yoder's participation in the European ecumenical dialogues on the problem of war provides valuable resources for that task. The task continues in the ecumenical discussions about social issues within the World Council of Churches and in the collaborative work of scholars and practioners in various ecumenical forums.

Chapter seven relates the task of just peacebuilding to ten basic principles of the "politics of Jesus" taken from Yoder's academic work. The task involves the concerted effort of scholars and practioners to build and contribute to the field of just peacebuilding in the same way that people work at other concerted and ongoing human efforts, such as healthcare and education. The task includes the formation and nurture of communities of faith that have the capacity to enter into and contribute to the nonviolent struggle for a just-peace. Another task is the formation of educational programs that teach peacebuilding strategies and skills.

Religiously oriented just-peacebuilding initiatives can especially learn from Yoder's work. The genius of his social ethics is the way he identified such ethics with Jesus and the life and practice of the Christian community. He then looked for practical opportunities to relate that praxis to analogous social processes in society. The "politics of Jesus" finds its natural home in the church and then becomes the basis of the church's witness to the world. That orientation to religious social ethics is applied in chapter seven but is evident throughout the book, including chapters two and three that research the particular Mennonite experience that helped form Yoder's thought.

As demonstrated by the chapters on Mennonite experience, Yoder took the separatist ethos that had characterized Mennonite communities in North America and gave it a twist—making it relevant beyond the borders of those communities. The truth of such separatism is that Christian ethics are rightfully rooted in the community of those who follow Jesus. The twist was helping such faith communities understand that they are called to give themselves *for the nations*—changing both church and society in the process.[81] What Yoder did was not new. He worked carefully within the Christian tradition, taking elements that had always been there, then reshaping them in ways that spoke to the situation facing Christians in his day.

Yoder talked about the intersection between Christian faith and life in the world. The theological analysis of social issues, in the narrow sense, begins with inquiring from Scriptures and tradition about how the will of God is revealed and interpreted in the community of faith. One needs to review and analyze how Christians have differed on such issues through the ages in many different situations. This can be studied on its own terms from within the community of faith. Nevertheless, the task is not complete until we study how such moral theology intersects with other debates about human nature and the shape of society. Yoder wrote:

> We cannot discuss theology alone but need to interface with the human sciences which are talking about the same phenomena from other perspectives. If the believer says that faith in Jesus Christ makes love of the enemy imperative and possible, is this not something that could be described and whose possibility could be measured by the psychologist? If love leads someone to go out and make peace with one's adversary, is this not an event which a sociologist could describe? When a preacher claims that "violence is always self-defeating," is that not a claim the historian could verify or refute? It is therefore appropriate, even imperative, as we flesh out the realism of the message of reconciliation that we attend to those other disciplines. There is no room here for the kind of dualism which would avoid such cross-references on grounds that they would represent unbelief or a confusion of categories.[82]

What Yoder proposed is a Herculean task that grows ever more challenging as our world becomes more complex. It is a task far beyond the capability of any single scholar, no matter how gifted she or he may be. All any single person can hope to accomplish is to add one's contribution to the effort. The effort to understand Yoder's theological language in chapter seven helps to elucidate the ways in which particular theological traditions and academic disciplines shape such work. Each discipline in itself requires the collaborative work of teams of scholars and practitioners. In short, it requires the collaborative effort of all who are concerned for human flourishing and the integrity of creation.

The motivation for the task of building flourishing and sustainable communities is the conviction that injustice and violence are not inevitable. Oppression and violence should not be understood as inherent in the nature of the universe or as part of the will of God. Unjust and violent social structures are human constructions. As such, they can be transformed. Progress in human history is made by those willing to struggle and suffer for the sake of life-giving social change. Yoder wrote:

> If children grow to fruitful adulthood, if fields are cultivated in such a way as not to lose fertility, if carefully coordinated labor achieves large goals, it will be because ways have been found to hold violence to a minimum. Finding those ways is the object of sociology and psychology where they intersect. There are better and worse ways to handle conflict. The differences can be studied. We can generalize from them and extrapolate from them. This is a descriptive science, challenging the best intelligences to observe and analyze.[83]

The descriptive scientific task is one element of such work. Another task is to inquire about the convictions and values that shape the way we participate in that struggle. How we are engaged matters deeply because means always affect ends. It is here that Yoder made his major contribution. He devoted his life to the theological task of asking how God's purpose, as seen in the "politics of Jesus," informs the task of building just and peaceable communities.

NOTES

1. Gustavo Gutiérrez, *A Theology of Liberation* (Maryknoll, N.Y.: Orbis Press, 1988), 5.

2. Hans-Georg Gadamer, *Truth and Method,* 2nd. ed. (New York: Continuum, 1994), 309. I am especially indebted to the late Stephen Happel for the masterful way he helped me and his other doctoral students in his hermeneutics class at the Catholic University of America grasp the implications of the relationship between the interpretation and application of texts in theological reflection.

3. Perry B. Yoder, *Shalom: The Bible's Word for Salvation, Justice, and Peace* (Newton, Kan.: Faith and Life Press, 1987), 10-16.

4. My understanding of just peacebuilding is deeply indebted to John Howard Yoder's "politics of Jesus." It also reflects the work and perspectives of the Center for Justice and Peacebuilding at Eastern Mennonite University. An excellent resource on peacebuilding as a sustained, multi-faceted praxis is the book by Lisa Schirch, *The Little Book of Strategic Peacebuilding* (Intercourse, Pa.: Good Books, 2004). Schirch conceptualizes peacebuilding as a set of values, as relational skills, as the analysis of conflict and violence, as a set of processes, and as peacebuilding principles. She applies this to various just-peacebuilding efforts that seek to wage conflict nonviolently; to reduce violence; to work at trauma healing, building relationships, and doing justice; and to build human capacity through such things as development and education.

5. The United States military has increased by 30% from 1998 to 2003. Its total military spending of US$322 billion in 2003 was greater than the military spending of the next ten highest nations combined. See Dan Smith, *The Penguin State of the World Atlas,* 7th. ed. (New York: Penguin Books, 2003), 74-75. The requested 441.6 billion budget for 2006 represents another 37% increase from 2003. And that amount does not include the cost of Homeland Security or the wars in Afganistan and Iraq. U. S. Military expenditures now approximately equal that of the rest of the world combined. See "U. S. Military Spending," *Global Issues That Affect Everyone;* available from *http://www.globalissues.org/Geopolitics/ArmsTrade/Spending.asp*; Internet; accessed August 23, 2005.

6. J. Milburn Thompson, *Justice and Peace: A Christian Primer* (Maryknoll, N.Y.: Orbis Books, 1997), 58-59.

7. I owe a special word of thanks to Mark Thiessen Nation for making these materials available to me from his personal Yoder collection.

8. Yoder, *For the Nations,* 3, n. 6.

9. Howard Zehr is a founding practioner and scholar in the field of restorative justice. See his book *Changing Lenses: A New Focus for Crime and Justice,* 3d ed. (Scottdale, Pa.: Herald Press, 2005). John Paul Lederach is a well known practioner and scholar of conflict transformation. See his book *Preparing for Peace: Conflict Transformation Across Cultures* (Syracuse, N.Y.: Syracuse University Press, 1995).

10. Some central texts in Yoder's later work where he addressed questions of theological process in a context of pluralism are: John Howard Yoder, "Walk and Word: The Alternatives to Methodologism," in *Theology Without Foundations,* ed. Hauerwas et al, 77-98; John Howard Yoder, "Meaning after Babble: With Jeffrey Stout beyond Relativism," *Journal of Religious Ethics* 24 (Spring 1996): 125-139; John Howard Yoder, "But We Do See Jesus," *The Priestly Kingdom,* 46-62. A central text in which he develops his argument for exile as a paradigm for the people of God in society is John Howard Yoder, "See How They Go with Their Face to the Sun," *For the Nations,* 51-78.

11. John Howard Yoder talked of Jesus as the bearer of a new possibility for social and political relationships. The word *new* does not deny Jesus' continuity with the Old Testament and especially the Hebrew prophetic tradition. Yoder especially emphasized this continuity in some of his later work. See Yoder, *For the Nations,* 66-70.

12. Yoder, *The Politics of Jesus* (1972), 11-25.

13. Yoder, *Anabaptism and Reformation,* 166-173; Yoder, *The Original Revolution* (1971), 58-74; and Yoder, *To Hear the Word,* 71-84.

14. Yoder, *Anabaptism and Reformation* 259-272; Yoder, "The Theological Basis of the Christian Witness to the State," in *On Earth Peace,* ed. Durnbaugh, 136-145; Yoder, *The Christian Witness to the State* (1964), 8-11; and Yoder, *For the Nations,* 51-78.

15. Yoder, *The Legacy of Michael Sattler,* 39; Yoder, *Anabaptism and Reformation,* 172-175; and Yoder, *The Politics of Jesus* (1972), 135-162.

16. Yoder, *The Original Revolution* (1971), 113-147, 177-182; Yoder, *The Politics of Jesus* (1972), 233-250.

17. Yoder, *The Christian Witness to the State* (1964), 5-44.

18. Yoder, memo to Mark Thiessen Nation, December 17, 1991, Mark Thiessen Nation, Yoder Collection, Eastern Mennonite Seminary, Harrisonburg, Virginia. See also Yoder, *To Hear the Word*, 47-70.

19. Yoder, *The Priestly Kingdom*, 46-62.

20. Ibid., 58.

21. Yoder was careful about theological arguments based on natural theology because such arguments have often been used historically in ways that ignore the social ethics of Jesus and the witness of the church. However, in his later work he would occasionally relate Jesus' way of suffering love to creation. In an unpublished lecture at the United Theological Seminary in Dayton, Ohio, he discussed this conviction in relation to Gandhi's principle of *Satyagraha* and Martin Luther King's argument that love is the most enduring power in the world. See Yoder, "The Political Meaning of Hope," May 1983, Mark Thiessen Nation Yoder Collection, Eastern Mennonite Seminary, Harrisonburg, Virginia.

Yoder also made the statement "people who bear crosses are working with the grain of the universe" in "Armaments and Eschatology," *Studies in Christian Ethics* 1 (Edinburgh, T. & T. Clark, 1988): 58. Stanley Hauerwas subsequently borrowed the phrase for the title of his book and further developed the argument in *With the Grain of the Universe: The Church's Witness and Natural Theology* (Grand Rapids: Brazos Press, 2001). For another more developed theological and scientific argument that agape or sacrifice is intrinsic to nature see Langdon Gilkey, *Nature, Reality, and the Sacred: The Nexus of Science and Religion* (Minneapolis: Fortress Press, 1993), 131-141. See also Murphy and Ellis, *On the Moral Nature of the Universe*, 141-172. Even the Christian *realist*, Reinhold Niebuhr, recognized love as the highest transcendent religious ideal but came to very different conclusions because of his understanding of human depravity. See Reinhold Niebuhr, *Moral Man and Immoral Society*, 71-76. For an early critique of Niebuhr's positon, see G.H.C. Macgregor "The Relevance of an Impossible Ideal," in *Peace is the Way: Writings on Nonviolence from the Fellowship of Reconciliation*, ed. Walter Wink (Maryknoll, N.Y.: Orbis Books, 2000), 17-29. Macgregor's essay in this volume is reprinted from *Fellowship* (June 1941).

22. Yoder, *The Politics of Jesus* (1972), 248.

23. Yoder, *The Original Revolution* (1971), 159-166.

24. John Howard Yoder, *When War is Unjust: Being Honest in Just-War Thinking*, rev. ed. (Maryknoll, N.Y.: Orbis Books, 1996), 5-7.

25. *Gaudium et spes* (*Pastoral Constitution on the Church in the Modern World*), no. 78, Austin Flannery, O.P. ed., *Vatican Council II: The Conciliar and Post Conciliar Documents*, new rev. ed. (Northport, N.Y.: Costello Publishing Company, 1996), 987.

26. "The Challenge of Peace," in *Biblical and Theological Reflections on the Challenge of Peace*, ed. John T. Pawlikowski and Donald Senior (Wilmington, Del.: Michael Glazier, Inc., 1984), 229.

27. Ibid.

28. John Howard Yoder, "Lambs War for Eerdmans Fall 97," Mark Thiessen Nation, Yoder Collection, Eastern Mennonite Seminary, Harrisonburg, Virginia, 86-87. This material is part of the book on nonviolence that Yoder was writing at the

time of his death.

29. Drew Christiansen, "A Roman Catholic Response," in Yoder, *When War is Unjust,* 102-103.

30. John Howard Yoder, "Lambs War for Eerdmans Fall 97," Mark Thiessen Nation, Yoder Collection, Eastern Mennonite Seminary, Harrisonburg, Virginia, 76.

31. Ibid., 77.

32. Ibid., 79-80. Yoder's stance in this exchange is a good example of his "politics of Jesus" in action.

33. Kenneth P. Hallahan, "The Social Ethics of Nonresistance: The Writings of Mennonite Theologian John Howard Yoder Analyzed from a Roman Catholic Perspective" (Ph.D. diss., The Catholic University of America, 1997), 364-366.

34. This simple teaching tool, which I have developed, does not seek to identify more than some of the most common positions on war and the use of lethal violence, nor does it seek to describe comprehensively the various positions that it identifies. It does seek to be honest in its descriptions. It is indebted to John Howard Yoder's even more limited delineation of various positions on war in *When War is Unjust,* 1-3.

35. One may ask if the notion of self-defense and just war are distinct positions. While defense against external aggression is generally recognized as a *just cause* within the just war tradition, it is still different than the common notion of self-defense based on the right to protect oneself or one's property. Traditionally the just war position has ruled out such self-defense as a justification for the use of lethal force. Augustine, one of the early developers of just war criteria, argued that private citizens are unable to defend themselves without undue passion, self-assertion, and a loss of love. See Bainton, *Christian Attitudes Toward War and Peace,* 87-100. According to just war criteria, even national self-defense must be justified in terms of the global common good. See Yoder, *When War is Unjust,* 152.

36. For an insightful discussion of making the just war tradition credible in relation to actual situations of war, see Yoder, *When War is Unjust,* 71-80.

37. Catholic acceptance of pacifism as a legitimate moral option includes both nonviolence as a social strategy and pacifism as a personal vocation but remains complex and ambiguous. Richard Miller writes that, despite the praise of nonviolence in official Catholic teaching, pacifism still remains anomalous within Catholicism. The commitment to pacifism remains vague and undeveloped even in ostensibly pacifist communities like the Catholic Worker movement. He notes that a pacifism that is merely permitted can hardly be passed on from generation to generation as a fixed tenet or practice. For such reasons, he encourages Catholic pacifists to structure and develop their ethics by drawing on just war tenets. See Richard Miller, *Interpretations of Conflict: Ethics, Pacifism, and the Just-War Tradition* (Chicago: The University of Chicago Press, 1991), 76-105.

38. Catholic theologian John Courtney Murray, who was a strong proponent of the just war tradition, also argued that just war had not been used for a long time or made the basis for a sound critique of public policies. See John Courtney Murray, *Morality and Modern War* (New York: The Church Peace Union, 1959), 15.

39. John Howard Yoder, "The Church and Change: Violence and Its Alterna-

248 / *Practicing the Politics of Jesus*

tives," lecture presented at the annual conference of the South Africa Council of Churches, Hammanskrall, July 24, 1979, Mark Thiessen Nation, Yoder Collection, Eastern Mennonite Seminary, Harrisonburg, Virginia, 4. Yoder's definition, given in the context of helping anti-apartheid activists consider nonviolent strategies, does not address all instances of systemic violence such as structural poverty, sexism, and racism. For a more comprehensive discussion of violence as "destruction or death by means that overpower consent," see Glen H. Stassen and Michael L. Westmoreland-White, "Defining Violence and Nonviolence," *Teaching Peace*, ed. J. Denny Weaver and Gerald Besecker-Mast (New York: Rowman & Littlefield, 2003), 17-36.

40. Ibid.

41. Ibid., 5.

42. Some of the literature referred to in this chapter uses the word "peacemaking" rather than "peacebuilding." While I prefer the latter for the reasons just mentioned, I use the words interchangeably.

43. Jeffrey Gros and John Rempel, eds. *The Fragmentation of the Church and Its Unity in Peacemaking* (Grand Rapids: Eerdmans, 2001), 2, 220.

44. Ibid., 7.

45. Marlin Miller and Barbara Nelson Gingerich, eds., *The Church's Peace Witness* (Grand Rapids: Eerdmans, 1994), 209-210.

46. Ibid., 210.

47. Ibid., 222-226.

48. Stassen and the group of scholars and practitioners who work with him use the phrase *just peacemaking*. Primarily for the sake of consistency with the rest of my writing, I change that phrase to *just peacebuilding*, which draws attention to the constructive nature of creating communities of peace.

49. Glen Stassen, *Just Peacemaking: Transforming Initiatives for Justice and Peace* (Louisville: Westminster/John Knox Press, 1992), 236-237.

50. Ibid., 239.

51. Ibid., 238-255. Glen Stassen sometimes makes it sound like Christian politics includes a mandate for Western-style democracy. While Yoder could also make "the Christian case for democracy," he was more critical of the naïve righteousness with which Western powers export their politics around the world. He debunked claims that nationalist democracies are a whole new style of governance. They are still characterized by the domination model of lording it over others that Jesus rejected (Mark 10:41) rather than his cross-and-servanthood alternative. At the same time, Yoder supported the relative claim of democratic governance in fostering liberty and providing useful structures for mutual service. See Yoder, *The Priestly Kingdom*, 151-171.

52. Yoder, *The Christian Witness to the State* (1964), 73.

53. Glen Stassen sees a threefold pattern to Jesus' teaching in the Sermon on the Mount. For example, Jesus' teaching on anger (Matt. 5:21-23) begins with a statement of traditional piety ("you shall not kill"), followed by identifying the mechanism of bondage (nursing anger or saying "you fool"), and culminates in a transforming initiative ("go, therefore, be reconciled"). See Stassen, *Just Peacemaking*, 42-51.

54. Glen Stassen, ed., *Just Peacemaking: Ten Practices for Abolishing War* (Cleveland, Pilgrim Press, 1998), 6-23.

55. Ibid., 19.

56. Ibid., 2.

57. For instance, I found it revealing to use the book *Just Peacemaking: Ten Practices for Abolishing War* as a text for classes in the Center for Justice and Peacebuilding at Eastern Mennonite University. Some students from other parts of the world were quite critical of what they saw as an American bias.

58. Robert Herr and Judy Zimmerman Herr, eds., *Transforming Violence: Linking Local and Global Peacemaking* (Scottdale, Pa.: Herald Press, 1998), 7-19.

59. Niall O'Brien, *Revolution from the Heart* (Maryknoll, N.Y.: Orbis Books, 1988), 4-5. Part of my knowledge of O'Brian's work comes from my years of mission service on the island of Luzon during the 1980s and early 1990s.

60. Naill O'Brien, *Island of Tears, Island of Hope: Living the Gospel in a Revolutionary Situation* (Maryknoll, N.Y.: Orbis Books, 1993), 36, 44.

61. O'Brien lists Yoder as a source in the selected bibliography of *Island of Tears, Island of Hope* and is familiar with the work of the Mennonite Central Committee in the Philippines. See O'Brien, *Island of Tears, Island of Hope*, 82, 104, 116, and 230.

62. O'Brien, *Revolution from the Heart*, 98.

63. Ibid.

64. O'Brien, *Island of Hope, Island of Tears*, 126.

65. Ibid., 125-129.

66. I have used O'Brien's book *Island of Tears, Island of Hope* as a text for a course in the Center for Justice and Peacebuilding at Eastern Mennonite University. It has been one of the more popular resources for that course because of the way O'Brien integrates his pastoral experience and social activism in a context of desperate poverty and oppression.

67. Various church leaders and scholars are addressing such challenges for churches in secular societies. Among the books on the subject that have recently been published are these: Martin Copenhaver, et al., *Good News in Exile: Three Pastors Offer a Hopeful Vision for the Church* (Grand Rapids, Eerdmans, 1999); Michael Budde and Robert Brimlow, eds., *The Church as Counterculture* (Albany, N.Y.: State University of New York Press, 2000); Stanley Hauerwas and William Willimon, *Resident Aliens: Life in the Christian Colony* (Nashville: Abingdon Press, 1989).

68. J. Milburn Thompson, *Justice and Peace*, 29-59.

69. R. Scott Appleby, *The Ambivalence of the Sacred: Religion, Violence, and Reconciliation* (New York: Rowman & Littlefield Publishers, Inc., 2000), 13.

70. Ibid., 7.

71. Ibid., 297-301. Appleby devotes several pages in his book to the Center for Justice and Peacebuilding. He especially notes Center for Justice and Peacebuilding collaboration with Catholic Relief Services in peacebuilding efforts between Catholic and Muslim communities on the island of Mindanao in the Philippines. This is an example of the kind of interreligious peacebuilding efforts now taking place in various communities around the world.

72. For the theory and practice of restorative justice and a brief discussion of the

beginning of the Victim Offender Reconciliation Program, see Howard Zehr, *Changing Lenses: A New Focus for Crime and Justice* (Scottdale, Pa.: Herald Press, 1990. For a brief history of the MCC sponsored Mennonite Conciliation Service, various peacebuilding case studies, and an analysis of Mennonite peacebuilding, see Cynthia Sampson and John Paul Lederach, eds., *From the Ground Up: Mennonite Contributions to International Peacebuilding* (Oxford: Oxford University Press, 2000).

73. Updated Proposal, still very rough draft #3, 1992, Center for Justice and Peacebuilding (hereafter CJP) Archives, Eastern Mennonite University, Harrisonburg, Virginia.

74. Eastern Mennonite University Mission Statement, approved by the EMU Board of Trustees, March 23, 2002.

75. John Paul Lederach "Recollections and the Construction of a Legacy: The Influence of John Howard Yoder on My Life and Work," unpublished paper given at the Believers Church Conference, University of Notre Dame, March 7-9, 2002.

76. Ruth Hoover Zimmerman, "Center for Justice and Peacebuilding: History 1992-1995," 2002, CTP Archives, Eastern Mennonite University, Harrisonburg, Virginia.

77. Ibid. See also the "Center for Justice and Peacebuilding Annual Report, 1998-1999," CTP Archives, Eastern Mennonite University, Harrisonburg, Virginia.

78. "Center for Justice and Peacebuilding Annual Report," May 2003, CTP Archives, Eastern Mennonite University, Harrisonburg, Virginia.

79. Harry Mika, "CTP Evaluation Report," 2001, CTP Archives, Eastern Mennonite University, Harrisonburg, Virginia.

80. Bonnie Price Lofton, "You've Transformed Us: Parting Thoughts from CTP Students," *Crossroads* 84 (Summer 2003): 16-18.

81. Yoder, *For the Nations*, 15-36.

82. John Howard Yoder, "The Science of Conflict," unpublished lecture in the Warsaw series, May 10-20, 1983, Mark Thiessen Nation, Yoder Collection, Eastern Mennonite Seminary, Harrisonburg, Virginia, 1.

83. Ibid., 5.

BIBLIOGRAPHY

Primary Resources

Archives

The Archives of the Mennonite Church (AMC) at Goshen College, 1700 South Main St., Goshen, Indiana, houses the John Howard Yoder Papers which includes more than one hundred boxes of materials. Box 11, which contains personal letters and other papers from the 1950s, was an especially rich resource for my research. Other collections consulted at AMC were the Harold Bender Papers, the Guy Hershberger Papers, and the Albert J. Meyer Papers.

Another archival resource consulted was the Mark Thiessen Nation, Yoder Collection at Eastern Mennonite Seminary, Harrisonburg, Virginia. Nation has been compiling a comprehensive bibliography of the writings of John Howard Yoder. He is in the process of archiving some of Yoder's papers and is having others published. He kindly allowed me to consult these materials.

Published Books and Articles

Shank, David A. and John Howard Yoder. "Biblicism and the Church," *Concern* (1955): 55-64.

Yoder, John Howard. "Let Evanston Speak on War!" *The Christian Century* (August 8, 1954): 973-974.

_____."The New Testament View of the Ministry." *Gospel Herald* (February 8, 1955): 121-122, 124.

_____. "Reinhold Niebuhr and Christian Pacifism." *The Mennonite Quarterly Review* 29 (April 1955): 101-117.

_____ et al., "Barth on Hungary: An Exchange. From Dr. Barth's Seminar in Basel." *The Christian Century* (April 10, 1957): 453-55.

_____. "The Turning Point of the Zwinglian Reformation." *The Mennonite Quarterly Review* 32 (April 1958): 128-140.

_____. *Täufertum und Reformation in der Schweiz: I. Die Gespräche zwishen Täufern and Reformatoren 1523-1538.* Karlsruhe: Buchdruckerei und Verlag H. Schneider, 1962.

_____. "Why I Don't Pay All My Income Tax." *Gospel Herald* (January 22, 1963): 81, 92.

_____. *The Christian Witness to the State.* Newton, Kan.: Faith and Life Press, 1964.

_____. "The Hermeneutics of the Anabaptists." *The Mennonite Quarterly Review* 41 (October 1967): 291-308.

_____. *Täufertum und Reformation im Gespräch: Dogmengeschichtliche Undersuchung der Frühen Gespräche zwischen Schweizerischen Täufern und Reformatoren.* Zurich: EVZ-Verlag, 1968.

_____. "The Evolution of the Zwinglian Reformation." *The Mennonite Quarterly Review* 43 (January 1969): 92-122.

_____. "Anabaptist Vision and Mennonite Reality." In *Consultation on Anabaptist- Mennonite Theology: Papers Read at the 1969 Aspen Conference.* Ed. A. J. Klassen. Fresno, Cal.: Council of Mennonite Seminaries, 1970, 1-46.

_____. *Karl Barth and the Problem of War: Studies in Christian Ethics.* Nashville: Abingdon Press, 1970.

_____. *The Original Revolution: Essays on Christian Pacifism.* Scottdale, Pa.: Herald Press, 1971.

_____. *Nevertheless: Varieties of Religious Pacifism.* Scottdale, Pa.: Herald Press, 1971.

_____. *The Politics of Jesus: Vicit Agnus Noster.* Grand Rapids: Eerdmans, 1972.

_____. *The Legacy of Michael Sattler.* Scottdale, Pa.: Herald Press, 1973.

_____, trans. and ed. *The Schleitheim Confession.* Scottdale, Pa.: Herald Press, 1973.

_____. *What Would You Do?* Scottdale, Pa.: Herald Press, 1983.

_____. *Christian Attitudes to War, Peace, and Revolution: A Companion to Bainton.* Elkhart, Ind.: Co-op Bookstore, 1983. (Available in photocopied form from Cokesbury Book Store, Duke Divinity School, Duke University, Durham, N.C.)

————. *The Priestly Kingdom: Social Ethics as Gospel.* Notre Dame, Ind.: The University of Notre Dame Press, 1984.

————. "Biblical Roots of Liberation Theology." *Grail* (September 1985): 55-74.

————. "Armaments and Eschatology." *Studies in Christian Ethics* 1 (1988): 43-61.

————. "Withdrawal and Diaspora: The Two Faces of Liberation." In *Freedom and Discipleship: Liberation Theology in Anabaptist Perspective.* Ed. Daniel S. Schipani. Maryknoll, N.Y.: Orbis Books, 1989.

————. *Body Politics: Five Practices of the Christian Community before the Watching World,* Nashville: Discipleship Resources, 1992.

————. *The Royal Priesthood: Essays Ecclesiological and Ecumenical.* Ed. Michael G. Cartwright. Grand Rapids: Eerdmans, 1994.

————. "On Not Being in Charge." In *War and Its Discontents: Pacifism and Quietism in the Abrahamic Traditions.* Ed. J. Patout Burns. Washington, D.C.: Georgetown University Press, 1996.

————. "How H. Richard Niebuhr Reasoned: A Critique of *Christ and Culture.*" In Stassen, Glen, D. M. Yeager, and John Howard Yoder. *Authentic Transformation: A New Vision of Christ and Culture.* Nashville, Abingdon Press, 1996.

————. "Meaning After Babble: With Jeffrey Stout beyond Relativism." *Ethics* 24 (Spring 1996): 125-139.

————. *When War is Unjust: Being Honest in Just-War Thinking,* rev. ed. Maryknoll, N.Y.: Orbis Books, 1996.

————. *For the Nations: Essays Public and Evangelical.* Grand Rapids: Eerdmans, 1997.

————. "On Christian Unity: The Way from Below," *Pro Ecclesia* 9, No. 2 (2000): 165-183.

————. *To Hear the Word.* Eugene Ore.: Wipf and Stock Publishers, 2001.

————. *Preface to Theology: Christology and Theological Method.* Grand Rapids: Brazos Press, 2002.

————. *The Jewish-Christian Schism Revisited.* Ed. Michael Cartwright and Peter Ochs. Grand Rapids: Eerdmans, 2003.

————. *Anabaptism and Reformation in Switzerland: An Historical and Theological Analysis of the Dialogues between Anabaptists and Reformers,* ed.

C. Arnold Snyder, trans. David Carl Stassen and C. Arnold Snyder (Kitchener, Ontario: Pandora Press, 2004).

Secondary Resources

Archives

Center for Justice and Peacebuilding Archives, Eastern Mennonite University, Harrisonburg, Virginia.

Personal Interviews

Included in my research were interviews with various people who personally knew John Howard Yoder and worked with him in various ways. The persons I interviewed were Leonard Gross, Ray Gingerich, Glen Stassen, Albert Keim, Orley Swartzentruber, Irvin Horst, Paul Peachey, Calvin Redekop, and Howard Zehr.

Published Books and Articles

Appleby, Scott R. *The Ambivalence of the Sacred: Religion, Violence, and Reconciliation.* New York: Rowman & Littlefield Publishers, Inc., 2000.

Arendt, Hannah. "The Aftermath of Nazi Rule." *Commentary* (October 1950): 342, 345.

Bainton, Roland H. *Christian Attitudes Toward War and Peace: A Historical Survey and Critical Re-evaluation.* Nashville: Abingdon, 1960.

Barnett, Victoria. *For the Soul of the People: Protestant Protest Against Hitler.* Oxford: Oxford University Press, 1962.

Barth, Karl. *Against the Stream: Shorter Post-War Writings 1946-52.* New York: Philosophical Library, 1954.

_____. *How to Serve God in a Marxist Land.* Trans. Henry Clark and James Smart. New York: Association Press, 1959.

_____. *Church Dogmatics,* vol. 3, part 4. Ed. G. W. Bromiley and T. F. Torrance. Edinburgh: T. & T. Clark, 1961.

Bauer, Arndt, and Gingerich. *A Greek-English Lexicon of the New Testament and Other Early Christian Literature.* Chicago: The University of Chicago Press, 1979.

Bender, Harold. *Conrad Grebel, c. 1498-1526: The Founder of the Swiss Brethren.* Scottdale, Pa.: Herald Press, 1971.

Berkhof, Hendrik. *Christ and the Powers.* Trans. John H. Yoder. Scottdale, Pa.: Herald Press, 1962.

Blanke, Fritz. *Brüder in Christo.* Zürich: Zwingli-Verlag, 1955.

Bonhoeffer, Dietrich. *The Cost of Discipleship.* New York: Macmillan, 1949.

Brandon, S. G. F. *Jesus and the Zealots: A Study of the Political Factor in Primitive Christianity.* Manchester: Manchester University Press, 1967.

Brown, Raymond. *The Death of the Messiah.* Vol. 1. New York: Doubleday, 1993.

Brunk, Emily. *The Mennonite Central Committee Shares in Community Building in a New Settlement for German Refugees.* Karlsruhe: The Mennonite Central Committee, 1951.

Budde, Michael L. and Robert W. Brimlow, eds. *The Church as Counterculture.* Albany, N.Y.: State University of New York Press, 2000.

Cahill, Lisa Sowle. *Love Your Enemies: Discipleship, Pacifism, and Just War Theory.* Minneapolis: Fortress Press, 1994.

Carter, Craig. *The Politics of the Cross: The Theology and Social Ethics of John Howard Yoder.* Grand Rapids: Brazos Press, 2001.

Casanova, José. *Public Religions in the Modern World.* Chicago, The University of Chicago Press, 1994.

Chafe, William H. *The Unfinished Journey: America Since World War II,* 3rd. ed. Oxford: Oxford University Press, 1995.

Copenhaver, Mark, et al. *Good News in Exile: Three Pastors Offer a Hopeful Vision for the Church.* Grand Rapids: Eerdmans, 1999.

Cullmann, Oscar. *Christ and Time: The Primitive Christian Conception of Time and History.* Trans. Floyd Filson. Philadelphia: Westminster Press, 1954.

_____. *The Early Church: Studies in Early Christian History and Theology.* Philadelphia: Westminster Press, 1956.

_____. *The State in the New Testament.* New York: Charles Scribner's Sons, 1956.

_____. *Jesus and the Revolutionaries.* New York: Harper & Row Publishers, 1970.

Dear, John S. J. *The God of Peace: Toward a Theology of Nonviolence.* Maryknoll, N.Y.: Orbis Books, 1994.

Demerath, N. J. III and Rhys H. Williams. *A Bridging of Faiths: Religion and Politics in a New England City.* Princeton, N.J.: Princeton University Press, 1992.

Driedger, Leo and Donald B. Kraybill. *Mennonite Peacemaking: From Quietism to Activism.* Scottdale, Pa.: Herald Press, 1994.

Dun, Angus and Reinhold Niebuhr. "God Wills Both Justice and Peace." *Christianity and Crisis* (June 13, 1955): 75-78.

Durnbaugh, Donald F., ed. *On Earth Peace: Discussions on War/Peace Issues Between Friends, Mennonites, Brethren and European Churches 1935-1975.* Elgin, Ill.: The Brethren Press, 1978.

_____. "John Howard Yoder's Role in 'The Lordship of Christ Over Church and State' Conferences." *The Mennonite Quarterly Review* 77 (July 2003): 271-386.

Dyck, Cornelius J., ed. *An Introduction to Mennonite History.* Scottdale, Pa.: Herald Press, 1967.

Epp, Frank H. *Mennonite Exodus, The Rescue and Resettlement of the Russian Mennonites Since the Communist Revolution.* Altona. Man.: Canadian Mennonite Relief and Immigration Council, 1962.

Evans, Craig and Bruce Chilton, eds. *Studying the Historical Jesus.* Leiden: Brill, 1994.

Friesen, Abraham. *Erasmus, the Anabaptists, and the Great Commission.* Grand Rapids: Eerdmans, 1998.

Friesen, Duane. *Artists, Citizens, Philosophers: Seeking the Peace of the City.* Scottdale, Pa.: Herald Press, 2000.

Gadamer, Hans-Georg. *Truth and Method,* 2d, rev. ed. New York: Continuum, 1994.

Gandhi, M. K. *Non-Violent Resistance (Satyagraha).* New York: Schocken Books, 1951.

Gilkey, Langdon. *How the Church Can Minister to the World Without Losing Itself.* New York: Harper & Row, 1964.

_____. *Nature, Reality, and the Sacred: The Nexus of Science and Religion.* Minneapolis: Fortress Press, 1993.

Girard, René. *Violence and the Sacred.* Baltimore: The Johns Hopkins University Press, 1977.

Godsey, John D. "Reminiscences of Karl Barth," *The Princeton Seminary Bulletin* 23, no. 3 (2002): 313-324.

González, Justo L. *A History of Christian Thought,* vol. 3. Nashville: Abingdon Press.

Gros, Jeffrey and John Rempel, eds. *The Fragmentation of the Church and Its Unity in Peacemaking.* Grand Rapids: Eerdmans, 2001.

Gustafson, James. *Ethics from a Theocentric Perspective*, vol. 1. Chicago: University of Chicago Press, 1981.

Gutiérrez, Gustavo. *A Theology of Liberation: History, Politics, and Salvation*, rev. ed. Maryknoll, N.Y.: Orbis Books, 1988.

_____. *Essential Writings*. Ed. James B. Nickoloff. Maryknoll, N.Y.: Orbis Books, 1996.

Halberstam, David. *The Fifties*. New York: Fawcett Books, 1994.

Hallahan, Kenneth P. "The Social Ethics of Nonresistance: The Writings of Mennonite Theologian John Howard Yoder Analyzed from a Roman Catholic Perspective." Ph.D. diss., The Catholic University of America, 1997.

Hallie, Phillip. *Lest Innocent Blood be Shed*. New York: HarperPerenial, 1994.

Hauerwas, Stanley and William Willimon. *Resident Aliens: Life in the Christian Colony*. Nashville: Abingdon Press, 1989.

Hauerwas, Stanley. *Against the Nations: War and Survival in a Liberal Society*. Notre Dame, Ind.: University of Notre Dame Press, 1992.

_____, Mark Thiessen Nation, and Nancey Murphy, eds. *Theology Without Foundations: Religious Practice and the Future of Theological Truth*. Nashville: Abingdon Press, 1994.

_____. "Remembering John Howard Yoder." *First Things* (April 1998): 15

_____, et al. *The Wisdom of the Cross: Essays in Honor of John Howard Yoder*. Grand Rapids: William B. Eerdmans Publishing Company, 1999.

_____. *With the Grain of the Universe: The Church's Witness and Natural Theology*. Grand Rapids: Brazos Press, 2001.

Hengel, Martin. *Die Zeloten*. Leiden: E. J. Brill, 1961.

Herberg, Will. *Protestant Catholic Jew: An Essay in American Religious Sociology*. Chicago: University of Chicago Press, 1983.

Herr, Robert and Judy Zimmerman Herr, eds. *Transforming Violence: Linking Local and Global Peacemaking*. Scottdale, Pa.: Herald Press, 1998.

Hershberger, Guy F. *War, Peace, and Nonresistance,* 2nd. rev. ed. Scottdale, Pa.: Herald Press, 1953.

_____, ed. *The Recovery of the Anabaptist Vision: A Sixtieth Anniversary Tribute to Harold S. Bender*. Scottdale, Pa.: Herald Press, 1957.

_____. *The Way of the Cross in Human Relationships*, Scottdale, Pa.: Herald Press, 1958.

Hillerbrand, Hans. "The 'Turning Point' of the Zwinglian Reformation: Review and Discussion." *The Mennonite Quarterly Review* 39 (October 1965): 309-312.

Historic Peace Churches and the Fellowship of Reconciliation. *Peace Is the Will of God: A Testimony to the World Council of Churches.* Amsterdam: J. H. De Bussy Ltd., 1953.

_____. *The Christian and War: A Theological Discussion of Justice, Peace and War.* Amsterdam: J. H. De Bussy, 1958.

Hooper, J. Leon and Todd David Whitmore, eds. *John Courtney Murray and the Redemption of History: Natural Law and Theology.* Kansas City, Mo.: Sheed & Ward, 1996.

Horsch, John. *Modern Religious Liberalism.* Scottdale, Pa.: Mennonite Publishing House, 1921.

Horsley, Richard A., ed. *Paul and Empire: Religion and Power in Roman Imperial Society.* Harrisburg, Pa.: Trinity Press, 1997.

Hunsinger, George. *How to Read Karl Barth: The Shape of His Theology.* Oxford: Oxford University Press, 1991.

Juhnke, James C. *Vision, Doctrine, War: Mennonite Identity and Organization in America, 1890-1930.* The Mennonite Experience in America, vol. 3. Ed. Theron F. Schlabach. Scottdale, Pa.: Herald Press, 1989.

Kauffman, Daniel, ed. *Doctrines of the Bible: A Brief Discussion of the Teachings of God's Word.* Scottdale, Pa.: Mennonite Publishing House, 1929.

Kiem, Albert N. *Harold S. Bender, 1897-1962.* Scottdale, Pa.: Herald Press, 1998.

King, Martin Luther Jr. "Pilgrimage to Nonviolence." In *Nonviolence in America: A Documentary History.* Ed. Staughton Lynd and Alice Lynd. Maryknoll, N.Y.: Orbis Books, 1995.

Lasserre, Jean. *War and the Gospel.* London: James Clark & Co. Ltd., 1962.

Lederach, John Paul. *Preparing for Peace: Conflict Transformation Across Cultures.* Syracuse, N.Y.: Syracuse University Press, 1995.

Lehman, James O. *Creative Congregationalism: A History of the Oak Grove Mennonite Church in Wayne County, Ohio.* Smithville, Ohio: Oak Grove Mennonite Church, 1978.

Lehman, J. Irvin. "Teachers and Teachings." *The Sword and Trumpet* 11 (July 1943): 28.

Lofton, Bonnie Price. "You've Transformed Us: Parting Thoughts from CTP Students." *Crossroads* 84 (Summer 2003): 16-18.

Lonergan, Bernard. *Method in Theology.* Toronto: University of Toronto Press, 1994.

Lovin, Robin W. *Reinhold Niebuhr and Christian Realism.* Cambridge: Cambridge University Press, 1995.

Lynd, Staughton and Alice Lynd, eds. *Nonviolence in America: A Documentary History.* Maryknoll, N.Y.: Orbis Books, 1995.

Marsden, George. *Fundamentalism and American Culture: The Shaping of Twentieth- Century Evangelicalism 1870-1925.* Oxford: Oxford University Press, 1980.

McClendon, James. *Ethics: Systematic Theology,* vol. 1. Nashville: Abingdon Press, 1986.

McKim, Donald K., ed. *How Karl Barth Changed My Mind.* Grand Rapids: Eerdmans, 1986.

Meier, John P. *A Marginal Jew: Rethinking the Historical Jesus,* vol. 2. New York: Doubleday, 1994.

Migliore, Daniel L. *Faith Seeking Understanding: An Introduction to Christian Theology.* Grand Rapids: Eerdmans, 1991.

Miller, Keith Graber. *Wise as Serpents, Innocent as Doves: American Mennonites Engage Washington.* Knoxville: The University of Tennessee Press, 1996.

Miller, Marlin and Barbara Nelson Gingerich, eds. *The Church's Peace Witness.* Grand Rapids: Eerdmans, 1994.

Miller, Richard B. *Interpretations of Conflict: Ethics, Pacifism and the Just-War Tradition.* Chicago: The University of Chicago Press, 1991.

Miranda, José. *Marx and the Bible: A Critique of the Philosophy of Oppression.* Maryknoll, N.Y.: Orbis Press, 1974.

Morris, Charles R. *American Catholic: The Saints and Sinners Who Built America's Most Powerful Church.* New York: Random House, 1997.

Murphy, Nancey and George F.R. Ellis. *On the Moral Nature of the Universe: Theology, Cosmology, and Ethics.* Minneapolis: Fortress Press, 1996.

Murray, John Courtney. *Morality and Modern War.* New York: The Church Peace Union, 1959.

_____. *Religious Liberty: Catholic Struggles with Pluralism.* Ed. J. Leon Hooper. Louisville: Westminster John Knox Press, 1993.

Nation, Mark Thiessen. *A Comprehensive Bibliography of the Writings of John Howard Yoder.* Goshen, Ind.: Mennonite Historical Society, 1997.

_____. "The Ecumenical Patience and Vocation of John Howard Yoder: A Study in Theological Ethics." Ph.D. diss. Fuller Theological Seminary, 2000.

_____. "John Howard Yoder: Mennonite, Evangelical, Catholic." *The Mennonite Quarterly Review* 77 (July 2003): 357-370.

Niebuhr, H. Richard. *Christ and Culture*. San Francisco: Harper & Row Publishers, 1951.

Niebuhr, Reinhold. *Moral Man and Immoral Society: A Study in Ethics and Politics*. New York: Charles Scribner's Sons, 1932.

_____. *Christianity and Power Politics*. New York: Archon books, 1940.

_____. "Why is Barth Silent on Hungary?" *Christian Century* (January 23, 1957): 108-110.

O'Brien, Naill. *Revolution from the Heart*. Maryknoll, N.Y.: Orbis Books, 1988.

Ollenburger, Ben C. and Gayle Gerber Koontz, eds. *A Mind Patient and Untamed: Assessing John Howard Yoder's Contributions to Theology, Ethics, and Peacemaking*. Telford, Pa.: Cascadia, 2004.

_____. *Island of Tears, Island of Hope: Living the Gospel in a Revolutionary Situation*. Maryknoll, N.Y.: Orbis Books, 1993.

Packull, Werner O. *Mysticism and the Early South German-Austrian Anabaptist Movement, 1525-1531*. Scottdale, Pa.: Herald Press, 1977.

_____. "Mennonites in 1954: An Appraisal. *Gospel Herald* (March 1, 1955): 193- 194, 196.

Pawlikowski, John T. and Donald Senior, eds. *Biblical and Theological Reflections on the Challenge of Peace*. Wilmington, Del.: Michael Glazier, Inc., 1984.

Peachey, Paul. "Toward an Understanding of the Decline of the West." *Concern* 1 (June 1954): 8-44.

Phillips, Kevin, ed. *Peace, Politics, and the People of God*. Philadelphia: Fortress Press, 1986.

_____. *American Theocracy: The Peril and Politics of Radical Religion, Oil, and Borrowed Money in the Twenty-First Century*. New York: Viking Penguin, 2006.

Rasmussen, Larry. *Reinhold Niebuhr: Theologian of Public Life*. Minneapolis: Fortress Press, 1991.

Rasmusson, Arne. *The Church as Polis: From Political Theology to Theological Politics as Exemplified by Jürgen Moltmann and Stanley Hauerwas*. Notre Dame, Ind.: University of Notre Dame Press, 1995.

Redekop, Calvin. *Mennonite Society.* Baltimore: The Johns Hopkins University Press, 1989.

Reimer, A. James. "The Nature and Possibility of a Mennonite Theology." *Conrad Grebel Review* (Winter 1983): 33-55.

Said, Edward W. *The World the Text and the Critic.* Cambridge, Mass.: Harvard University Press, 1983.

Sampson, Cynthia and John Paul Lederach, eds. *From the Ground Up: Mennonite Contributions to International Peacebuilding.* Oxford: Oxford University Press, 2000.

Sawatsky, Rodney J. and Scott Holland. *The Limits of Perfection: A Conversation with J. Lawrence Burkholder.* Waterloo, Ont.: Institute of Anabaptist Mennonite Studies, 1993.

Schirch, Lisa. *The Little Book of Strategic Peacebuilding.* Intercourse, Pa.: Good Books, 2004.

Schlabach, Theron F. *Gospel Versus Gospel: Mission and the Mennonite Church, 1863-1944.* Scottdale, Pa.: Herald Press, 1980.

Sharp, Gene: *The Politics of Nonviolent Action:* "Part One: Power and Struggle." Boston: Porter Sargent Publishers, 1984.

Smith, Dan. *The Penguin State of the World Atlas,* 7th. ed. New York: Penguin Books, 2003.

Snyder, Arnold. *The Life and Thought of Michael Sattler.* Scottdale, Pa.: Herald Press, 1984.

Stassen, Glen H. *Just Peacemaking: Transforming Initiative for Justice and Peace.* Louisville: Westminster/John Knox Press, 1992.

_____, ed. *Just Peacemaking: Ten Practices for Abolishing War.* Cleveland: The Pilgrim Press, 1998.

Stayer, James, Werner Packull, and Klas Deppermann. "From Monogenesis to Polygenesis: The Historical Discussion of Anabaptist Origins." *The Mennonite Quarterly Review* 49 (June 1975): 83-121.

Stayer, James M. *Anabaptists and the Sword.* Lawrence, Kan.: Coronado Press, 1973.

_____. *The German Peasants' War and Anabaptist Community of Goods.* Montreal & Kingston: McGill-Queen's University Press, 1991.

Steinfels, Peter. "John H. Yoder, Theologian at Notre Dame is Dead at 70." *The New York Times* (January 7, 1998).

Sturzo, Luigi. *Church and State.* Trans. Barbara Barclay Carter. Notre Dame, Ind.: Notre Dame University Press, 1962.

Toews, Paul. "The Concern Movement: Its Original and Early History." *The Conrad Grebel Review* 8 (Spring 1990): 109-126.

_____. *Mennonites in American Society, 1930-1970: Modernity and the Persistence of Religious Community.* The Mennonite Experience in America, vol. 4. Ed. Theron F. Schlabach. Scottdale, Pa.: Herald Press, 1996.

Thompson, J. Milburn. *Justice and Peace: A Christian Primer.* Maryknoll, N.Y.: Orbis Books, 1997.

Tracy, David. *The Analogical Imagination: Christian Theology and the Culture of Pluralism.* New York: Crossroad, 1991.

Trocmé, André. *Jèsus-Christ et la Revolution Non-violente.* Geneva: Labor et Fides, 1961.

von Muralt, Leonhard and Walter Schmidt. *Quellen zu Geschichte der Täufer in der Schweiz,* vol 1. Zürich: Hirzel Verlag, 1952.

Walton, Robert C. "Was There a Turning Point of the Zwinglian Reformation?" *The Mennonite Quarterly Review* 42 (January 1968): 45-56.

Weaver, J. Denny. *Becoming Anabaptist: The Origin and Significance of Sixteenth- Century Anabaptism,* 2nd. ed. Scottdale, Pa.: Herald Press, 2005.

_____. *Anabaptist Theology in Face of Postmodernity: A Proposal for the Third Millennium.* Telford, Pa.: Pandora Press U.S., 2000.

_____. *The Nonviolent Atonement.* Grand Rapids: Eerdmans, 2001.

_____. "The John Howard Yoder Legacy: Whither the Second Generation?" *Mennonite Quarterly Review* 77 (July 2003): 451-471.

Weaver, J. Denny and Gerald Biesecker-Mast, eds. *Teaching Peace: Nonviolence and the Liberal Arts.* New York: Rowman & Littlefield, 2003.

Wenger, J. C. *Introduction to Theology: A Brief Introduction to the Doctrinal Content of Scripture Written in the Anabaptist-Mennonite Tradition.* Scottdale, Pa.: Herald Press, 1954.

Wink, Walter. *Engaging the Powers: Discernment and Resistance in a World of Domination* Minneapolis: Fortress Press, 1992.

_____. ed. *Peace is the Way: Writings on Nonviolence from the Fellowship of Reconciliation.* Maryknoll, N.Y.: Orbis Books, 2000.

Wright, N. T. *Jesus and the Victory of God.* Minneapolis: Fortress Press, 1996.

Wuthnow, Robert. *The Restructuring of American Religion: Society and Faith Since World War II,* Princeton, N.J.: Princeton University Press, 1988.

Yoder, Perry B. *Shalom: The Bible's Word for Salvation, Justice, and Peace.* Newton, Kans.: Faith and Life Press, 1987.

Zehr, Howard. *Changing Lenses: A New Focus for Crime and Justice,* 3d ed. Scottdale, Pa.: Herald Press, 2005.

Zimbelman, Joel Andrew. "Theological Ethics and Politics in the Thought of Juan Luis Segundo and John Howard Yoder." Ph.D. diss., University of Virginia, 1986.

THE INDEX

Calvinism, 113
Capito, Wolfgang, 148, 167n18,
    167n31
Carlstadt, Andreas, 145, 147, 155,
    167n17
Carter Center, 230
Carter, Craig, 65n46, 134n14,
    136n41, 166n9, 198, 206n26
Cartwright, Michael, 27, 143,
    206n26, 209n88
Catholic
    moral theology, 27
    social teaching, 223, 225, 233
    See also Just War
    U.S. Catholic Bishops, 221, 223
Catholic Relief Services, 239, 249n71
Center for Justice and Peacebuild-
    ing, 20, 236-241, 244n4,
    249n66, 249n71
Chafe, William, 38-39,
Christian Century, 84-85, 89-90
Christiansen, Drew, 222
Christendom, 16, 34, 109, 131,
    176, 186
    post-Christendom, 131, 154
Christology. *See* Barth, theology
Church. *See also* ecclesiology
    as body of Christ, 91-93, 111,
        119-120, 164, 192, 213, 232-
        233
    and society, 37, 46, 58, 90, 103,
        137n69, 142, 144, 151, 159-
        161, 187, 192, 242
    and state, 55, 112-122, 127,
        131, 137n69, 142, 152, 157-
        162, 170n88, 193
    polity, 12, 46-50, 79, 111
Church of the Brethren, 36, 76,
    99n59
Church World Service, 239
Civilian Public Service, 36, 52,
    63n13

Cold War, 25, 35-39, 74-76, 108-
    109, 230
Communion, 147, 225
Communism, 39, 74, 84-85, 108,
    110, 132
Confessing Church, 83-84, 188
Conflict transformation, 29, 215,
    218, 236, 238
Conscientious Objection, 35-36, 77
Constantinianism, 98n44, 142, 154,
    186-187, 198
Creeds, 166n9, 187-189, 221
Cross, 177, 188-189, 216
    way of the cross, 90-91, 120,
        125, 162, 189, 193, 197,
        246n21, 248n51
Crusade, 223-224
Crysdale, Cynthia, 19
Cullmann, Oscar, 113, 137n33,
    biblical studies, 114-118
    on church and state, 124-130,
        139n90
    and Jewish religious parties,
        123-125, 138n70
    as mentor to Yoder, 27, 95, 101-
        105, 131, 133, 144, 176-177,
        184
    and reign of Christ, 116-119,
        123
Culture, 46, 52, 80, 160, 241
    Christ and, 119, 135n37, 187
    Christian faith and, 30n4, 181-
        182,
    Mennonite adaptation to, 35,
        56, 82

D
Dalai Lama, 214
Day, Dorothy, 214, 221
Democracy, 18, 40, 157, 194, 197,
    210n105, 218, 223, 229,
    248n51

THE AUTHOR

Earl Zimmerman is Assistant Professor of Bible and Religion at Eastern Mennonite University, Harrisonburg, Virginia. He is also a core teacher in the Justice, Peace, and Conflict Studies Program at EMU. He began teaching at EMU in 1998.

Zimmerman is an ordained pastor in the Central District Conference of Mennonite Church USA. He is a member of the pastoral team at Shalom Mennonite Congregation in Harrisonburg, Virginia.

He and his family spent eight years in the Philippines with Eastern Mennonite Missions and Mennonite Central Committee. There he was involved in theological education, various peace and development initiatives, pastoral work, ecumenical and interreligious conversations, and a regional Asia facilitator. He is co-editor of *Telling Our Stories: Personal Accounts of Engagement with Scripture* (Cascadia, 2006).

Zimmerman was born and grew up in Myerstown, Pennsylvania. He is married to Ruth Hoover Zimmerman. They are the parents of Krista, Stephen, and Sara.

Printed in the United States
80536LV00005B/226-252